TO KILL A TIGER

TO KILL A TIGER

A MEMOIR OF KOREA

Jid Lee

THE OVERLOOK PRESS
NEW YORK

This edition first published in hardcover in the United States in 2010 by
The Overlook Press, Peter Mayer Publishers, Inc.
141 Wooster Street
New York, NY 10012

PHOTO CREDITS:
The images of the man eating corn, on page 22; men harvesting rice,
on page 65; children skating, on page 85; and a view of the Korean countryside, on page 268 are used courtesy of Homer Williams, © 2010
Homer Williams.

The images of Seoul Station, on page 161; Seoul City Hall, on page 167;
the Korean country village, on page 209; men pushing a cart through
Seoul streets, on page 275; and the view of Seoul metropolis, on page 334
are used courtesy of Gary A. Helsene, © 2010 Gary A. Helsene.

All other images are from the author's private collection.

Cataloging-in-Publication Data is available from the Library of Congress

Book design and typeformatting by Bernard Schleifer
Manufactured in the United States of America
FIRST EDITION
2 4 6 8 10 9 7 5 3 1
ISBN 978-1-59020-266-1

*To my father
(1920–1989)*

CONTENTS

Be silent in that solitude,

    Which is not loneliness—for then

The spirits of the dead who stood

    In life before thee are again

In death around thee—and their will

Shall overshadow thee: be still.

          —EDGAR ALLAN POE,
          Spirits of the Dead

A Note on Authenticity

WHILE I TRIED TO BE AS ACCURATE AS POSSIBLE IN MY RECOUNTING OF historical events, I added some fiction to the personal lives of the people affected by these events. The names of the characters, too, except those of well-known historical figures, were changed, and some of the facts, including the contents and dates of the incidents in their lives, were altered to accommodate the narrative integrity and consistency. That history is fiction is a cliché, and trying to explain why I attempted to fill in the blanks in modern Korean history with the information I gathered on my own would be a waste of time. The truth was intentionally cast out of the official version to be replaced by lies and propaganda, so the only way to arrive at the truth again is an exercise of disciplined imagination, and this I tried to do. I must acknowledge the random power of memory to select what remains in a nation's or an individual's psyche, but it is with certainty that I can say that I did my best to take into account the unreliable nature of what I remember.

Since the history of my country has to be thoroughly interpolated into the re-telling of my personal childhood, what I know now must remain entirely mixed with what I remember as my distant past. I must give an adult's sharp language to a child's inarticulate thoughts. Since it is equally true, however, that the retrospective reassessments that I gained as a grownup gave me newly born layers of interpretation, it was necessary as well to make them distinct from the narratives regarding my past.

I have now lived in the United States for twenty-eight years, for several years longer than I did in Korea, and I can finally look at the little Korean girl I used to be with a sense of humor. Still, however, unable to abdicate the Korean custom of not calling one's older siblings and parents by their names, I use birth orders and generic nouns to refer to them. Perhaps, I wrote this memoir to let this custom go with laughter.

*My family in 1956. I am the baby, and that is my mother
holding me. Right of her is Father, and in front of him,
holding hands, are my two brothers.*

A Woman Who Wished to Be Eaten Alive by a Tiger

MY NIGHTMARE—AND MY DREAM—STARTED WHEN I WAS SIX years old, a child sick in bed.

"Your great-great-great-great-great-great-grandmother—she was quite a woman," Grandmother said. "She volunteered to be eaten alive by a tiger for her descendants."

I couldn't afford to be bored by the only story Grandmother had to tell me. I had been ill for half a year from renal paralysis, and there was nobody else who could stay by my bedside except the old woman. Mother was busy with housework, Father was at his job, and my brothers and sisters were in school, so Grandmother was stuck with me, and I was stuck with her same old story. With my silence, I invited Grandmother to start from the beginning.

"That great-grandmother of yours was always ready to do anything—anything—for her posterity. She prayed, so that her descendents would prosper forever under the auspices of the gods. And one day suddenly her long-awaited chance came." Grandmother sighed with pride and sadness. Her delivery was always a mix of glee and melancholy, what she actually felt creeping through how she thought she was supposed to feel. "When she had just turned twenty, with two sons and one daughter, she had a visitor, a Buddhist monk from a temple in a distant city. He came to tell her that there was a way she could place her children, their children, and these children's children under the gods' eternal good will.'"

"What did he say she should do?" I inquired, already knowing the rest of the story.

"If she chose to be eaten alive by a tiger, he said, her offspring would be promised good health, high offices, long lives, riches, talents, good looks, and many loyal friends and servants.'"

"Did she decide to be a tiger's meal, then?"

"Yes," Grandmother said. "The Buddhist monk didn't tell her exactly when the tiger would strike the house and take her away, but he said it would be in the night, about when the eighth half moon of the year started to wane into a crescent shape. She, her husband, and her parents-in-law figured it would be around the beginning of August, the time of the year when bamboo forests grow the tallest and willow trees wear the longest leaves. Such a young, pretty lady waiting to be carried away by a tiger's teeth, prepared to leave a suckling girl behind her!"

"What happened to her?" I pretended not to remember. "Did a tiger come for her?"

"On the third day of lunar August, she was washing her hair in the backyard. Since the Buddhist monk had told her that the tiger would come in the night, she thought she would be safe during the day, so she boiled a big basin of water to wash herself clean for the gods. I think the tiger came sooner than the gods had planned because she smelled so good." Grandmother dropped her head, dabbing her teary eyes on her skirt. "So young, so pretty, with a baby in her arms!"

"The tiger come in broad daylight?" I made my voice sound shocked.

"Yes." She blew her nose in her skirt. "He sank his teeth into the nape of her snow-white neck. He snatched her away, her beautiful hair dragging down behind her like a long, black painting brush, wet and lustrous in the sunlight."

I touched the nape of my neck with the palm of my hand, feeling my blood congeal. The vision of the lady being carried away between a tiger's teeth choked me. In my imagination, she became me. I was screaming, but as if in a dream, my tongue was dead. My body, separated from my face by the tiger's mouth, was limp like a rag doll.

"You said they later found parts of her body in the mountain."

"Yes, they searched the mountain for days and found one of her breasts, half-eaten, under a tall oak tree, and a hand with three fingers on the grass near the trail." Grandmother had regained her composure. "Your great-great-great-great-great-great-grandfather and his parents buried the remains in the clan cemetery and performed a ritual of gratitude every year for a century on the lunar day of her death."

"Did her descendants prosper?"

"Yes, they did, for two hundred years, until your Grandfather ruined it all."

"I know what Grandfather did," I interrupted to prevent her from slipping into her usual bitterness. "Tell me about his ancestors."

Matter-of-factly, she began to list family accomplishments. "The brave woman's son, your great-great-great-great-great-grandfather, became a minister of education at the age of twenty-five, and his son at twenty-one achieved the honor of being the youngest to serve as the finance secretary for the king. To follow them, this son's son rose to be the governor of one of the largest provinces at only twenty-six, and this man's son in turn responded to their ancestors' call by becoming a nationally celebrated calligrapher and writer. Lastly, your great-grandfather, as you might have heard, was a renowned scholar. Although he couldn't hold a title in the government as his forefathers had, he was just as talented. If the exams for Confucian bureaucrats had not been abolished in his adolescence, he probably would have earned the highest scores."

In my clan, such a brilliant record was routine, not an extraordinary achievement. "You will get it all back—whatever your grandfather ruined," Grandmother concluded. "You, my grandchildren, my flesh and blood. You will make something of your lives and make it up to the young lady who was gladly eaten alive by a tiger." I thought

I saw tears in Grandmother's eyes. "Women in your clan have all been so brave and firm. They never hesitated to do anything for the good of the family, just like the tiger woman. They were warriors. You, my dear, are going to be a fighter, following them. You will bring honor to your family. You will make your husband and children proud."

"I will have to be eaten alive by a tiger, then," I squeaked. But inside, I was thinking, *If a tiger comes for me, I will cut the beast in half with a sword.*

I remembered a story Mother had told me about her mother's father, who had scared a tiger off with a pair of flint stones on a pitch-black summer night. His village was a basin surrounded with thickly forested mountains, and tigers often roamed into people's houses to forage. When he saw a tiger blocking his way, he wasn't surprised a bit. Undaunted, he dropped his sacks, took the flint stones out of the pouch of his summer hemp coat, and struck them against each other. His voice echoed against the mountains. "Hey you, you bastard! Get away from me, or I'll cut you down!" The tiger skulked away, and the old man picked up the sacks and resumed walking, whistling all the way home.

"You're not going to be taken by a tiger, dear, not these days," Grandmother replied. "You will honor your family and country by holding a prominent post in the field of letters."

I had nothing to tell her in response because I had never thought I was clever. It seemed that my brothers had taken all the talents of the family. And Grandmother had never treated me as a warrior. Whenever Big Brother and Less Big Brother beat me up, she merely clicked her tongue at me, smiling. Grandmother was an elderly matriarch in the most classical sense, and she did everything she could to reinforce our classical boundaries. Every evening, she drew a holy demilitarized zone down the middle of the dinner table, dividing freshly cooked food from the leftovers. The former was for the men, the latter for the women. When I refused to eat my brothers' leftovers, she called me a "worthless chick" and a "goody monster" and hit my wrist as it tried to reach over the DMZ.

Grandmother was also the one who established a seating chart for the family. At dinner, Father sat at a small table perched beside the big, round one for his wife and children, and Big Brother and Less Big Brother sat side by side next to Father. I was placed at the opposite end from them with Big Sister, the oldest child, because the girls had to be closer to the kitchen to serve the men. Mother squished into the spot next to Big Sister, and facing her, between the boys and girls, Grandmother enforced the DMZ. She didn't have to watch Big Sister because Big Sister was a good kid, helpful and obedient. But I was different, always trying to poach from the fresh food and asking for more than I should. While the younger women ate the men's leftovers, the older women scraped what was stuck at the bottom of the dishes. According to Grandmother, this hierarchy was a perfect system for a Korean family, whose success was dependent on the men's strength and intelligence. Our destiny was in the hands of the Three Men of the Family—Father, Big Brother, and Less Big Brother.

Yet this very same woman believed in my ability to achieve greatness, and I was confused. I felt I was in a tiger's stomach. I wanted to get out. I realized that my dreams of achieving were made possible by my nightmares.

The Stolen Grapes

I CANNOT DESCRIBE HOW MUCH I DREADED BEING ASKED TO HELP MY MOTHER around the house. The worst of her chores by far was the charcoal briquette.

Although well built by 1962 standards, my family's house was hot in summer and cold in winter, with four small bedrooms for the eight of us. Because each room had to be heated with the coal briquette that was pushed in through the rail under the floor, the air in the house was unbearably cold while the floor we sat on was hot enough to burn our behinds. Twice a day, Mother walked into the basement with a long, thin prong to run it through the four different rails, pull the old coal briquette out, and put new briquettes on top to keep the fire going. To protect herself from the poison gas and the black soot, she wore a large cotton mask on her face, and a long, wide apron over her body. Emerging from the basement, she was met by the icy air, which choked her throat and always forced her to stand in shock for a full minute or so to recover her breath.

Summer was more welcomed than winter, since she could dispense with this excruciating labor, but summer had its own unpleasant chores. Mother had to cook on a stove of coal briquette in burning heat, squatting on the ground to watch the soup boil. She always had sweat pouring down her face. In less than forty years, coal briquette would be a national legend, used only by paupers and by some restau-

*The Susongdong marketplace area of Taegu,
the city where I was born.*

rant owners who wanted to attract customers with a sentimental relic.
It would be replaced almost entirely by a highly sophisticated indoor
heating system that used burnt refuse, but when I was a child, it was
a challenge to avoid freezing to death in our own house.

Shaped like a large English letter L, our house had three rooms
in a long line and one room on the short side. In the center was the
living room with a wooden floor, which could not be heated safely
by coal briquette and so was never used in the winter. Our front
yard was a rather narrow strip of cement ground, following the
straight walls of the rooms belonging to the next house. The back
yard, too, was narrow, its long, walled edge bordering the front
yard of the next house on the other side. A persimmon tree grew in
the middle of the sparse lawn, which showed patches of bare soil
here and there. The kitchen was right behind the one room on the
short side, connected to the living room through a small swinging
door. In summer, we could eat in the living room, with a fan turning 180 degrees.

My family lived in one of the safest, coziest areas in the munici-
pality of Taegu, where children were kept clean and well dressed and
men rarely went to work without a suit and a tie. I knew that my
upwardly driven neighbors, who were so concerned with proper

appearances, would have been shocked to learn that I snuck out into the dark streets when I should have been studying with my parents' blessing. But I felt liberated. I was escaping all the wholesomeness of my house and street.

For many reasons, I felt uncomfortable in my middle-class neighborhood. My family struggled to maintain the same quality of life as our neighbors, but mostly we failed, running out of money at the end of each month as certainly as we drained the water out of our pump. It was painful to watch Mother run around in a panic to borrow grocery money from our relatives and friends, to see her count with her fingers the number of the days we had to wait until Father would bring his paycheck home. Even as a child I though it was ridiculous that we spent our money to live in a house in a nice neighborhood, but didn't have enough for food. Our neighbors' children dressed well, in new clothes and solid shoes; beside them, we looked ragged. It was obvious that by choosing to live where we lived, my family was making a desperate statement: *We are actually better than we appear to be.*

It was the impulse of fallen nobility that drove my family's frantic search for the "right environment." Drummed into us was Grandmother's sermon that we were descended from a once powerful clan that had occupied a whole village but had ceased to exist at the turn of the century. Westernization was the culprit, according to her. It felled the Confucian system of social order and therefore brought down all the wealth and prestige that had been ours for centuries. To fulfill our family's destiny, which was to recapture our ancestors' glory, we needed a home where we could "breathe the air from clean people" and learn to speak a cultured language. "It's worth it," Grandmother declared. "We wear cheap clothes and eat bland food today, so that we'll have fancy clothes and delicious food tomorrow. Those who don't know how to sacrifice the present for the future don't go too far." She reminded us constantly of our duty to make our great-great-great-great-great-great-grandmother's sacrifice worthwhile. Her grandchildren were meant to fly away to somewhere much higher, to a place where there was no more longing or deprivation.

My first fight to escape the tiger's stomach happened over a tiny bunch of shriveled grapes. One summer when I was seven years old, Mother handed each of her boys a bunch of grapes as long and thick as my calf, doling out portions only half that size to Big Sister and me. I swallowed my saliva, coveting the fat, dark purple ones in my brothers' hands. Big Brother tilted his head up and lifted the grapes over his mouth to bite the soft, juicy bulbs one by one, laughing at me. Less Big Brother taunted me, too, dangling his grapes in front of my eyes. I felt my hands clenching into fists, my nose-tip tingling with tears, my silent outrage instantly melting into sadness.

But I didn't want to cry. I knew Less Big Brother would launch into a tirade about girls being weak. Instead, I threw my shabby cluster of grapes out of the window, grabbed in both of my little hands the biggest clump, which was reserved for Father, and ran out of the room toward the gate of the house. But before I could crash the gate open, I felt Mother's hand pulling my ponytail and Grandmother's curse petrifying my legs from behind. "You stupid bitch! Don't you dare fool yourself!" Grandmother shouted after me. "Why do you think you deserve a man's portion of grapes?"

Mother, still gripping my disheveled hair, whispered, "I gave you the few grapes I could afford. You forgot to see that Grandmother and I couldn't even split one bunch between the two of us, didn't you?" Her right hand smacked back and forth from my right to left cheek, making sharp, metallic sounds, forcing tears to well up in my eyes. Her legs and arms were shaking with outrage, her face was livid, and her eyes bore into my terror-stricken face like a spear. "Look at your sister. She enjoys what's given to her, just like other girls. Some girls even give their meager shares away to their brothers. Why are you so different?"

Holding the bunch of mushed grapes, I walked out of the house and turned onto the street. I wanted to leave my home forever. I couldn't go back to the room where Big Brother, Less Big

Brother, and Big Sister were eating their unequally distributed shares. I wanted to plod on to a distant place where grapevines covered every roof and wall. I kept walking until I had left the protected confinement of my middle-class neighborhood and reached a main street.

Although it was getting dark and prostitutes were stealing out of their dens, I didn't stop walking. Home seemed worse than the maze of reflected neon lights in half-dark streets, which offered adventure if nothing else. Wandering along streets frequented by lonely men looking for love, by pickpockets ferreting out unguarded back pockets, by bar brawlers crashing beer bottles on each other's shoulders, and by passionate women trying to conceal their desires with shy, intermittent glances at their men, I realized that I liked moving about in a tiger's stomach. If my home was a small jungle with seven familiar people, the street was a large wilderness with a thousand nonchalant strangers crossing each other's paths, a throng of spirits forever rushing toward the unknown. These spirits, I thought, were my kindred souls, running, but doomed to fall back into the same old, dreaded place where they would be again locked up. The street was a bigger stomach of a bigger tiger, where I was free to discover scenes forbidden to a child at home.

Although in my heart I was far from my parents' middle-class neighborhood, it took me only forty-five minutes to walk west to the downtown, where the typical seediness of a city abounded. As the third largest city in South Korea, Taegu in 1962 boasted a little over seven hundred thousand people and about 180 square miles, but the downtown lay only within a mile of the residential district where my home was. Because most houses in Korean cities were built with no space and walls in between, they could house an incredible number of people in a small area, and Taegu was no exception. Half of the city's middle-class population lived in the eastern edge of the downtown, spread over a dozen or so square miles. At a brisk pace, a healthy adult could cover the dozen miles from one end of the city to the other in just a couple hours. Like most cities in Korea, Taegu was a congested metropolis with its business centers heavily concentrated in the downtown, its residential districts dotted with small, crowded circles of schools and markets. Densely populated and basin-shaped, it suffered extremes of hot and cold weather. The entire city became a giant stove on hot days, with concrete buildings packed in like a row of matchboxes. People in Taegu jokingly said that they could roast their meat by leaving it in the sun for half an hour.

But thanks to its inclement weather and its location, Taegu had its share of fame. Tucked in at the southeastern tip of the country, its scorching summers produced an abundant harvest of delicious red apples in fall, which attracted tourists from all over the country. "Taegu women are pretty because they eat a lot of apples" was one of the flattering lines tourists liked to repeat whenever they came to visit. These happy visitors, of course, never had a chance to stumble into the other side of the city, where endless files of slum houses lay like a vast swamp sucking in its inhabitants. Women in these squalid neighborhoods, married to jobless men who seldom brought home enough money for groceries, rarely ate delicious red apples. The children, who begged and stole for food, spent more time in police custody than at home. Secretly, they studied the geography of the city to plan where they could successfully snatch a lady's purse and pick a gentleman's back pocket.

Although I had never met this type of child myself, Mother had one story about a personal encounter with a street ragamuffin. "Until you were born," she told me, "I used to take your Less Big Brother to Susong Market with me. On his third birthday, I bought him a red bean cake from a peddler, a hot, steamy one he could barely hold in his hand, but as he was ready to take a bite, a little boy with black soot all over his face showed up out of nowhere and snatched it away from him, darting away like an arrow. Your Less Big Brother screamed for half an hour, kicking his legs on the ground. The special treat he had been anticipating for days was gone, and he knew I didn't have the money to buy him another one. How could a three-

A man eating roasted corn in front of a corn vendor in a Korean marketplace in 1972.

year-old child understand what I was trying to explain: 'He needs it more than you do. He comes from one of those neighborhoods where people are starving.'"

The parents and grandparents of these little boys flocked into the bustling quarters of the city during the day—fighting the sub-zero temperatures in winter and sweating in summer—to sell fruits, vegetables, dried fish, and homemade cookies under the little tents they pitched on the sidewalks. Sidewalks were six feet wide to accommodate the lines of people standing in front of the bus stops and taxi signs, but the instant shops the peddlers set up zigzagged over half of the space. Few people complained, though, because these merchants were adroit enough to avoid blocking the precise spots at which the vehicles stopped. Most people, in fact, appreciated them because they could pay less for fresher produce and pick up, with just a few coins, some tasty snacks to munch on while waiting in line. All day and all night until the national midnight curfew, the downtown sidewalks were packed with little carts and basins offering a quick feast.

Most buyers knew that these merchants were the unfortunates from the outskirts of the city. If incensed, the merchants were desperate enough to pull a knife on anyone or spit out the kind of foul language that would make one's ears go deaf in shame. Taegu was a polarized metropolis with a sharply pronounced division between the blessed and the wretched, with a tiny breathing area in the center where the wealthy lived, encircled by layers of airless habitats, mostly slums. The two rarely met except in the markets and on the sidewalks in the bustling quarters, where the latter sold what they had made and the former enjoyed the privilege of buying it.

Few people in these two different worlds harbored any genuine curiosity about each other. As a child, my curiosity about those on the other side bordered on fear. I knew only what my neighbors told me about how violent they could be when provoked. But I enjoyed watching them and their little street shops. I was in the presence of something that was forbidden to me, right in a tiger's stomach.

I scrutinized the street. The chaos was hauntingly familiar. It seemed one could discover a whole universe in just one busy block in downtown Taegu. The plaza in front of Taegu Train Station, with its extremes of good and evil, was a microcosm of a nation in transition. There were gangsters extorting money from peddlers, street thugs exacting "protection" fees out of the tiny stores built inside the walls, pimps beating up frail teenage prostitutes, small-time merchants selling teddy bears and stuffed animals on carts, errand boys carrying trays of fried vegetables, elderly women roasting chestnuts and corn on a round metal tube over burning coal briquettes, and young men in soiled T-shirts cutting thick chunks of hard toffee into knuckle-sized pieces. Each time a train arrived and belched out a load of travelers, prostitutes rushed to accost them, chanting virtually in unison, "It's only a dollar per night!" And whenever parents with small children passed by, the food peddlers shouted hyperbolic sales pitches: "If you don't feel you're in heaven after you've eaten three of these roasted chestnuts, I'll give you the money back," or "This toffee is so sweet that you'll miss it in your grave."

There were rich people, too, whose pants and skirts cost more than the yearly earnings of all the food sellers combined. Some carried their poodles and Chihuahuas in their arms, with packets of choice dog food containing roast beef, boiled peanuts, and fried fish. A few wore knee-high leather boots on a burning summer night just to show off; their shoes alone would have cost the equivalent of my father's monthly salary. I wondered, with the vague, inarticulate questioning of a seven-year-old, why on earth some were blessed with so much money and others cursed with so little.

I imagined gangsters abducting struggling merchants and putting knives under their chins. "Park Chung Hee is working to get rid of the organized crime and street bullies to restore the so-to-speak order in this country, but what an irony! He is the godfather of a mafia himself," I remembered Father saying to my brothers. "He took over Syngman Rhee's regime, and now he wants to clean up the mafia. Only a mafia knows how another mafia operates and can figure out how to wipe it out. In a couple years, most likely, we won't see gangsters on the street anymore. They'll have to either leave Korea or go underground. But until then we'll see them threatening poor people in the back streets. They'll wield their knives on the powerless, leaving the powerful alone to their big-time theft."

It was 1962, nine years after the Korean War had ended and a year after Park Chung Hee had come to power through a military coup d'état. After ousting a democratically elected president and his cabinet, Park seized the country and reignited the war for the same arbitrary dictatorship. Like his predecessor, he kidnapped, assassinated, tortured, and imprisoned anyone who dared to voice disagreement, but the brutality during his regime reached a new level. In addition to a strong national security and devout anticommunism, which had been Syngman Rhee's pretext for unmitigated murder, Park promised a rich country and a bright political future for Korea as a global player. He also promised a society operated by law alone, a nation of perfect order where citizens would volunteer to obey the authorities.

Park turned out to be an effective ruler in a way, fulfilling his promise to bring the country out of postwar poverty, building the foundation for the industry that made Korea the seventh largest economy in the world in the late nineties. In all fairness, it was partly he who expedited the process of democratization in South Korea, if not quite in the way we might have hoped. Thanks to the absolute power he exercised, the country's economic groundwork was laid out quickly and became one of the most efficient forces in generating the politically democratic system. For example, Park made it possible for most middle-class Koreans in 2004 to consider a brand new Hyundai Sonata a necessity. In 1962, before his overhaul, cars were a luxury only rich people could afford, and I still remember gawking as a child at a black sedan parked at the side of the alley behind my neighbor's house. Back then, nobody owned a colorful car; the owners deliberately chose somber colors, afraid to attract attention and provoke resentment.

But the Three Men of the Family knew better. They knew that the law and order Park had promised would be of the sort that Al Capone's Chicago had to endure—a quiet surface masking a crackdown on differing views. "A gangster's wealth," Father would explain to his sons, "is what Park is going to dole out to us. Be prepared to see a whole lot of bloodshed on this land, my boys." Father was soon proven right. Life for the Korean working class was characterized by the highest number of industrial accidents in the world, a total disregard for the workers' rights, shameless exploitation of young girls' and women's labor, forced seizures of private properties, a world record in human rights violations, and the mainstream media's fearful vows of silence.

Hypocrisy ran rife during Park's regime. Certain high-class prostitutes who served rich American customers were granted exemption from the midnight curfew and were praised by the government as patriots for bringing foreign currency into the nation. The foretold magical economic revolution—or the "miracle at the Han River," as Park's regime dubbed it—was created by the people's blood. What I was watching at the age of seven was the violent beginning of this criminal miracle. After Park's death in 1979, historians would speak in consensus: Park had made himself into a god, and if a man who made himself into a god couldn't accomplish that much, it would have been ridiculous indeed. But in 1962, petty thieves still lingered, waiting to be struck down by the Korean Al Capone and his henchmen.

I could very well understand why the rich people—with their two-hundred-dollar suits and three-hundred-dollar dresses—looked so proud and righteous, and why the owners of the fruit stands and the old women roasting the chestnuts and corn were so anxious and fearful. The former didn't have to worry about being harassed by organized crime, while the latter was always on edge. With no Robin Hood, their only hope was the increasing weight of the change in their pouches, and part of this had to go toward "protection" fees. With a child's instinct, I sympathized with these petty merchants who hungered for a fuller stomach and a better tomorrow. I, too, felt hunger at the moment, coveting one of those yams on the coal briquette. My stomach growled.

In front of the station, two uniformed police officers strolled by with batons and notepads in hand. All the peddlers bowed deeply, while a shoeshine boy whose little shop was propped up at the entrance of an alley yelled out an offer to shine the officers' shoes for free. Some police officers accepted—or rather extorted—bribes from these paupers, working in covert allegiance with organized crime and common thieves.

There were always dozens of hoodlums hanging around in the plaza, never to be arrested by the corrupt cops. These hoodlums, posing as free escorts hired by the city, preyed upon gullible-looking old men and women who had just arrived in the city and took them to shady ghetto inns. There, they robbed the newcomers of everything, including the chewing gum in their mouths, to use a Korean idiom. The scenario was so familiar that the eyewitnesses in front of the station just laughed, silently wishing for the victims' safe return from the rather surprising journey. I found myself laughing, too, as one of the thieves kindly guided an old man in a traditional Korean costume, cooing, "You must be tired, so I'll take you to a fine hotel where you can crash after a great dinner. Let me be your son tonight."

But the oddest thing I saw was a Buddhist monk hitting his *moktak*, his chanting instrument, on the sidewalk. He was sitting in the lotus position, his eyes unmoving and his back as straight as a concrete wall, facing a short birch tree planted like a little island in the middle of the paved road. Beside him, an elderly woman with a wrinkled dark-brown face squatted on a low stool with a plastic basin, hoping to earn a few dollars for the dried brackens, short flowering plants eaten in stir-fry. It was hard to tell why the monk was there, but one thing seemed clear: he couldn't help any of the sinners on the street. Didn't he know I was resisting an impulse to steal a fistful of those shining coins from his paper box, where a few generous believers had thrown their change? Even at seven, I felt pity for him, and for the beggars and prostitutes around him. I longed for a world where no priest would have to sit on a straw mat on the ground.

My Little Dog

WHEN THE CROWDS OF THE NIGHT BEGAN TO DISPERSE AND THE LIGHTS started to thin out, fear replaced my dream for adventure. The curfew was drawing near and I couldn't tell where I was. My plan had been to walk along the Central Boulevard, the mile-long main avenue running through the center of the downtown, but I had lost my sense of geography while absorbed in scrutinizing the street. It seemed I had come so far that I would have to walk all night to get back, although I'd strayed only a mile or so from home.

Three drunken men approached. One hollered, "Hey, kiddo, hurry back to your parents. There's no bed for you out here." "I can spread myself for her, hee-hee-hee," another man giggled. They all smirked and stumbled on, dropping curious glances at me. Their wives, I thought, were probably awake past midnight seven days a week, used to waiting for their brute husbands with bowls of hot, spicy beef soup and steamed rice to wash the alcohol out of their systems.

According to Mother, Father was a gentleman among gentlemen compared to these men. Although he occasionally complained about her cooking, he never—literally *never*—became involved in a compromising situation, and he never visited the bars where teenage girls called "delicious chicks" wore miniskirts and served men potent drinks. Father, in fact, was a total abstainer. "His father was a heavy drinker and ruined his family," Mother told me once. "He doesn't want to repeat his mistake."

Me in the doorstep of my childhood home.

A harmless-looking old man was coming toward me from the opposite direction, but I didn't dare to ask him for directions. I was afraid that if he knew I was lost, he might try to pick me up and sell me to a pimp. I had heard about girls—hundreds of them—being kidnapped and taken to secret places, never to be returned to their families. Even when they were found by the police, they didn't want to go home, afraid that they might be disowned. I was aware, even as a seven-year-old, that men wanted to marry virgins, that a man never married a prostitute, and that once a prostitute, a woman was forever a prostitute.

I sat beside a dumpster in a narrow alley between packed rows of houses. Nobody could see me. The odor from the trash, the flies feeding upon it, the mosquitoes swarming around me were too much. At first I sobbed quietly, for fear of being heard by a dog and causing him to bark. But ever the slave to my stomach, when another wave of hunger came over me, I abandoned my fear of discovery and started to screech. I was frightened by my own cry echoing off the still walls of the houses, "Help, help me!" After a while, an elderly woman opened the gate of her house and stuck her head out to ask, "Are you lost, child?" I managed to gasp, "I . . . want to go . . . home!"

When she took me into her house and offered me rice and vegetable soup, I saw the bunch of mushed grapes in my hands for the first time since I had left my house. I had been carrying it like a chalice, with both hands pressed against my chest. The grapes were smeared on my blouse, crushed into clouds of mucus. But I shook my head when the old lady suggested I throw them out in a trashcan and change into a clean top.

"You can't eat them anymore, child," she coaxed, concerned but amused. "Your parents wouldn't want to see you dirty like this. They're coming soon to pick you up." I said nothing, and let my head drop. She handed me an old newspaper to put the mushed fruit on. "Eat first. You must be starving."

I picked up the spoon and chopsticks with stained hands and started to eat. The old woman went over to another room, where her grandsons were sleeping, to unravel the ends of the mosquito nets tangled in between their legs. Then she came back to watch me eat, to smile at my voracious appetite and to bring me a second bowl of rice and more soup.

"When's my mother coming?" I asked.

"Soon, child, soon. I told the night patrolmen on this block to drive over to your house and tell your mom and dad that you are here and safe. Since you don't have a phone, the men had to go to your house." How I wished we had a phone! I had never resented my parents so much for being poor as I did at that moment in a stranger's house. "You've been carrying the grapes all night along. You are a strong girl. If you carry your life hopes the way you've carried those grapes tonight, you will be bound for success." Seeing my frozen face thawing into a faint smile, she inquired, "How did you get those grapes?"

"I didn't steal them from a store!" I declared. Against her soft laugh, my voice was so loud that it seemed to rip my ears apart. "I stole them from my father!"

I told her how I grabbed the biggest bunch, ran to the gate of the house, and was slapped in the face by Mother and cursed by Grandmother. I told her how Big Brother, Less Big Brother, and Big Sister quietly listened to the sound of their heinous Little Sister being punished. I became a volcano of words. By *saying* I had stolen the grapes from Father, I realized what I had done for the first time.

"Your mother loves you very much," the old woman told me. "She didn't eat any of the grapes to give you her share."

"She loves my brothers more than me!"

"Someday, you'll see how much she loves you."

She closed her eyes and started to pray, "Lord, you brought this child to me tonight. Please let her see how much her family loves her and how much she loves them. Please open her eyes toward You and lead her to use her words for love, Lord!"

Exhausted, I fell asleep on the floor, waiting for my parents. When I woke up, I felt someone shaking my shoulders gently and saw Mother's face, smeared with tears. She was sobbing convulsively, and I was surprised.

"I'll buy you a bunch of grapes as big as your face tomorrow," she cried.

"Let's go." Father tried to be curt. He wasn't weeping, but his eyes were red. As he squatted down on the floor to pick me up on his back, Mother said to the old woman, "I don't know how to pay you back. You found my child."

"She will find *you* someday. The Lord will see to it." She handed Mother the grapes wrapped in old newspaper.

Sitting on Father's back, my arms wrapped around his neck, it took only half an hour to get to our house; I hadn't gone far at all. "A flea can't jump too far," Koreans often say. "No matter how far it jumps, it still is a flea."

When Father dropped me on the floor of the living room, Grandmother was awake. To my surprise, her eyes were red with tears. She stretched her arms wide toward me. "Come here, my little dog."

But I didn't go to her. All I could remember was that I wasn't a boy.

"What do you want to do with your grapes?" Mother asked.

"Throw them out," Father ordered. As I shook my head, he frowned for a moment, but then suddenly roared into laughter. "You are my girl, indeed! You have a bulldog's teeth!" Turning to

Mother, he said, "Why don't you spread them for her in the sunlight on the cement rack beside the water pump? Leave them there until they turn into raisins and give them to her."

Mother and Grandmother laughed as well. "She's going to be a fighter," Grandmother said. "She's my little dog."

Mother took the grapes from me and went outside to the water pump. When she came back, I could hear her whisper to Father, "Do you think your second daughter will become somebody? That old Christian lady thought so."

"If her tenacity is combined with a decent brain, she will," Father whispered back. "I'm sorry she's not a boy."

"If you look at the way the world is changing, a girl might make it as well as a boy."

"I wish I weren't paying so much for what I did as a young man. If I were in a better position, I might have a lot more money by now to give the girls what they want. As it is, I can't even give the boys what they want," he groaned.

"Once Park Chung Hee gets out of power, things may change."

Father was silent. Even cats and dogs knew Park wasn't going to be leaving the Presidential House except as a corpse. Father changed the subject, laughing in a falsetto to show he was done with serious topics. "Well, we met a good Christian, didn't we?"

"She said she'll pray for your little girl." Mother, too, turned chatty. "She gave me an idea."

The following Sunday morning, Mother gathered all the children in her room. She had bought a mountain of Beggar Moons, cheap cookies that came packed in long, thin, coarse cardboard and loaded side by side in a bulky hemp bag. Each bag, containing a dozen rolls of seventeen cookies, was less than a dollar fifty, much cheaper than a tiny bunch of grapes, so cheap nobody had to be careful about dropping crumbs on the table. They were called Beggar Moons because even beggars could afford to throw them out when they were tired of them. Shaped like a two-inch full moon, they were light brown and flat on top, paper-thin and unsweetened. One ate them to stay alive, to stuff one's empty stomach between meals. Nevertheless, they were cookies, and children were fond of them.

I vividly recall sitting in a circle with Mother and my siblings, my eyes fixed on the cardboard pack and my hands clutching the edge of the round table. I had been appointed by Mother as the official cookie distributor, and was waiting to divide them equally among us. Fearful that I might err and give someone the wrong number, I counted the cookies over and over again, creating little heaps on the table. "You can see she has a two-digit IQ," Less Big Brother grunted. "It's taking her forever to count."

"Hurry, hurry," Big Brother growled at me.

But I didn't hurry.

"I think you've got the right numbers," Mother said, ever patient. "Four for each. You can keep that extra piece for yourself."

"No, the extra is for her Big Brother," Grandmother snarled, but Mother silenced her with a frown.

"Come on!" Less Big Brother threatened again. "Mom's not going to let you divide the cookies again if you drag it on this long."

Afraid of his fist, I put four pieces on four different spots on the table, counting each share carefully for the last time. They began to eat immediately, but I was busy cutting the extra piece into four tiny pieces.

"Look how greedy she is!" Big Brother sneered. "She doesn't want to give that one piece to anyone. She has to go through all that trouble cutting it apart. It's going to be smashed." I ignored him, and managed to cut it in four perfectly even pieces without breaking a corner or dropping any crumbs.

"Astonishing!" Big Sister exclaimed. "She could break those little cold pills of mine in four easy pieces with her naked fingers."

"Eat them. She cut them for you." Mother laughed, a hearty laugh echoed by everyone. My cookie distribution was a comedic show now, and they all looked forward to having me cut the extra piece the following Sunday. That evening, Father called me in to his room. He motioned for me to sit down, his entire face puckered.

"Don't ever let those fingers of yours rust," he advised, trying not to laugh. "But don't use them too much, either."

Many years later, Mother reminded me how Father had massaged my little hands. He wanted to assuage the wrist ache I felt after the miracle I had performed with the cookies. "He took your hand, small enough to be curled up in his like a marble, stretched it, and rubbed it with his fingers. He murmured, 'Hands that'll change the world! My daughter has the hands that'll change the world!'" Decades later, when my hands were tired from too much typing, I'd close my eyes and picture his fingers holding mine, my hands getting smaller and smaller until they would be buried in his like a pair of marbles. How tricky memories are. Until Mother reminded me, I'd forgotten how the cookie ritual had lasted six months, and how often Father had held my hands. Why is it we remember cruelty and heartache, but find it so easy to forget love?

When I was very young, a nameless old woman, a fish peddler who used to come to our house to sell what was left in her plastic basket, once told me, "You are loved plenty, I can tell. An unloved child doesn't grow tall, but love made you grow tall." How long it took me to see this simple truth! My own brain cheated me into seeing only the bad and none of the good.

Love Thy Enemy, They Say

I WAS THANKFUL FOR THE GOOD OLD CHRISTIAN WOMAN WHO TOOK me in and inspired Mother to create the cookie ritual. But I had mixed feelings about Christians in general. Father had always condemned Christians in Korea, calling them toadies for Syngman Rhee and Park Chung Hee, the dictators in South Korea, and lackeys for the "Yankee bastards" who supported them. He would lecture his sons, "It's the Catholic Church the French brought to Vietnam that paved the road for the Americans. Christians work for the big guys."

I learned most of the things a child wasn't supposed to know from eavesdropping on conversations among the Three Men of the Family. I would listen as they were talking amongst themselves at the dinner table or discussing the North Korean radio news, the one thing able to infiltrate South Korea over the DMZ. With my ears pressed against the thin wall of my room, I could hear the fierce voices of North Korean newswomen condemning "the South Korean puppets for Park Chung Hee and his ilk, servants of the American imperialists." The "big noses" (Americans) were crafty, Koreans who flattered "big noses" were scum, and Christians were the worst scum among all of these flatterers.

It was the memory of the good old Christian woman—the woman who wrapped my torn grapes in an old newspaper—that kept me from being rude to the Christian missionaries who occasionally came to our house to try to convince us of their God, who they said would

My father as a young man in his study.

eventually destroy all the nonbelievers on the day of judgment. I also kept myself silent in front of two young Mormon missionaries. On a blazing summer day when the trees were sweating from heat, these young men came to our house in black suits and navy blue bow ties. Even to a child, it seemed strange that they should be wearing black suits in burning hot weather. With their sky blue eyes and corn-silk hair, they frightened my two-year-old Little Sister so much she couldn't stop crying.

"God will forgive you if you change your mind now and prepare to enter his heaven," one said from his trance of over-rehearsed evangelism.

Mother smiled, tossing Little Sister lightly up and down in her arms. She was too nice to ask them to leave. "My husband lived in America for a couple years and told me a lot about your country." Mother somehow couldn't dissociate Christianity from America. "He said it's a big country full of generous, kind people."

They nodded. "It's God's blessing," the other said. I couldn't tell them apart; they both looked like Jesus in the paintings I had seen.

"He has been corresponding with a professor of his for ten years, since he came back to Korea. His name is John Ellison, and now he is teaching at a university in Florida." John Ellison was the kind professor who took Father's poor English into account and gave him a generous grade. His wife once asked Father to cut a huge watermelon at a party. "It was an honor to be picked by her among all those men present," Father would reminisce every time he ate a slice of watermelon.

"The Lord was directing that professor," one of the men said. They sat on the floor like Koreans, their legs folded, speaking fluent Korean with Mother. They didn't seem to be bothered by the smell of the kimchi she had just made and left in the corner of the living room to let sour.

"My husband would very much like to go back to America."

"The Lord will see to it, I'm sure."

"Bring two glasses of water for them, will you?" Mother ordered me, setting the electric fan in their direction.

I went to the kitchen reluctantly, wishing they would leave. I was disappointed with Mother, who didn't have the gumption to say good-bye to them. I deliberated what to do, and came back with two glasses of water on a tray that I thumped down on the floor. Water spilled from one of the glasses and soaked the pants of one of the men.

"Behave yourself, child," Mother cried, picking up the glass. Little Sister's cry receded into a convulsive, feeble sob.

"That's okay," the man with the wet knee said in haste. "The girl has spunk. I like her." I stared at him with all the antagonism I could marshal, but he gazed back with engaging curiosity rather than with disapproval.

"You make my Little Sister cry." I spoke furiously. "The Lord wants you to leave, don't you see?"

"I believe so," the other man agreed. I was afraid that he might call me the devil's child, but he, too, smiled at me. Were they flattering Mother and me so that we would convert? Why were they suddenly nice to me after talking about the heathens who will end up burning in hell?

"I am terribly sorry." Mother asked them to leave by standing up with the baby in her arms.

"Your daughter will see the Lord someday," the man with the wet knee prophesied quietly. "When she sees Him, He will give her more than He ever has to anyone who once refused to accept Him."

It was always strangers who spoke well of me and who foresaw a promising future my family never seemed to see. All the more, I felt puzzled by America, a country where the "Jesus devils" and the folks who recognized my potential cohabited in an infinite continent. It seemed a formidable tiger with a boundless stomach. I wanted to be with those who looked just like the men I spilled water on, and to live in houses just like theirs.

In 1963, I was too young to understand that my ambivalence toward Christians was deeply rooted in the Koreans' collective experience of Christianity. Christianity was a historical force responsible for many scars on our national psyche, a perpetuator of the right-wing dictatorship in South Korea and massive-scale conflicts in the Korean Peninsula before, during, and after the Korean War.

In October 1950, the UN army was advancing north. In Sinchon, a division of the North Korean army arrested and shot a number of Christian leaders, whom they suspected of being spies for the United States. To retaliate, the Christian youths seized the town as soon as the UN army marched into the city. According to North Korean sources, Korean Christians tortured, raped, and slaughtered thirty-five thousand civilians, some of whom were organizers and agitators for the Communist Party, but many of whom were women and children. To the best of our knowledge, U.S. troops did not participate in this violence, although the United States did have supreme command over both UN and South Korean forces, and it is possible they turned a blind eye.

Of course, we will never know the whole truth about what happened at Sinchon; American sources have their politicized version of events, and South Koreans theirs. The North Koreans of course have theirs, since the horror happened in North Korea, but how many people can ever travel to North Korea to verify or research the facts? The truth will remain shrouded in mystery, at least for the near future, since North Korea has done such a good job of exaggerating it, and the United States and South Korea have done such a good job of hiding it. Thirty-five thousand murdered might be an overstatement, given the fact that the town's population was a little over a hundred thousand, but the town was decimated. At the time it occurred, the soon-to-be-forgotten holocaust was shocking enough to catch Pablo Picasso's attention—he painted *Massacre in Korea* in 1951.

It wasn't until the year 2003, however—fifty-three years after the event, and fourteen years after Father's death—that the magnitude of violence was widely acknowledged. Because of the right-wing dictators' suppression of information, the people of South Korea were kept in the dark about what historians would call the Sinchon Holocaust.

"It is true that the communists started the killings, but the retaliation was on a whole different level," Mother told me, shaking her head. "Hundreds of innocent Sinchon residents were locked in a bomb shelter and burned alive. The bomb shelter still stands in Sinchon as it was in 1950, preserved as a memorial."

Mother and I watched the story unfold in 2003 with sadness but not shock. Horrific as it was, Sinchon came as no real surprise to people of Mother's generation. Christians and communists in North Korea had been fighting like mortal foes for a long time before it boiled over.

"It wasn't just the communists who disliked the Christians," Mother continued, an angry edge in her voice. "Most Koreans who were aware of what was going on in the Korean Peninsula at that time found it difficult to like them."

To understand Sinchon, one must understand the history of Christianity in Korea. Korea was at once blessed and cursed by Christianity, passionate in both embracing and rejecting it. In the nineteenth century, Christian missionaries from the West, most from the United States, brought their particular brands of science, medicine, and technology to Korea, where they found a small but mushrooming army of zealous converts. In the missionaries' philosophies, modernization through scientific advances was wrapped up together with belief in the Christian god, and the new Korean adherents saw this path as a means of modernizing their country to keep it abreast of global developments.

With the Christian god and the philosophies of his white adherents came a complete rejection of traditional Korean values, including the Confucian patriarchy that built our family structures, the Buddhism we called upon for birth, death, and wedding rituals, and the ancient shamanism we respected for protecting the living and communicating with the dead. Christians denigrated ancestor worship—perhaps the most sacred Korean tradition, at the intersection of Buddhist and Confucian traditions—by deeming it a superstition. Some went as far as to condemn it as devil worship.

Of course, there were certain social advances that could not have been made under the traditional Korean system—feminism is one of the best and most contentious examples—and even non- and anti-Christian Koreans acknowledge the contributions Christians made toward positive social change. But in the meantime, the Christian converts attacked everything, good and bad, that Koreans held dear. It is no surprise they inspired intense ambivalence among those who did not convert.

"Your father gave two thumbs up to the Christian missionaries and their Korean loyalists," Mother told me. "They built schools and hospitals for us, the beginnings of the best we've got. But they did it with such arrogance. They condemned what we cherished." Mother shook her head. "You cannot imagine their intolerance for their former culture. Your father used to say, 'Political violence is one thing, and cultural violence is another. The Christians committed both in this country.'"

Sinchon was exemplary of the clash between capitalism and socialism, between the two warring ideologies in the Korean Peninsula. Simply put, it was a bloody combat between landowners and sharecroppers, between the rich who had absorbed the concept of private property from the Christian missionaries and the poor who had accepted the commuist belief of community land ownership. The Christian missionaries had pitched their power base by approaching the most privileged upper class in Korea, so the majority of Christian converts were landowners. In North Korea, where the communist government initiated a sweeping land reform, landowners were justly afraid. They were condemned and sometimes unfairly persecuted by the Communist Party.

As a result, some North Korean landowners used Christianity to guard their self-interest and preserve their economic supremacy. They cast themselves as Christian warriors fighting the Communist Party's atheism, but the root reason for their crusade was landownership. In Sinchon, Christianity became as wicked a tool as communism.

Christianity arrived in Korea strapped to Uncle Sam's back, and stayed, holding onto his coattail. Christians put themselves under the tutelage of the Americans who actively supported the right-wing dictators in South Korea. Christians in South Korea remained the most vocal force for blind anticommunism. They provided the biggest boost for the right-wing dictators, who used the red scare as an excuse to consolidate their power. Of course, although they didn't change the tide of public opinion, there were some Christians who participated in the campaign for a peaceful reunification of the Korean Peninsula. They even risked going to prison. Moon Ik Hwan, a minister whom Father used to admire very much, spent the last two decades of his life in solitary confinement. He had been to North Korea in an effort to persuade the two states to talk. Unfortunately, individuals like him were only a fraction of the Christian population, which comprised an active and conservative political force.

"Maybe they are still traumatized by what happened in

Sinchon," I suggested. "For them, it would be impossible to forget that the communists started the killing."

"But the Christians' revenge seems to have been on a much bigger scale," Mother replied. "What is even more shocking is that the U.S. Army is suspected of having been involved. There is no evidence, but there might have been tacit sanction from the U.S. Army, which controlled everything during the war. The Americans held the key for every operation, no matter how small."

"Christians say 'Love they enemy,'" I remarked. "They were even worse than the communists."

Mother nodded. "They were, and that's why progressive Christians, who are fighting for democratization and peace talks between the North and South, are frustrated with their fellow Christians, who volunteered for decades to serve as toadies for the right-wing dictators and still support the Cold War factions in South Korea. Since 1992, we've had democratically elected civilian governments, so they don't have the same clout they used to have. But their Cold War voice is still loud."

"They're behind the times."

"There's no way one can measure the degree of their intolerance." Mother paused, struggling to keep her rising voice down. We Koreans have cherished our ancestor worship for six centuries, but some of them call it 'devil worship.'" Most of them believe it should be condemned. To them, even Buddhism, Korea's number one religion for two thousand years, is a superstition."

"And the ones who disagree are shunned by the majority." I knew that for these progressive Christians, life in Korea must have been challenging. "I wouldn't be surprised if they harbor the same ambivalence Father felt toward the United States. How could they not feel troubled by the fact that their religion came to us via the American oppressors?"

Mother and I have spoken often of this strange history, of how the United States, supposed champions of democracy, set up and boosted the right-wing dictators in Korea. It was all done under the guise of protecting the world from the spread of communism, although some of the dictators the United States supported were among the most atrocious and notorious in world history. "The government worked so hard to cover the truth," Mother said. "But your father was so attentive and well-informed. He never gave up thinking critically about these things."

When Mother spoke of Father, I found myself listening with eagerness I had not shown while he was alive. Having left Korea for America immediately after I graduated from college, I spent most of my adult years away from home, and my adult knowledge of Father remained limited to bits and pieces. I finally broached the subject of Father with Mother, who became his chief storyteller, a decipherer who would spell out the intricate parts of his life, the pieces that had made him who he was. As the historian who made me *remember*, Mother was the one who planted in me the passion to speak the truth to the world. If Father was the can of oil in a lamp, she was the book of matches, and I became the catalyst striking the matches into the oil to bring the two to light.

As a preteen, I couldn't hear anything but confusing dissonance in Father's words about Americans and Christians. The "Yankee bastards" who wreaked so much havoc upon my country didn't seem to be the same as the kind professors who had shown him the bright, caring side of Americans and the warm Christian lady who had invited me in to her house. How enchanted I was by the tolerance and generosity that made the big country so magical, and how disturbed I was by the brute military power that made it so destructive! I wished I could do something to persuade the Americans, to convince them to exercise their might for the innocents instead of against them. I longed to go to America to talk to its people.

But I knew I couldn't. Only girls from rich families could go to America to study, and my family wasn't rich. Also, I felt a little scared. From what my brothers told me, Korean women who went to America were corrupted by loose, beer-drinking American women and eventually became whores for the Yankee bastards. Promiscuous women who couldn't find husbands in Korea, my brothers told me, were sent to America by their parents to cover up the family shame.

What discouraged me the most, however, was Father's story about the five Korean women who had studied with him in America. Now, twenty years later, four of them were still single in their forties, and the fifth was married to a wife-beater. All of them, according to Father, lived lonely, miserable lives, full of regrets about having received so much higher education that they intimidated men. "Women who 'drink the American water' for too long are the most wretched lot on earth," he would sigh. "They don't enjoy a woman's life. They live with nothing but books! What a stupid waste! When they marry, they don't learn how to be good wives, and they provoke their husbands to use a whip. Mind you, girl, don't be too smart."

At the same time, it was Father who constantly inspired my dreams of going to America. Watching the American Forces Korean Network (AFKN) news on TV, he would turn to me and ask, "You think someday you'll be able to understand every word of the news on American TV?" Being in grade school, I didn't even know the English alphabet, but he would go on, his eyes shimmering, "One of these days, you're going to beat me with your English. I'm sure of it." He confused me. He knew that without "drinking the American water," it would be impossible for me to reach that level of command of English. Was he wishing I would fulfill what seemed to be an unnatural destiny for a woman?

Peppers

~ ❦

I HATED LIVING IN MY HOUSE.

One day, after we'd each received our fair share of cookies, Less Big Brother wrenched my arm to snatch my share away, I screamed and cried, looking at Mother for help. But she just turned away and said sharply, "Why don't you eat them faster? Because you keep them so long, you end up inviting trouble."

After that, I ran from home whenever I had cookies, clutching them tightly until they were reduced to tiny fragments. I would squat down beside a dumpster on a dead end or lean against the wall of a stranger's house to chew them. My favorite hiding place was under a bridge where I would listen to old, noisy cars wheezing by above me.

One freezing winter day, I was escaping to consume my cookies in peace when I came across a group of boys clustered under the bridge, in one of my usual snacking spots. A thin layer of ice floated on the water burbling underneath. The stream was named Crystal Waters and had once been famous for being clean and pure, but the waters now were pitch black with pollution. As I approached the boys and tried to make sense of their flurry of activity, I realized they were huddled around a crying naked baby, which had apparently been abandoned under the bridge, not an altogether uncommon occurrence at that time. The boys were stoning the crying infant to death.

I didn't even know that I was horrified. I just observed, munching the crumbs, hearing the boys' whoops and yells and the metallic drone of the cars on the bridge, wincing occasionally at the baby's

Here I am surrounded by my older siblings. From left to right, Big Brother, Big Sister, me, a boy cousin, and Less Big Brother.

piercing cries. The attackers, children themselves, sounded like dogs yelping over a piece of meat, and I felt glad they weren't interested in robbing me of my cookies.

It occurred to me to imagine what the woman who dumped her baby must have been like. "An unmarried woman who gets pregnant will be scourged by the gods," Grandmother always told me. I knew to disparage women who hung around with men before they got married. "If you are smart, you'll be able to chase boys off," Grandmother would say. "Boys leave smart girls alone. The best way to avoid nature's punishment on a loose girl is not to try to look pretty." I understood that if I went out with boys, I would get pregnant and have to throw my baby beside a frozen river, where he'd be stoned to death.

While I licked the last residue of cookie powder off of my palm, the baby's nasal gasp made the same shooing, gurgling sound of a stream rushing into the hole of a sewer. A map of blood covered his face; his tiny penis, curled like a half moon over his pale groin, was the only zone untouched by the red.

"See his fucking pepper!" one of the boys shouted. "Seems like it's still good, hee-hee-hee."

"Let him take a piece of his pepper off for you!" another boy giggled. He was referring to a game older women played with little boys. First, the boys would pull their pants down and show off their "peppers," then stroke their genitals with their hands and let the women kiss their palms to breathe in—that is, worship—the phallic energy transmitted through the contact.

"Yeah, yeah!" the other boys yelped.

"Wait," a boy with a high-pitched voice shrilled, "we need a woman to do that kind of stuff! Men don't do that!" Then, he turned around and looked at me with an ear-to-ear grin that made his eyes pucker, and all the boys stared at me, their eyes teeming with the sheen of malicious joy.

"I'd better drag her here," a boy with an orange wool hat declared. "You know how women are. You have to push them to make them admit they want it." He strode toward me through the gravel.

"Get her, yeah!!" The boys clapped their hands in glee. For a moment I was paralyzed with fear.

But I surprised myself by regaining control of my legs and running up the slope to the levee as fast as the wind. I didn't know how close behind the boy was, but when I got on to the flat part of the levee, I could hear him turn back and holler something to the others. As a broad, busy street flashed up in front of me, they fell completely out of earshot. I squatted down on my feet, with my back on an electricity pole near the traffic lights, wiping the cold sweat of my palms on my pants. The soot from buses made my eyes itch, and closing them, I decided to wait until my heart stopped pounding.

A scene I had only vaguely remembered floated to the surface of my memory. It was the previous summer, and Mother's elderly cousin, whom we called Big Aunt, had come by on her way home from the market where she sold fabric. "I just adore your little proof of manhood," she'd told Less Big Brother. "Now that you're nine years old, you must have a good size one. You ought to feel honored that I wish to enjoy a pepper game with you." Big Aunt was laughing, her raucous voice loud enough to shake the walls of the room.

"If you don't stop, I will kill you." Less Big Brother was livid, his lips trembling with shame and his eyes aflame with anger.

"He thinks he's not a kid anymore," Mother guffawed.

"If you're not a kid anymore, all the more reason to show it to me," Big Aunt persisted.

Less Big Brother's face had turned purple from rage. Like an arrow, he darted out of the room and came back with an ax in his hand, its blade pointed toward Big Aunt. Mother let out a scream and clung to one of his legs to keep him from moving. "Get out of the room! Hurry!" she shouted to Big Aunt.

Big Aunt looked startled but did not budge. She cackled, "You let me taste your pepper a year ago. You're only one year older and it's no longer delicious?"

Less Big Brother tried to wrench his leg from Mother's grip. Scared for my life, I opened the door to run out.

But Mother cried to me, "Hey, you, get his other leg! Grab it!"

"Grab his arms and take his ax away!" Big Aunt thundered. "He's not getting out of here until I get a piece of his pepper."

A sick feeling came over me. I wanted to stick a chunk of glass in her mouth. Instead, I swooped upon her and sank my teeth into her shoulder, trying to strangle her with my hands. Even her scream was coarse, I thought, and her fingers crude, entangled with mine on her neck.

"Drop the ax," Mother pleaded with Less Big Brother. She was sweating, her head pushed against his back, her arms clenching his thighs. She didn't move until Less Big Brother dropped his arm and lay the ax flat on the floor, panting.

"Take the ax back to the basement," Mother ordered.

Picking up the ax, breathing loudly, Less Big Brother seemed like a crazy old man who had just committed a murder and was leaving the scene of the crime with the weapon tucked at his side.

"What a ferocious little bitch!" Big Aunt exclaimed, coughing, after I released my arms and teeth. "I can't believe she's only six. What do you feed her?"

"When I was pregnant with her, my stomach was twice as big as it should have been," Mother said. "I felt so heavy that I had to eat twice as much kimchi as usual to keep myself awake, and all that spice and garlic got into her head to make her such a tenacious little bugger."

"When my girls get pregnant, I'll tell them to eat tons of kimchi. They'll all have peppy little fighters like yours!" Big Aunt roared with laughter, then groaned. Mother unbuttoned her blouse, found my teeth marks on her shoulder, and glared at me. "I told you never to lay your hands on an adult."

Mother seemed ready to strike me, but Big Aunt, to my surprise, growled at me with a touch of affection, "Get out of here before she beats the hell out of you. Don't lose your spunk!"

"Are you okay, child?" A voice woke me from the reverie. A police officer was standing in front of me by the electricity pole.

"I'm fine." I struggled to sound cheerful.

"Go home for dinner. Mommy's waiting for her little girl." He left, whistling.

I walked home like a zombie, my palms in a cold sweat, my nerves jangling. Less Big Brother's ax, Big Aunt's smirk, Mother's hand raised to strike me, the river bank boys' devilish grins, and the map of blood all over the baby's body whirled in my mind like a gruesome kaleidoscope. There was no doubt in my mind that the boys had committed a perfect crime, but I was more disturbed by what would have happened to me had I not succeeded in running away. I pictured what the boys would have forced me into: In my imagination, I knelt on the pebbles, stroking the nearly dead boy's "pepper" with my fingers. I kissed my fingers, breathing the phallic energy in deeply until I couldn't anymore. The boys, human monsters, pressed my shoulders down, exhilarated, and I clenched my teeth. In my mind, I refused to give them the pleasure of beating a girl down to nothing.

A week later, I went back to the scene of the crime, the Crystal River, this time without cookies. I wanted to feel the nightmare all over again, to have it inscribed in my memory one more time. But the baby was gone, and the trail of blood I expected to see was not there. The ice in the river had melted into lacy layers, and the water was pitch black, as if it had swallowed everything that had happened there.

Where did they throw the baby out? I wondered. It was only then that all the questions assailed me. *Should I have called the police? Could I have saved the baby? Why didn't I run to tell people that they were killing him? Shouldn't I have told someone so that they could have buried him somewhere?*

As the guilt was starting to overwhelm me, I could almost hear Grandmother say, "It serves that mother right. Whores and trouble travel together. She deserved to see her baby stoned to death." I imagined the face of a mad woman with disheveled hair in half-torn clothes looming over the dark river. Sex, which I only knew made babies, seemed to be an unspeakable crime. Curiosity and fear, spurred by ignorance, created the murky mystery surrounding the topic among the children of my generation.

After the day at the Crystal River, I started to paint a house whenever I played with my pastels. It was a lovely red home covered with round green leaves growing from vines, and an egg-shaped fishpond, its beautifully carved granite stones displaying the owner's immaculate taste. With rose bushes at one corner and golden-bell trees at another, the garden was filled with flowers of all sizes and tall, luxuriant bushes. In the front, a low wooden fence flanked both sides of the gate, behind which a gravel path led to the entrance, dividing a lush green lawn into a perfect symmetry.

Sometimes I painted the inside of the house. In a sunny room, a man and a woman were lying down together on a cotton mattress, and a dog was watching them attentively with its head cocked, waiting to be invited to sit between them. Through the windows of their rooms, the couple's two children—both of them boys—watched squirrels slide on the electric wires in the back of the house. In the family, sex was sacred and good—completely the opposite of the sordid encounters that would create babies who deserved to be stoned to death. This couple made children whose eyes were so pure that they could suck in all the dirt out of the world. I painted the same house over and over again on cheap notebook paper, experimenting only with colors, never content.

But my house of sex—pure, clean sex—was brought to an abrupt end. One day when I came home from school, I found out that Big Brother had doodled on several pages in my notebook with his magic pen, letting the marks soak through my paintings and blot out the green leaves. The sight of "red tears" in the boys' eyes made tears start to roll down my own cheeks. The debris of my twenty-nine masterpieces—months of my dreams of sacred sex—were scattered. Big Brother had destroyed them all. I knew he had made a mistake, thinking they were no more than my silly experiments. But he had not respected my privacy and I was angry. No matter how insignificant my work seemed to him, it was *mine*. I wanted to stick a knife into his throat, to see red tears sprouting out from his eyes, to let the boys witness their tears in his.

But Big Brother was the oldest son, and nobody dared to cross him. He was the one to whom Father was preparing to pass his family throne, and the one in whose kingdom the rest of us would thrive. His whims were as unavoidable as the air we breathed, and his actions—even the slightest slant of his eyes—were heeded as divine will. When he sneered, "She painted the same house over and over again. She has no imagination," Less Big Brother chimed in, agreeing girls were stupid, and they giggled and chuckled as my face turning ashen with shame and anger.

I knew going to Mother to report Big Brother's "crime" would be of less than no use. I could predict her scolding me, "Why didn't you hide the notebook in a safe place?" I went to the outhouse and dropped all the paintings in it. The house of clean, pure sex was gone, mixing with mounds of human excrement. But I didn't let go of my thoughts about sex.

Big Brother had a nearly mystical power over me. I was amazed by the glow of his eyes. They were the eyes of a warrior who, had he been born a thousand years before, would have united kingdoms and conquered nations. Envying him, I looked hard into the mirror, striving to imitate the expression of his eyes. My big, round eyes gave me the look of a scared rabbit, but after much work I produced his lancing gaze. I felt electrified, but nobody noticed me. This new ability was my secret, and with it I felt I could carry anything from a feather to a steel mountain.

Although he was often cruel to me, I would have defended Big Brother to the death. I once took on a neighbor girl to defend his honor; one day she and I were playing on the seesaw together when she saw him walking back from school. "Your brother looks like a yam," she said.

"Yours looks like an eggplant," I fired back.

"An eggplant? If mine looks like an eggplant, at least he doesn't look rotten. But yours looks like a yam eaten by worms."

"A rotten yam still has the color of living flesh, but an eggplant looks like a dead rat." Then I leaped to my feet and ran toward my house, hearing her end of the seesaw thump down on the sand. She chased me and grabbed my ponytail, but I swung back and managed to drag her backward toward her house, with her hands on my hair. I pushed her against the wall, pinching her cheeks with my fingernails until the ribbon on my hair came off in her hands and she released her grip. Snatching the ribbon, I dashed to my house and closed the gate, looking back to stick my tongue out at her.

The truth was, Big Brother's face did look a bit like a yam, but by the wisdom of Korean physiognomy—already familiar to me, as young as I was—he had fine and auspicious features. His face was long, with a broad, sloping forehead and a narrow but round chin, his lean cheeks unmarked by hollow lines. His lips were just the right thinness, not so thin as to damage his masculine energy, but showing he was neither too talkative nor, like thick-lipped people, too reticent. His brows were straight, the ends curving down almost imperceptibly. This indicated he would be a productive man with plenty of novel ideas and inspiring thoughts, all of which he would pursue with a single-minded zeal. The downturn at the ends showed he would be able to accommodate the wills of others, and would make himself into an honest, modest overachiever. I worshipped his face, and thinking about it reminded me of what mattered the most—I had a role model to follow in my family.

But to Big Brother, I was the same old stupid girl. I was too slow to catch his quick tongue, too dull to grasp the meanings of his witty jokes, too selfish to give my share of the cookies to Less Big Brother. To make it worse, I was ugly to him, and being ugly was the most heinous crime a girl could commit. Once, when he was angry that I had accidentally broken some of the new crayons Mother had bought him, he grabbed my neck and pushed me into the wall of his room. He thundered, "You tried them without my permission! A plain-looking girl like you should at least be polite!"

But I was loyal to him. Praying I would be blessed with just a fraction of his excellence, I set my attention on books, hoping the printed letters would creep into my brain. With half his brilliance, my teachers would give me rave reviews and I would enjoy the privilege of some of the fresh vegetables and meat reserved for Big Brother.

Big Brother possessed a steadfast mind, sound judgment, and a reservoir of knowledge astonishing for a boy of fourteen. How natural it was, I thought, for Mother and Father to show preferential treatment for him over Less Big Brother. Undoubtedly, Less Big Brother was as bright as his older brother, but he was bereft of one critical attribute: the discipline to accomplish what he was set out to do. Routinely, he had to be ordered to finish his homework. "Look at your brother," Mother or Father would chide. "He doesn't have to be told to do his homework. Why can't you be like him?"

Less Big Brother in his daily behavior reinforced the preferential love culturally destined for Big Brother, the oldest son. "I couldn't help it," Mother recalled years later. "When your uncles and aunts gave the boys little bills, your Big Brother kept them in his pocket for weeks. He wanted to save them until he would need extra money for school. But your Less Big Brother spent them right away. He bought worthless things like little colorful marbles in a painted metal box because he liked to hear the sound of them rolling. Sometimes he would even buy ice cream cones for his buddies, so that he could enjoy the taste of being a hero for a while."

Whatever their differences, my two brothers were inseparably linked together in my mind, provoking the same spectrum of emotions: fear, adoration, jealousy, resentment. They were buddies, members of the superior gender and bearers of my parents' hopes and expectations. Sharing the same language and aspirations for the future, my brothers were of one mind, comprising a phalanx that filled me with awe. Although Big Brother scolded his little brother for being wasteful and negligent, he nevertheless made it clear that he was fond of him. Less Big Brother always lowered his tail in front of

Big Brother, which demonstrated their almost instinctual kinship toward each other. No wonder I do not remember Big Brother ever defending me from Less Big Brother's cruelty. According to Big Brother, I was willfully disobedient and reckless.

Still, his every word seemed to me to have the ring of divine truth. Even when he was being entirely irrational, he sounded right to me, and I feared being one of those women of whom he staunchly disapproved. To this day, I vividly recall a conversation I overheard when I was about thirteen years old. Big Brother came back from school and declared to Less Big Brother his loathing of the girl who had sat next to him on the bus. "She looked like a mashed potato," he grumbled, lowering the corner of his mouth with disgust.

"I heard an ugly girl has bad karma," Less Big Brother chimed in. "If a man does horrible things in this life, he is born as an ugly girl in his next life because being ugly and being a girl are the worst combination one can ever endure."

"What about pretty, dumb girls?"

"They were professional liars in their previous lives," Less Big Brother said, confident in his knowledge. "In this life, they don't have the brains to lie."

Big Brother chuckled. "How were pretty, smart ones?"

"They were the ones who put honesty above everything else. They make good-looking, intelligent children. I hope you get one of them as a wife."

"But I don't want a short, pretty, smart girl. I prefer a tall, smart, pretty girl."

"You'll get one who was so virtuous in her previous life that she is everything a man wants. She'll be tall, smart, and pretty, I promise."

"But to be dedicated to a man, she shouldn't be too strong." Big Brother turned serious. "I need a woman who'll want things for her man, who believes my business is her business."

"If she's that smart, she'll be able to manage your affairs. She'll be independent, but devoted to you exclusively."

"What about you, my brother?"

At sixteen, Less Big Brother had clearly thought this through. "You know my name is that of a famous emperor during the Tang Dynasty in ancient China who had two hundred wives. Since I share his name, I'm entitled to at least twenty wives. But the law prohibits it, so I'll have scores of girlfriends before I get married."

"What kinds of girls?"

"Pretty and dumb, ugly and intelligent, pretty and smart. There will be a spectrum. For the sake of diversity, I will have fat ones as well as gangly ones, and I won't mind pudgy or athletic ones once in a while. I'll have them all. And when I'm thirty-five, I'll marry a twenty-four-year-old virgin who has never held a man's hand." His face glowed with prospective joy.

I overheard this conversation as a teenager, but since the time I was in grade school I had caught numerous exchanges between Big Brother and Less Big Brother about the "sins" of ugly girls. As a child, I was pained. Neither smart nor pretty, I would have to work hard to do as well as smart girls, and be especially sweet to make up for my lack of beauty. My bad karma, I silently feared, would bring my family and me bad luck, and I would have to pay for all the crimes I had committed in my previous life. In tears, I recalled Grandmother's rueful theory of her own past life. "I was doomed to have a tragic life," she told me, "because in my previous life I was a warrior who raped hundreds of innocent women wherever I went."

I knew that clothes from costly department stores and long, well-nourished hair would help me to look better. But Father didn't make enough money to feed his children, never mind clothe them fashionably, and Mother was too overworked to pay attention to my appearance. Even as a third grader, I sensed that Father, a high school teacher, was without money or prestige, and I was slightly ashamed of his occupation. Even though Mother was constantly supportive and encouraging, I could see he wasn't nearly as illustrious as she presented him to be.

I lived with the fact that I was poor. Every afternoon, I felt sorry for myself as I watched my classmates enjoy fashionable dime jelly candies after lunch, chatting amongst themselves in a cliquish manner. The candy came in a small plastic can the size of my thumb, and I could tell how delicious it was. Watching them greedily dig their tiny spoons into the cans made me salivate. To avoid the sight, I left the classroom to roam around the block surrounding the school, counting my steps one by one, five hundred paces every lunch hour. I convinced myself the cute little plastic can was a trifle that only silly girls indulged in, that I was beyond such foolish luxuries. Being strong enough to feel proud of one's poverty was a virtue, I thought, and anything other than oxygen and three meals a day meant absolutely nothing to me. "Those poor girls," I muttered. "They don't know how to deny themselves sweets. They're going to have rotten teeth."

I feared being reminded how poor we were more than anything else. I tried to stop thinking about the undersized pants I had to wear because Mother couldn't afford to buy me a new pair, or about the TV we didn't have and the embarrassment I felt when I couldn't participate in my classmates' discussions of the most popular shows. I remembered Father once said with a sigh, "If we had more money, we could treat boys and girls equally. We could buy the girls what they want." I could clearly connect our poverty with what had made Big Brother so angry when I touched his stationery: he knew it would be a long time before Mother could buy him another set of pencils if he broke them. She bought him things she couldn't buy me because she didn't have the money for both of us.

Because my family lived in a middle-class neighborhood, we were sent to middle-class schools that were also attended by rich people's children. These children boasted their parents' money with brand-name clothing and shoes, with fancy snacks and stationery that made them envied by everyone. I knew I wasn't one of them, but I convinced myself that I was. I was from a family of fallen nobility, and I wanted to prove it to myself as well as to them. I deserved to wear new and different pants every day, to watch TV on a giant screen, to eat the choicest items on a king's table, and to have my hair curled at a beauty shop. How it tortured me to be told I couldn't be who I thought I was! It was this dissonance that nearly killed me.

At the same time, we weren't extraordinary in our poverty. Although there were some rich children, most of my classmates, just like me, carried roasted locusts and pieces of boiled potato and cabbage, doused only in the cheapest sauces, in their lunch pails. Sharing our lunch in a circle, we would laugh, listening to the sound of our teeth cracking the wiry locust wings. But I was hurt inside, believing I was entitled to the expensive ham and chicken the rich few girls ate. I felt so poor.

Guilt added to my anger. Didn't Mother have to give up her share for the boys because there wasn't enough? Didn't Grandmother tell me she hadn't tasted a single grape all summer because they were too expensive for us? And yet, a year after that summer day when my wish for a boy's portion of grapes had driven me from my house, I would not eat them. I threw out my portion of shriveled grapes even though they were my favorite fruit. This summer, I drifted along the Taegu streets with neither grapes in my hands nor fear in my heart. I was reducing my body to thin air, so I could go anywhere I wanted to go.

As my appetite disappeared, so did the temptation to move my chopsticks over the holy DMZ on the dinner table. I realized that I had not eaten anything all day, but I felt no appetite. I was going to turn into a piece of wind, a stream of white smoke that didn't need pretty clothes and jelly candies. I was going to surpass Mother and Grandmother in self-denial and become in the history of my family a woman as remarkable as my great-great-great-great-great-great grandmother. To keep myself barely alive in the tiger's stomach, I picked at whatever fruit was placed on the table, so long as it wasn't grapes.

"Child, you look sick. Ask your mother to take you to a doctor," my neighbors started to say. It wasn't strange that they noticed how thin and pale I was before Mother, to whom I was invisible. She was too busy worrying that the heat might make my brothers sweat away weight. After trying in vain to tell her about my tiger's stomach, I closed my mouth.

Father, too, was rotting in his own tiger's stomach, a vortex of struggling to feed his family while railing against political persecution and the failures of his government. In 1964, I was only a third grader, and I couldn't understand all the stresses on him. Together, the Three Men of the Family talked about evil men like Syngman Rhee, Park Chung Hee, and the Yankee bastards who supported them. They also talked about good men like Yuh Un Hyung and Kim Ku, patriots who, until they were assassinated or disappeared, did everything in their power to keep the disease of corruption from spreading. Father compared these men in terms of their capacity for either great good or extraordinary evil. I listened to him talk about the tyranny of Syngman Rhee's successor, Park Chung Hee, although many of Father's words were beyond my comprehension. Father encouraged his sons to support the same friends and condemn the same enemies identified by the passionate North Korean woman on the radio, and I felt the impulse to stand up and announce my agreement. As he explained to them why Korea was divided, who were responsible, and how North and South Korea could be reunified, I wanted to comfort him.

Some of the things the Three Men of the Family discussed were personal. Mother's brother and sister were in North Korea, and my parents had been waiting for almost ten years for the moment they would see them again over the demolished DMZ. Occasionally, Mother shed tears when Father mentioned her siblings' names. My uncle and aunt's escape to North Korea was a closely guarded family secret. Another secret I was to keep to myself was that Father had been involved in some kind of political movement with my uncle. If it became public knowledge, it would get him into some serious trouble. Without anyone telling me, I learned I was to remain silent about what I heard. Everyone in the family was carrying their own personal pain; they were all writhing in a tiger's stomach.

*In this picture, I am flanked by a male relative and
a female relative, whose father was killed
by Syngman Rhee's police.*

None of them, however, had the claws to cut the stomach into
pieces and get out. The more wrath Father unloaded on his boys,
the more helpless they seemed, and the longer his rituals of
denouncement lasted, the shorter their tempers became. When
Less Big Brother hit me in the head because I refused to hand him
one of my apples, when Big Brother humiliated me in front of the
entire family by calling me a "dog head," they were acting out the
victimization and frustration they felt toward the villains
abhorred by Father. Being a third grader, I couldn't understand
why I had to become an object of their revenge. The reasons they

gave me—that I was stupid, ugly, greedy, spoiled, disobedient, and rebellious—I tried to accept, but I knew that I didn't deserve that much punishment.

Twenty-six years would pass before I could figure out the details of Father's life, and understand the extent of my brothers' rage. At thirty-five, I finally learned the historical context of their secret conferences over the North Korean radio, and that they had every right to condemn those whom they condemned. The crimes of the right-wing dictators who seized and perpetuated their hegemony through terrorist-style operations—and the crimes of the Americans who led and orchestrated the conspiracy of these dictators—became as clear to me as the shape of a tree in the sun. Because he had once expressed his opposition to the tyrants, Father was buried for the rest of his life, stuck with a job far below his qualifications. At the peak of his youth, his resume was smeared with a black mark, and he was systematically excluded from career opportunities. If allowed to pursue his talents, he would have risen to be the chancellor of a university. But he found himself a high school teacher, underpaid, underappreciated, and surrounded by colleagues and students who couldn't relate to him.

Exiled in His Own Country

HISTORY, AS THEY SAY, IS WRITTEN BY THE WINNERS. BECAUSE OF the suppression and manipulation of historical data, popular impressions of the Korean War are of a one-sided, unprovoked attack by communist North Korea against democratic South Korea, and of the United States marching in to defend the world against the growing threat of communism. The truth, of course, is more complicated, and even more tragic.

It is difficult to sum up the origins of a war—a massive-scale conflict—that was really part of a continuous conflict. In East Asia, the twentieth century was an umbrella of crisis. Moreover, being historically sandwiched between the global crisis of World War II and the political juggernaut of the Vietnam War, the Korean War is typically overlooked by Western historians, and is often referred to as "The Forgotten War." For Koreans, of course, the war is anything but forgotten. It was *the* pivotal moment in Korean history, a blood-soaked calamity that leveled our civilization, killed off a large portion of our population, and split our one nation into two. It was the point at which families were permanently divided, and the reason that people like my mother still don't know—sixty years later—whether their siblings, cousins, and friends are alive, whether they have nieces, nephews, and grandchildren, or whether they will ever have a chance to see their families again during this lifetime.

My father, an idealistic young man.

Where does one begin to attempt to describe a war? In the case of the Korean War, any description can amount to little more than an attempt, since there has been so much political rewriting of state histories on all sides. The surviving histories of the war are, of course, more about perspective than fact. When the war broke out, the ally troops were told they were marching to Korea to drive the evil communists back to where they had come from, to help the innocent South Korean people defend themselves. The soldiers were given to believe the North Korean regime had disobeyed the Korean people's wishes to create a democratic republic and had established a separate renegade state across the 38th parallel. The theory was proliferated that the communists had invaded South Korea in an attempt to reunify the peninsula and to turn the whole country into a state reigned by "red terror."

Since the truth about the origins of the Korean War was deliberately destroyed by North and South Koreans and Americans alike, those of us who wish to know what really happened are left with little besides the oral recounting of those who survived.

It was Mother, as always, who told me the history of the struggle that Father took part in for his people and the high price he was forced to pay for the rest of his life. Listening to her, I could put the pieces together and identify the origins of his shadows. The fragments I held in my memory gradually fell into place like in the puzzle.

To explain where Father's life had begun and ended, Mother started with the posters he had placed on the campus bulletin boards at his university. "The posters said in calligraphy: 'Protest the U.S. military government's dictatorship. Keep Korea for Koreans.' These words summarized the opinions of the overriding majority of the students at Seoul National University (SNU), who were opposed to the U.S. military conspiring with the right-wing terrorist-style dictators in Korea."

In 1945, the year Korea was emancipated from the Japanese occupation, the American government, in an attempt to establish its toady regime in the Korean Peninsula, set up its own military administration in Seoul. Headed by General Hodge, the administration was awarded the power to preside over public affairs in the country, to control, manipulate, and govern the political process through which the future leaders of Korea were to be selected. Naturally, the most vocal opposition to foreign domination of Korea came from the intelligent, politically conscious young men—most of whom attended Seoul National University, then a nest for progressive ideas in Korea.

To seize control of the university and silence the students, General Hodge and his men decided to merge SNU with other colleges and vocational schools in Seoul. They believed that once they consolidated them, they would be able to wield power over all the schools in the capital, and crack down upon the perceived and real dissidents with ease. The U.S. military called this plan the "nationalization" of SNU.

Since the "nationalization," however, was a euphemism for the plot to suppress the outcries against the right-wing totalitarian faction in

Korea, which was being nurtured by the U.S. government, SNU students started to build their own case. When a U.S. Army colonel, Harry B. Ansted, was named to be the chancellor of the consolidated SNU, the students chose a Korean man who had been a resistance leader in Yenan against the Japanese occupation to run against Ansted. Mother explained to me that while the American colonel knew nothing of Korea, let alone anything about running a university, the Korean candidate was thoroughly conversant with his country's needs. His skills as a college administrator were as yet untested, but his track record in the resistance movement was in clear agreement with the students' wishes and principles. He stood for "Korea for Koreans." He would make decisions and choices in the interests of his country.

That he was on the left politically didn't upset the students. In 1945, most bright, well-educated, and righteous-minded citizens in Korea knew that the socialist camp held true patriots. The overwhelming majority of the students themselves were on the left ideologically. The socialists were the only group who had actively and effectively fought against the Japanese occupation, which lasted

Men threshing rice in a Korean village. Korea has been an agrarian society whose community and politics are derived from peasant cooperation—the very nature of grassroots socialism. This picture was taken in 1972.

from 1910 through 1945, so it was natural that the students picked a leader from the left.

Socialism in Korea during and after these years wasn't an import from the Kremlin or Peking. It was instead a set of principles created by Koreans who wished to protect their country from a foreign conquest. Korean socialists wanted to implement policies beneficial to the disenfranchised masses, to extirpate the Japanese colonial presence, and to eliminate those legacies of feudalism responsible for the gross gap between rich and poor.

Because Korea was traditionally founded on family-centered, community-oriented peasantry, Mother explained, the socialists believed it was unfit for the culture of individualism on which capitalism was based. To modernize itself, Korea had to mobilize its collectively based lifestyle and achieve an equal distribution of wealth for everyone, including landlords and peasants. In an effort to avoid the violent transition to capitalist concepts of private property, the socialists set up plans for a speedy, yet cautious revolution. They were ready to wage a sweeping land reform, to abolish the ancient class system by leveling out the wealth of the landed nobility and the incipient urban ruling class, and to institute massive grassroots programs to educate former slaves, peasants, and women. They were determined to oust the rich who had accumulated their wealth by actively supporting the Japanese.

On the other hand, the right was unfit to govern. Very few of the public office candidates had ever been actively involved in the resistance against the Japanese occupation; they were alienated from the masses and out of touch with the circumstances of their people in the years following 1945. With degrees in higher education from European and American universities, they were well versed in Western civilization, but that hardly qualified them to practice Western-style democracy. As the residue of factions that had loyally served the Japanese colonial government and thrived as a ruling class under the Japanese occupation, these right-wing elements formed a small, rich, and privileged few who worked for the foreign interests. Without the support of the masses, they befriended the U.S. military when the Japanese left Korea after World War II, latching on to another foreign power to perpetuate the advantages they had obtained by ingratiating themselves with the Japanese. Grossly distorting representations of their rivals on the left, they played up to the Americans' fear of communism, thus winning from the United States entirely undeserved recognition as the only legitimate government in Korea.

The Americans did not bother to see that the uniquely Korean form of socialism was nothing like the tyrannical communism they feared, that in fact it was the only true democracy at that time in Korea. By aligning themselves with those who were once Japanese collaborators, they guaranteed the continued hegemony of the pro-Japanese powers and the ongoing oppression of the true patriots. The American regime would use Japan as a primary weapon for its anti-communism in Asia, and in the process crush the wishes of a people who had fought so hard to liberate their country from the colonizers. "The Americans made a deal with the Japanese," the few well-informed Koreans would whisper. "On condition that they be allowed to set up a U.S. military base on Okinawa, they guaranteed Japan a powerful presence over our country. Look how well the Japanese used our cheap labor to develop their economy."

Forty years later, America and Japan finally fulfilled the secret promise they had made to each other in 1905 to exercise total hegemony over Korea. By covertly signing the Taft-Katsura Agreement, which was not publicized until 1924, the two nations had decided to overlook each other's territorial ambition in Asian countries. On condition that Japan accept America's inheritance of the Philippines from the Spanish conquerors, America recognized Japan's occupation of Korea. Using the euphemism "sphere of influence," the two nations conveniently sealed their ties in sharing the pie. Although America and Japan became enemies during World War II, the two partners joined forces again in 1945 in virtually colonizing Korea one more time. In 1945, the "annexation" of Korea by Japan took place all over again in a way, because America not only condoned but also actively promoted Japan's lingering power over its neighbor. In appearance Korea was an autonomous country, but in reality it remained in Japan's shadow.

The Korean Democratic Party (KDP), as the undemocratic Korean allies of American imperialism were called, were authorized to build an empire of tyranny, a government with no connection to the people. Obsessed with their own definition of democracy—capitalism free from the taint of communism—the Americans ended up planting the exact opposite of democracy. They were indeed the "Yankee bastards," as Father called them.

As one of the SNU students actively involved in the protest against the U.S. military's decision to "nationalize" the university, Father was busy. With his peers in the movement, he printed and circulated fliers, drew up and pasted declarations on the walls of the buildings on campus, organizing meetings.

"He and his friends knew they could be gunned down by the right-wing police any time," Mother recalled. "But they were young men with convictions. Nobody could stop them."

When the U.S. military came in 1945 to build a right-wing toadies' regime, the Americans were surprised to see that there was already an independent government in Korea. Created immediately before the Japanese withdrawal in August 1945, this state was a loosely constructed entity without a solid infrastructure. But it was a grassroots administration of socialist nationalist democracy founded on legitimate, well-deliberated plans. Named the KPR—the Korean People's Republic—it was a federation of like-minded leaders who possessed track records in the resistance against the Japanese occupation and whose reputation was firmly rooted in their people's approval.

The Japanese surrendered on August 15, 1945, and General Hodge and his men entered Korea in early September. With less than a month to officially proclaim the birth of their republic, the representatives of the KPR had to publish the list of their cabinet members on September 8, the same day as the American general and his troops arrived. Wishing to be inclusive, they listed names from both the right and the left, choosing people from all walks of life; they even included some pro-Japanese right-wing elements. Undoubtedly, the cabinet leaned toward the left, but since their top priority was "Korea for Koreans," the KPR founders were sensible enough to invite the opposite camp to join. Considering how little time they had, it was a careful, scrupulous proposal, and considering it was their blood being shed on the battlefields against the Japanese, such an invitation was a generous gesture.

It is conceivable that, had it not been for the American government's championing of the right, Korea would have become a social-ist state. The grassroots socialist republic might have kept the country intact from an ideological division. Kim Il Sung, the North Korean leader, who has been blamed by the South and the United States for the job of splitting the country in two, may have been spared the need to establish a separate regime in the North. It is possible, too, of course, that he was motivated by territorial ambitions of his own and would have proclaimed an independent communist state in the North under any circumstances. He later denounced not only the American military government but also the KPR for its failure to build broad political support among the masses. But at no time dur-ing the first five months after the emancipation from the Japanese did Kim overtly declare his intentions to redress that failure. He had the Soviet Union on his side while the South had the United States, and given the irremovable presence of the two superpowers in the peninsula, the division might have been inevitable. But the sequence remains clear. Kim did not strike first. The North Korean Interim People's Committee (NKIPC) didn't come into being officially until the inclusive, moderate socialists lost power in the Korean Peninsula. Judging from the chronology of the events, the Koreans on the right, at the behest of their American bosses, initiated the moves leading to the eventual birth of the two separate states.

By killing the ones who tried to swim in the middle, the Americans permanently destroyed the meaning of the once-sacred word "socialism" in the Korean peninsula. The Americans made it represent only "communism," the brutal Stalin-style dictatorship that evolved in North Korea. As South Korea found itself heading for an extreme capitalism, North Korea plunged into an equally extreme socialism, polarizing the peninsula into a state that the moderate socialists could not have imagined. "Socialism," which had stood for justice and equality for all, became nothing but a cursed word in both North and South Korea.

In the minds of most Americans and South Koreans to this day, Kim Il Sung was a human monster with no consideration for anything but his own power. This image is true to life in every sense of the word. He was responsible for one of the most oppressive regimes on earth, where a thorough, brainwashing hagiography eliminated an individual's ability to think. For the torture and killing he committed in his own country, he deserved to be tried for crimes against humanity. Once in power, he purged everyone he perceived as a threat, including intellectual socialists who voluntarily migrated to the North and many of his former Japanese resistance fighters, as well as the hard-core socialists who participated in making the ideological infrastructure of the state.

But to reduce Korea's troubled post-World War II history to Kim and his regime leaves out three important facts: One, the right-wing dictators in South Korea, who maintained their power by propagating their dehumanizing picture of Kim, were hardly better. Two, Kim certainly was one of the primary culprits who created two different Koreas, but he was not the only one. Three, his pre-1945 life shows a solid record of resistance against the Japanese, so his infamy should be attributed to his post-1945 hegemony, not to his prior activities. The Japanese in fact tried to assassinate Kim because he was one of the most effective guerilla leaders for the Korean independence movement in Manchuria. Though little known to the world, Koreans throughout the Japanese occupation had a globally organized independence network, with unofficial but well-coordinated centers in China, the Soviet Union, and the United States. Domestically, they had broad, tightly knit underground bases, and organized national as well as local uprisings such as the 1919 March First Movement and the 1929 Kwangju Student Movement. The thirty-six-year reign of terror by the Japanese failed. Koreans remained incorrigibly Korean, and Kim was one of those who helped them to remain so.

Kim's right-wing counterparts in post-1945 South Korea didn't have gulags to which they could ship dissidents, and they didn't practice hagiography. But since the 38th parallel was drawn between the two Koreas, the South Korean dictators waged a ruthless campaign to eliminate individuals they saw as possible troublemakers. As one of those presumed "guilty," Father was arrested in 1949. When the police came, he was teaching at a teacher's college after having been expelled from SNU. They took him as a "thought criminal" and tortured him, threatening to kill him if he ever harbored any seditious thought against the "democracy." They hung him upside down from the ceiling, hitting him on the calves with a heavy baton. While forcing buckets of water down his throat, they also kicked him in the belly in an attempt to rupture his stomach.

Fortunately, Father had to spend only three months in prison. Mother's brother pulled strings on his behalf, and Father was released much more quickly than any of his peers. Although my uncle, too, was a socialist and was known as such in the intellectual circles he belonged to, he wasn't as yet a marked man and had clout with other lawyers on the right and left. Having passed the Japanese bar exams to become the first modern Korean lawyer, he was a celebrity among them, and they were eager to ingratiate themselves.

There were no modern lawyers in Korea until 1943, the year my uncle passed the bar exams in Japan, because the traditional justice system had just begun to be replaced by the Western-style court introduced by the Japanese. The Japanese had annexed Korea in 1910, and to firmly entrench their own rules of colonialism in Korea, they adopted modified German-style imperialistic laws. Authoritarian, hierarchical, and state-controlled, it was a far cry from the British-

American style court that allowed for citizens' participation. Lacking the jury system, weaker in its application of the concept of private property, and more considerate of the dictates of the government than of precedents, it was in no way based on a democratic, truly Western concept of justice. But the Japanese had to define it as Western in order to justify their occupation of another country.

Having invaded Korea under the false pretense of "civilizing the backward country," the conquerors had to convince themselves— and the rest of the world—that their imperialistic legal system was Western. The new legal system was in fact one of the most powerful weapons the Japanese could wield to keep Korea under their heels. The purpose of modernizing the Korean legal system was to make Korea into a smaller, weaker Japan, a very cleverly disguised means of maintaining Korea's slavery to Japan.

My mother described my uncle, the Japanese-style lawyer, to me. He served the Japanese law in appearance, but he remained a devoutly Korean young man, a brave, enduring spirit quietly accumulating knowledge under the reign of the colonizers; he was waiting for a chance to use that knowledge to benefit his people. Inside, he was holding hands with other socialist young men, the same quiet spirits hiding behind masks of compliance to maintain their inner faith. My uncle was a genius, one of those who shocked his conquerors by achieving the standards they had set to be unreachable. He had passed the Japanese bar exams back when such a feat was difficult for even the most well-educated, talented Japanese man.

But this genius uncle of mine, who delivered Father from prison, couldn't save Father's psychology. For the rest of his life, Father was traumatized by the torture he had undergone in prison. Because so many people were still being arrested and incarcerated on the grounds of vague suspicion or for their one-time activity in the past, Father lived in a constant state of fear. As an SNU student, Father had often been chased by the police, but after serving the prison term, he was hounded by the fear of being secretly captured and killed.

In the practice of political oppression, there was little difference between South Korea's "democracy" and the tyrannical communist regime in the North. After his inauguration in 1948, Syngman Rhee launched a nationwide "search and destroy" campaign, continuing to terrorize independent thinkers such as Father, forcing them to go underground to avoid being exterminated. Against the students' will, the "nationalization" of SNU had been accomplished, the Korean Democratic Party and the American government had won, destroying the Korean People's Republic and assassinating its leaders.

Exiled in his own country, Father plunged into a deep grief from which he would never recover. He mourned his former socialist classmates and colleagues who had gone to North Korea. "I imagine they are either dead or slowly dying in labor camps," he said. The radio propaganda from North Korea, which was full of manufactured good news about happy people and a thriving economy, made him laugh. From what was happening in the South, it was easy to guess that in the North, too, people like him were being exterminated as if they were lice or cockroaches.

Father's ordeal didn't end with being expelled from his position and being incarcerated. In 1950, in the midst of the paranoia during the Korean War, he was again arrested, on the common cover all charge of planning to join a "communist conspiracy." And in 1961, immediately after Park Chung Hee's coup d'état, Father was yet again interrogated by the police. Although he was released on both occasions because of insufficient evidence, he suffered from constant fear of sudden imprisonment and torture, which crippled his already broken sprit. He could ruminate only on the certainty that the right-wing dictatorship would continue to rule South Korea for generations to come, endorsed and often actively aided by the American government. More than the torture, more than the killings, and more than the destruction of so many talented youths, it was this eternal presence of the same pro-Japanese forces in his country that enraged him.

Having forsaken a life of guaranteed privilege for what was the morally right thing to do, Father was entitled to be called a leader.

During the last year or so of the Japanese occupation, he placed himself on the short list of the men who managed to pass the Preliminaries, exams that were the first step toward the Japanese bar exams. Had the Japanese occupation lasted a few years longer, Father most likely would have made it all the way to the final stage of the bar exams, to succeed in becoming one of the few modern Korean lawyers to practice under the Japanese rule. Fewer than a dozen were selected each year from all the regions under the Japanese reign, including Manchuria, Taiwan, Korea, and Japan itself. As his brother-in-law probably would have, Father could have risen to be one of the highest-ranking officials in the South Korean government, possibly to be a deputy head of the Justice Department or to be a vice chief of the National Prosecutors Office. With one slight nod toward the pro-Japanese regime, he would have won the national recognition, money, and power automatically granted to men with his qualifications. Instead, he gave it all up to take a stand for Korea, for his beloved country—a decision that, once made, could not be unmade for the rest of his life.

Stealing a Dream

I HAD BEEN STARVING MYSELF THE WHOLE SUMMER I WAS EIGHT years old.

"Why is she so thin?" Father asked Mother, pointing at me. "She looks like a spider. Is she eating at all?"

"She has a seasonal difficulty," Mother diagnosed, looking at me up and down. "She stops eating during the summer. Lots of kids have the same problem. She'll start eating again when the breeze turns cool."

"Oh, yeah? The boys seem to be affected by the heat a bit, too. Make sure they eat right, will you?" With nothing to worry about, Father went back to reading the newspaper's flattering report of Park Chung Hee's most recent conspiracy.

Maybe Mother was right. My summer anorexia was possibly a seasonal difficulty caused by the heat alone. But for multiple summers in a row, my illness was a form of protest I wielded against circumstances beyond my control.

"Child, you look like a skeleton," one of my neighbors said. "Your mother ought to take you to a doctor. You may die if she doesn't. Eat these, at least." She gave me two apples.

Carrying them home, I saw Less Big Brother. He demanded that I give him one, but I refused, ready to fight until death. To my relief, Big Brother sauntered out of his room. "Let her have both," he said. "She'll gain five pounds."

Me as a toddler riding piggyback on a girl cousin.

I resented him for using the word "let," because the apples were mine to begin with, but I didn't argue. I just walked away, taking bites alternately from each apple. If both of them had my teeth marks, Less Big Brother wouldn't want them and wouldn't come after me. That summer, those apples were the only thing I had for myself exclusively. They were a sign that my kind neighbor had taken notice of me. Although I was invisible to my own family, I was not invisible to everyone, and it thrilled me.

I desired to surpass Mother and Grandmother in self-denial, and I found myself looking for an additional burden. That was when I put Little Sister on my back. I lugged her around through the dead heat of summer, a weight almost as heavy as my skinny self. Little Sister was the only one in my family that I loved wholeheartedly; I loved her because Mother and Father had created her exclusively for me. I knew that, even if Mother and Father didn't.

Even before Little Sister was born, I had picked her up and put her on my back to roam around the block. I used Father's pillow, the largest in the house, to represent my future sibling, strapping it to my back like a baby, wrapping it horizontally with a long, wide towel. I felt desperate to love and be loved by someone, and I saw this someone in the unborn baby. She would receive all the love in me that could not be given to anyone else and, in turn, she would love me in her soul. She would be *mine*.

"There comes the child with the pillow on her back!" my neighbors used to exclaim, laughing. "She thinks she'll have a younger sibling if she pretends that pillow is a baby."

"Why won't you have another baby, Mom?" I complained habitually. "There must be something wrong with you."

For the first few months of my begging, M`other just laughed, but I didn't give up, and sure enough, along came a baby. The day Little Sister was born, I felt loved by my parents for the first time. If they could create such a perfect little creature for me, they must indeed love me very much. I knelt down beside her, a peachy lump of flesh squirming on a quilt. Beside her, Mother was fast asleep, with her mouth slightly open and her face tilted toward the wall. She was deathly pale. Half of her blood seemed to have gone out of her body.

Grandmother's metallic cackle cut into my silent joy: "Your mother had a worthless pussy this morning." I looked through the door crack. She was violently sweeping the floor in the living room while talking to Big Sister, who had just woken up.

How could she insult the baby—my baby—who was born to receive all my love and to give me all her love? A violent emotion flitted across my mind, and I darted out of the room to avoid the sound of her broom. Big Sister came in, raising the corner of her lips in an attempt to smile. She was the oldest child, the first in the family who had learned how to treat Grandmother like a barking dog. She was telling me with her eyes how foolish I would be if I gave the ugly old bitch the power to control me.

"You're panting like a dog," she said in that dry, detached voice that would teach me the benefits of equanimity for decades to come. "Sit down."

Trying to mimic her poise, I stepped into the backyard to catch some fresh air. But Father was standing there, his back to me, gazing at the dying half moon hanging over the branches of the persimmon tree near the fence. Without unclasping his hands behind his back, he looked back at me for a moment before returning his gaze to the sky. "I saw a blue dragon in my dream last night," he said in a low voice. "It was so huge, with its wings outstretched so very far I couldn't see the end of the sky. I thought it would be a boy. But the gods pulled a trick on me!"

I was surprised he talked to me so honestly; he was serious only with his boys. I cried out, in spite of myself, "I will be that dragon! I will be your son and bring you fame, fortune, and honor!"

"I wish you were a boy." He sighed. "You have a boy's mind. You're the kind of kid who goes out and gets what she wants." Pride tinged with sadness crossed his face. He was feeling sorry for me— and himself.

"What should I do to be a boy? Tell me!"

"Sweetheart, you can't be."

Tears welled up in my eyes. What I wanted to be more than anything else, I couldn't be. A convulsive sob shook me as I started to run to the family outhouse, where I could pour out my true feelings without being seen by anyone.

Pounding my fists on the cement wall, I bombarded myself with questions I couldn't answer. *Why is Father disappointed with girls? Why does everyone think boys are better than girls? Why do they think men are superior to women?* I wondered why nobody noticed the fact that a man could not be born without a woman. Father grew up to be a man because Grandmother had brought him into this world, fed him, changed his diapers, and picked him up. He could wear clean clothes because Mother washed his pants and socks and ironed his shirts every day at six o'clock in the morning before he woke up. I was puzzled as to how a man could accuse a woman of enjoying a "free ride" when she was laboring so hard at home. A husband worked to make money, but a wife had to raise his children and, in Mother's case, she even took care of her mother-in-law, who hated her.

I started to blame myself for not being resigned. By reproaching myself for perceiving injustices few children noticed, I was able to absolve those who practiced them without thinking. Making myself into a "good girl" by condemning "bad girls"—girls like me—became my weapon against myself, my instrument for survival.

At bedtime that night Little Sister was born, Big Sister brought Mother dinner on a plate. "Grandmother's still angry," she said softly to me. "She hasn't fixed dinner for Mother. I had to cook for her."

Mother's bleached face pained me. She was a tree without sap, struck down by a terrible storm, and, despite my resolve to be a good girl, I wanted to stick a knife in Grandmother's throat.

Instead, I walked to the yard in the back of the house to watch the moon. I stood, facing the persimmon tree, and stole the dream of the blue dragon Father had the night before. To him the dream was no longer useful, but to me it was invaluable. It was mine because I *said* it was, and I *was* the dragon endowed with all of its power and majesty, destined to grow up to cover the sky with its fully stretched wings. With the dragon in me, I would be able to make my descendants prosper forever and yet avoid the misfortune of being a tiger's meal.

But watching the moon, I felt that the power of a dragon alone would not be enough. People compared the moon to a beautiful woman, a being so ethereal she could walk between the drops of the finest rain. So airy, she could travel like light as far as any planet. I wanted to add her elegance to the dragon's energy, to bring beauty and power together, and to unite the man and the woman in me. To create such a self would require an enormous effort, but I would not give up. I stood in the yard, picturing myself combining a faerie queen's feathery lightness with a blue dragon's steel-heavy energy. I knew the gods disliked humans with overweening wishes, and I was afraid I might be one of those bound to invite their wrath. At eight, I had no specific idea of what my visions of the faerie queen and the blue dragon meant. I only knew that I wanted to be both, and I clung to this wish as a child would cling to her only toy.

The Good Vampires

As the breeze cooled that summer, I felt happy as a child should. I stored memories of ordinary but beautiful moments — accompanying Mother on her visit to relatives; walking with her to parks and alongside the trees on the roads; Little Sister jumping up and down in a basin of warm water and Grandmother washing her with a bar of baby soap; Big Sister, Big Brother, Less Big Brother, and I splashing our faces at the water pump with Mother pumping on and on for us; Father coming home from a long-distance trip with a box of cookies wrapped in a red ribbon. Grandmother loved Little Sister, although she never stopped lamenting that she wasn't a boy, and Mother loved me and tried to show me her love out of Grandmother's sight.

Mother would sneak me out to a market to buy me rice cakes, creating one of the shining moments in my life. Alone with her, I could feel her compassion and catch her tender gaze. In her eyes, I got a glimpse of the love she wasn't allowed to express to me and of the circumstances keeping her from showing it. Often, she would sneak into my room to see me fall asleep and say, "Your face is so intense, even when you're asleep. I'm afraid you think too deeply." "It's because I have strange dreams," I would assure her. "But they disappear when I wake up." As the hard, worn knuckles of her fingers stroked my hair and braided it, I could feel her devotion touching me. The covert but clear manifestations of her love became the life buoys that kept me floating on the ocean of painful memories.

Big Sister clutches me as a baby in front of our house. Big Sister was always the model oldest daughter, or "family capital"—she looked after her younger siblings as if she were our mother; she sacrificed endlessly on our behalf; whip-smart, she came in top of her class at school; and she quietly submitted to the will of the men of her family.

How I wished we had more money! With a refrigerator to reduce her labor, central heating to lessen her back pain, and a washing machine to protect her hands from constant wear and tear, she would have had so much more time to spend with her children and to learn new ways of life. But she had to spend all of her time on just surviving.

Although far more moderate than Grandmother, Mother was bound to traditional practices as much as any woman of her age, and I knew she *couldn't* stop putting her boys above her girls. How could she treat gods equally to people? Big Brother was the one to set up the table for ancestor worship, the one to bow to her and her husband's names pasted on the folding screen, to recall their struggles for their children, and to pass on their names to his sons. She couldn't defy the system she had learned from her mother, who in turn had inherited it from her mother. Even as a fourth grader, I was aware of the forces working against Mother.

Still, Mother loved us all. On some Sundays, whenever there were only women around, we were a happy family, and Mother was devoted to her girls. No one was better or worse than anyone else, and even Grandmother seemed to put her bitter tongue on hold. We shared some gourmet dishes we normally couldn't, including freshly cooked meat and fish and vegetables, and Grandmother smiled and laughed with us over the comedies on the small TV we borrowed from a neighbor, clapping her hands and cheering.

Our favorite show was about cartoon vampires who fought bad people in the hopes of becoming human someday. The nine-inch black-and-white TV gave us an opportunity to unite ourselves against the villains on the screen. While our eyes were glued on it, we were happy. "Good job! Well done!" we shouted, applauding the vampires, who lashed their long, black leather whips at the loan sharks who "drained the blood" from poor people.

All the women in the family identified with the vampires—Vam, Vera, and Vero—who could choose to be male or female as they wished. We whooped with joy at the screams of the villains, gasped with anxiety at the hazards facing the heroes, and sighed with relief at their final victory, oblivious of everything else in the world. We felt sad because they worked so hard to earn the right to turn human, doing all the dangerous work for people. It wasn't fair for them to have to wait for a full hundred years before having a chance to be judged and approved by the gods. But every Sunday afternoon, we were happy to witness them moving, if at a snail's pace, toward the eventual day of glory. We could celebrate freely because the Three Men of the Family weren't at home to tell us how foolish women were to enter such a heated discussion over a silly cartoon movie.

"Women like to cry. They like to be sentimental," Father would sniff whenever Mother emoted over her favorite TV dramas. "They like to waste their emotion and throw out their reason." He spent his Sunday afternoons catching up with his friends, while my brothers spent weekends playing basketball. Less Big Brother would jeer, "You women stay in a dark room all day, doing nothing but watching that stupid TV and gabbing about it."

Still, Sunday afternoons in 1965 were ours, and we spent them freely with Vam, Vera, and Vero. Occasionally, I thought I was Vera, lashing her serpentine whip around a villain's body, smothering and paralyzing him. I thought of Big Sister as Vam, whose whip, slightly shorter and thicker than Vera's, would fasten around a swindler's torso, turning him into a dummy with a broken back. Mother was Vero, the smallest and pudgiest of the three and the one with the most common sense and strategic wisdom, responsible for the harmony between hot-tempered Vera and reserved Vam. I fantasized about her binding a hoodlum's body with her whip, pulling him in all directions, and finally striking him down on the ground with circus-style adroitness. Although too little to be a fighter yet, Little Sister was one of the vampires, too. I added an imaginary character, Vira, to include her, making her a trainee and potentially the most powerful combination of everyone's merits. At nine, I thought I could take an active part in vanquishing the evils of the world.

That winter, as the cool breeze changed into icy winds, my brothers taught and encouraged me, and helped me to do better in school.

Spending days tutoring me in math, giving me science pop quizzes, and explaining geometric axioms in detail didn't seem to tire them at all.

"You know my friend Dongil. His sister is going to the best junior high school for girls in Seoul," Big Brother said. "You'd better go to the best in Taegu at least."

"You've got to do better than you have so far," Less Big Brother joined in. "You can't make your family ashamed." I didn't understand I was a pawn for their competition with their peers, but had I known, I would have been grateful nonetheless. In my mind, my brothers awakened in me a passion for knowledge and a desire to push myself much as the fairytale prince woke up the sleeping princess. It was the princes in them that made it possible for me, as an adult, to forgive them for their other cruelties, to replace the sharp edges of my anger with the softening power of gratitude.

At fourteen, Big Brother had a constantly full schedule and was entrusted with the most respected—and demanding—duties a teenage boy of his age could be charged with. He was the student body president for a junior high school of fifteen hundred boys, an amateur painter who won awards for his school in national fine arts contests, and a young critic who was invited to lead after-school discussions of classical Korean and world literature. He hardly had an evening free of commitments. After going to school all day, working intensely to keep his number one spot among his five hundred peers in all twenty subjects in liberal arts and math and sciences, he dedicated his extracurricular hours to helping his peers as well as to improving his own leadership skills.

That winter, Big Brother spent several of his packed evenings painting the "twelve most important foods of our lives" for my class, sacrificing precious homework and sleep hours. A poster in watercolors, his painting was pasted on the board in the back of my classroom for one whole semester, serving as a guidepost for my teacher whenever she needed to explain nature and nutrition. I won celebrity status in school as the sister of the great watercolorist, and it made me glow with pride I had never felt before. The potatoes, apples, meat, cabbage,

Children skating on a makeshift ice rink in 1973.

rice, barley, eggs, and tomatoes in the painting looked so real and delicious that children from other classes came by to look, throwing envious glances at me. The fame Big Brother brought me was the only visibility I ever had a chance to enjoy in my grade school years, and for this I was eternally grateful to him. I could bear a million sarcastic remarks if I could have one more round of that reflected glow.

Less Big Brother, too, planted a sparkling memory in my mind. When he was twelve, he taught me how to skate on the Crystal River, where some merchants had poured liquid nitrogen from a truck into the half-frozen water to set up a tent house. They charged about a quarter for unlimited use of the rink and less for renting a pair of skating boots.

"My friend Jay Ho's sister skates real gracefully," Less Big Brother goaded me warmly. "My sister should do just as well."

I was so overwhelmed to be the focus of his attention that the pressure to do well seemed only an additional blessing. He held my hand and helped me to stand on the blades, pulling me slowly, doubling up his energy on his feet to maintain his balance against my struggling legs. His hands were an oasis of warmth in the frosty ring. They were just like the small radiator in my classroom, around which girls fought to occupy a spot to escape the icy drafts creeping through the poorly insulated walls. I realized he loved me, and my entire world seemed to stand on that moment in that cheap tarpaulin tent house pitched up by some poor merchants trying to scrape children's coins together.

But the liquid nitrogen had become less effective because the weather was getting warmer, and the ice beneath my feet cracked when I had barely made three stiff rounds of the ring. Suddenly, I was almost entirely immersed in the cold water. I cried hysterically, swinging my arms in vain, trying to grab the ice above me. Pandemonium broke loose on the ring and children ran in all directions, screaming. Some of them lay flat and crawled to the outside beneath the tarpaulin and others rushed to the exit at the end of the tarpaulin sheets. In total panic, I pawed the air, wriggling my arms to and fro, my head barely above the water and my legs numbed by the freezing water, until Less Big Brother darted toward me, followed by two of the merchants carrying metal poles. By the time Less Big Brother reached me, I had almost lost mobility in my arms. I felt a burning pain, as if I were dissolving in heat in the midst of icy water, and when Less Big Brother squatted down on the ice near the hole and extended his hands to me, my arms grabbed them with desperate energy.

"Get away from there, boy!" one of the merchants cried to him. He thrust one end of his metal pole in front of Less Big Brother, blocking him from the broken part of the ice.

"Don't go any further!" the other hollered to his partner. "Give him the end of the pole! Hurry!"

The ice beneath Less Big Brother had cracked. Falling into the rapidly expanding hole of water with me, he began to kick his legs and swing his arms, clenching his teeth to fight the pain. But he refused to scream, playing the big brother comforting his screaming little sister, and he was soon able to gain his balance in the water after a few erratic strokes. Struggling to keep a stoic face, he held my waist up to help me to get hold of the metal pole extended by one of the merchants, and when my torso came safely above the water, I climbed up on the pole. Relieved, the merchant swung around and walked toward the entrance to drop me on the gravel outside, coming back to help his friend, who was doing the same thing for Less Big Brother. They were at ease with the whole rescue mission, as if we were as light as a pair of balloons; I thought they had probably done it before.

Stamping our feet on the gravel, we tried to stop the chattering of our teeth. "Get on my back," Less Big Brother ordered. "I can carry you home. It'll be faster." He squatted. Reluctantly, I sat on his back and wrapped my arms around his neck, laying my face flat between his ribs. I was afraid that people might see me, nearly grown, on my brother's back and laugh at me. But we were home much sooner than we would have been had I walked.

"Your Father told you not to go skating on temporary rings like that!" Grandmother yelled. "If you don't come down with some awful chills, I'll be surprised."

Begging her not to tell Father, Less Big Brother and I changed our clothes and sat on the warm floor to thaw our toes. Then I fell asleep to the sound of Grandmother washing our clothes in the bathroom. When I woke up, I was lying in another room, beside Little Sister. I could hear Grandmother grumbling to Mother, "The merchants would have got her out anyway. He was stupid enough to try to rescue her himself. Why should a boy get sick for a worthless chick?" Mother didn't respond, her eyes fixed on the shirt she was ironing. "I'm glad it happened during the break, though," Grandmother muttered. "I would have cried if he had missed school because of a stupid flu he didn't deserve."

For once, Grandmother's tirade didn't bother me. My heart had no room to feel anything other than gratitude toward Less Big Brother. Crooning to Little Sister in my arms and watching Less Big Brother slowly recover, I felt free from the grip of a tiger's stomach. I was happy because I felt loved. Less Big Brother had risked his safety for me.

Summer Perils

Summer had perils of a different kind, most of them stemming from my curiosity. I couldn't help myself; I was desperate to *know* everything. And *knowing* could be ugly.

One boiling hot afternoon in July, I had a chance to see a junkyard, where starving paupers retired from ration stores with pouches of barley and flour, and beggars sat on dirt to eat morsels of food from the bowls they carried from house to house. The yard was fenced off with wires from a row of wooden shacks. A professional junk collector, a thin man in a torn army uniform, was sorting through the heap of broken utensils. People with his job—those who ransacked dumpsters of the city with hemp sacks on their backs—were a totally foreign lot to me, known only by whispered tales of murder, robbery, rape, and most often, self-destructive, vicious violence. They belonged to a world beyond my reach, and I took a step into the yard out of curiosity.

The junk collector lunged toward me. The scar on his cheek, running from beneath his eye through the edge of his mouth, gave him the face of a leper. The loose sleeves of the torn army uniform hung in tatters over his hands, and his eyes were bloodshot, his nose tip red.

"What are you trying to steal in my yard?" he yelled, his tongue thick with liquor. "Before you steal, you'll die."

I ran, panting, and as soon as the bellowing Frankenstein was out of sight, I threw myself down under a tree, ready to faint.

From left to right, front row: me, Father, my maternal grandfather, Little Sister, and Mother. Back row: Big Brother, Less Big Brother, Big Sister.

That summer's adventures weren't entirely solitary and sinister. One of my favorite memories of that time was frog hunting with my brothers. Any frogs they could catch in the field were free meat supplements in our always scanty diet. Usually my brothers went off by themselves, but this time, much to my surprise and delight, they invited me to come along.

"Don't lose this," Big Brother instructed, putting Big Sister's straw hat over my head. "It's scorching out there. If you walk around uncovered, you'll turn into a chunk of roast beef in five minutes."

I trotted along to keep pace with my brothers, pressing the top of the hat down with my right hand. Walking slowly for my sake, they each carried a thin but sturdy wooden stick for striking frogs and a small tin bucket to gather them in. When they started whistling and shaking their weapons in the air, I wished I could, too.

At the rice paddies on the edge of the town, my brothers took separate ways through the furrows between the patches, while I sat on the grassy path beside a brook, clapping my hands. Each time they hit a frog, I shrieked with excitement, jumping up and down on the wet soil.

"Wow! Look at this big sucker!" Less Big Brother shouted, holding a dead frog by its hind legs.

"Good job!" Big Brother shouted back. "It looks as big as your foot."

I cheered, too, thinking it was the size of my shoe. Then, I felt a sudden gust of wind across the paddies and saw my hat floating on the brook beside me. Before I could reach the brook, it was swept away. The recent heavy rain had made the water fast and high.

"Wear this," Less Big Brother said, handing his straw hat to me. "Don't clap your hands and jump, and don't take your hand off of the rim. If I were you, I would just sit and wait until we're done."

"After a while, she can wear mine and you can get yours back," Big Brother suggested.

"Do you think there's anyone else in this world who can wear your hat?" Less Big Brother teased. "If there is, his head must be as big as a mountain."

"My head is as big as a mountain," I cried. "I'll wear it!"

In fact, I had secretly tried on his hat on numerous occasions. I wished so much to have his brain—which gave him the nickname "The Einstein of K High"—that I became almost superstitious. I nearly convinced myself that if I could wear the same size clothing and shoes as his, I would eventually end up being like him. Having heard from other superstitious children in my grade school that the physical size of one's head corresponded to one's intelligence quotient, I was also determined to increase the size of my brain. While he was out, I would sneak into his closet to grab his hat and snatch his running shoes out of the family shoe rack, and putting them on in a hurry like a thief, I would steal away to the backyard. Shuffling in the giant shoes, both of my hands tightly pressed against the rim of his huge straw hat, I couldn't resist being impressed by myself. Convinced that my head and feet were getting larger every minute, I would circle around the persimmon tree a dozen times in a row with a wicked, delicious smile on my face.

"If you can wear his hat, that means we have another genius in the family," Less Big Brother joked. "Are you going to follow in Big Brother's footsteps?"

"I am!"

"You'd better protect your genius head from this sun then. Sit beside the tree there." Big Brother pointed at a lean, tall tree on the gravel path running along the brook.

Big Brother and Less Big Brother seemed to have forgotten the sun. Bent on catching frogs, they stole along the furrows with their backs stooped and their faces lowered, like a pair of huge, two-legged cats intent on a mouse-chase. I laughed, delighted at the loud swishes of their sticks, watching the arches drawn in the air by their arms, listening to the dim drone of the traffic on the roads far from the paddies and their exhilarated cries as they displayed their prizes. The frogs were as big as my fist, dangling from their fingers.

It wasn't until the light faded that we started for home. Big Brother and Less Big Brother whistled all the way, feeling as accomplished as workers going home after a long, productive day, their buckets full of frogs with thick, fat legs. I tried to keep up with them but fell behind, much to my disappointment.

"I'd better carry her home. It'll be a lot faster," Big Brother announced. "Father will get mad if we don't get home in time for dinner." Crouching down on the ground, he picked me up and started to walk at the speed, it seemed to me, of lightning. He was going to carry me on his back for many years, but I didn't know it back then.

Since the frog legs had been obtained at no cost, even Grandmother had no objection to me eating them to my heart's content. But when Less Big Brother complained about the headache he got from the searing sun, she chided me for having gone with the boys to the fields. "Thanks to a worthless chick, he got sick." I surprised myself, however, by smiling. Once again, Less Big Brother had proved that he loved me enough to ignore Grandmother, and I loved him. Together we could crush her, I thought.

At the age of ten, I wasn't eating, and had no spare energy. But no one else had any energy for me, either. "I want to die, Mom," I confessed to Mother one day on the way from the outhouse to the kitchen. "I feel sick with fear all the time."

Mother looked at me, dumbfounded, but her face turned blank again after a moment. "I've never heard a child say anything like that. You're an odd one, you know that?" She turned her back on me, hurrying to the kitchen with the coal briquette.

"Why are grapes purple?" I asked Big Brother, who was intent on his physics homework. "What makes dust settle on our furniture? What makes trees green?"

"You are so stupid," he snapped, his eyes fixed on the book. "Don't you know nobody asks questions like that?"

Father certainly had no energy for me. Recently, he had plenty to say about things I didn't understand, things like "Ulsan Pollution Center," "Kuro Home of Industrial Waste," "Kyongin Nest of Hazard," "Kumi Haven of Bad Air," and "Pohang House of Poison." These were the names of planned industrial complexes, sites where cheap, mass goods would be produced at the cost of clean air and the most basic workers' rights. I didn't feel for the impoverished workers on whose behalf Father ranted. Nor did I have the ability to imagine the consequences of the pollution and the hazardous waste. I just wished Father would turn off the radio and listen to his daughter rather than to a North Korean woman condemning American imperialists and their South Korean lackeys.

As I grew old enough to challenge him, Father would curse me, "Those feminist bitches you imitate! They're nothing but a pack of dogs for the Yankee bastards! They're in cahoots with the right-wing hounds who do witch-hunting for their American owners."

My mother's sister, on the left, was a social feminist. She and my mother's brother left South Korea for the new socialist republic in the North—and were never heard from again. To this day, my mother does not know if she lives, or if her children live.

For Father and other Korean men of his generation, progressiveness and socialist ideals did not connect with a feminist agenda the way they often have in other countries. Father was being a traditional man, a model of a stoic Korean husband, trained not to show affection for his wife. His daily sexist behaviors were anything but deliberate. But Father did believe Korean feminists were, in a way, traitors.

When I was growing up in the sixties, the voices of Korean feminists were only just starting to be heard. I knew nothing of these women's existence except through the famous names mentioned by the adults around me. Mother repeated to me what Father had told her about the history of the women's movement in South Korea, and I was able to trace his words back to where they came from. I found myself not only understanding but also sympathizing with him.

As a small, determined army of women who arrived in the arms of the right-wing dictator and his American champion, the first-generation South Korean feminists, exactly like their male counterparts, had no power base among the female masses. They were a privileged few, a select number of well-educated, English-speaking elite, alienated from the needs of the majority of Korean women. As part of Syngman Rhee's constituents, they took over the mainstream women's movement in South Korea in the forties and fifties, governing its center through the sixties and well into the seventies.

"The socialist feminists fought to keep Korea for Korean women, while the right-wing feminists served American interests," Mother explained. "The former made the women's movement accord with the people's wishes, but the latter betrayed the masses to promote their own agenda, catering to the Americans' anticommunism and playing direct or indirect roles in destroying the socialist grassroots republic. Like the socialist men, the socialist women lost power and some of them had to flee to North Korea, where they probably suffered the same fate as their male comrades. As you know, my sister was one of those socialist feminists. She went to North Korea with my socialist brother."

Father was embittered against the early feminists in South Korea for other reasons as well. They espoused beliefs in direct contradiction to deeply ingrained Confucian ideology, disrupting time-honored traditions made possible partly by keeping men and women in separate places. There was a personal reason he disliked them, too. The feminists reminded him of Grandfather's illegitimate wife, the liberated woman with a feminist lifestyle who took his father away from his mother, as I was to find out shortly, when I was in middle school. But the primary reason for his aversion to the feminists was political.

"It is unfortunate—and tragic—that the socialist feminists were wiped out by the right-wing camp," Mother said. "But history is made by contradictions, and sometimes by violent contradictions. The right-wing feminists had to be lackeys for Uncle Sam in order to be pioneers for women. To establish *their* democracy, they betrayed everyone's democracy. By riding on the American side, they brought American women's feminism to Korea. America is the hub of global feminism, and without the models established by American women, Korean women wouldn't have had much guidance."

Despite what they did wrong, the right-wing feminists deserve credit for what they did for Korean women. They created Ewha University, the first institution of women's higher education in Korea, and one of the leading women's universities to this day. Analogous to Radcliffe or Smith in America, Ewha University, founded in 1886, was the first pioneering institution of women's higher education in Korea. Initially, it was started as a small school-house for girls by a Methodist missionary woman from Ohio, but in 1946 it became a university with several subsidiary schools. Since, it has blossomed into the world's largest university for women and one of the centers of the women's movement in Asia.

Its first president, Helen Kim, was a devout Christian right-wing feminist whose alliance with right-wing dictators in South Korea invoked intense ambivalence among socialist men of Father's generation. As one of the handful of the early feminists who fought to replace age-old Confucian ideology with newly imported Christianity, Kim did not hesitate to place herself in the hands of Americans and the Korean toadies conspiring with them. Although Christianity, too, was a patriarchal religion, it seemed to be a creed relatively kinder to women than traditional Yi Dynasty norms. Judeo-Christian countries, for instance, enforced monogamy at least by law, while Confucian countries practiced legally sanctioned, one-sided polygamy for men. For this difference alone, Christianity was worth fighting for.

To this day, I remember the chapter in her autobiography in which Helen Kim proudly recalls the party she organized for American army officers during the Korean War. To boost the morale of soldiers fighting to preserve "democracy" in another country, she called in the teachers' pets at Ewha to pair them with the officers. I was disturbed by the absolute certainty with which she described her party.

"She claimed she just wanted to comfort the soldiers far away from home," one of the feminist professors at my university, who knew all about Kim's life as an educator, said in class. "But there was a rumor that the party didn't end where it should have. Some people heard that some of the students and officers went further than expected, going out on regular dates and making frequent, possibly sexual, contact. 'She doesn't think there are enough whores and prostitutes in this country right now,' people whispered in anger. 'She thinks we need more, and she's the chancellor of a university dedicated to promote women's rights and equality.'" The professor paused to control her rising voice. "Regardless of the hearsay, Kim's party was morally reprehensible. Given that it was wartime, when the GIs' prostitutes filled the U.S. army base in the night, she should have abstained from anything that would reinforce the fallen image of Korean women. The selected Ewha students weren't poor, starving prostitutes, but in terms of the role they played for the army officers, they were members of a conquered race eager to please the conqueror. They were high-class one-night geisha, bluntly speaking, who were picked to serve the soldiers of a superpower. In peaceful times, when a man and a woman of different nationalities can sustain a relationship as equal individuals, such a gathering wouldn't be frowned upon. But in a country where so many of its women were made into playthings for soldiers from a conquering nation, Kim's party was a disgraceful idea, to say the least."

Kim didn't think about the consequences. Knowing that most of the prostitutes—and decent ladies—who consorted with American military men were left behind in Korea, never sent for by their boyfriends who returned to America, she took the risk of throwing her students into the officers' arms. She wasn't concerned that they might become casualties of the war. The rumor that some of them went further than expected was very possibly groundless, but taking this chance during the war was not only morally questionable but also unpatriotic.

In another chapter of her autobiography, Kim confesses to having pledged an allegiance to Park Chung Hee, the military general who took over Syngman Rhee's dictatorship through a coup d'état in

1961. With pride, she writes how she was summoned into his office immediately after the takeover and how unfalteringly she promised loyalty to him. As long as she was allowed to keep running Ewha University, she gladly shook hands with the dictator. It is impossible for me even now to shake off the disappointment that taints my admiration for her, admiration I believe she deserves for her ultimate achievement. The name Helen Kim provokes in me the same ambivalence that many people—men who had good reasons to distrust her, and other feminist women who had doubts about her integrity—admitted to feeling before and after her death.

But history must be examined with a sense of irony, as Father himself often insisted. *Because* Helen Kim so willingly made those shady compromises, she was able to keep what was to become the single largest institution of women's education, a haven for millions of Korean women who came after her. Because she spared nothing to preserve her cause, she was able to help rescue half of her country's population from ignominy and servitude. And because she pandered, she could help her fellow women to be free from pandering. Democracy is a strange beast. In my mind, her greatest achievement was to leave the next generation of women the weapons with which they could criticize her. She empowered them to become informed and able to sort right from wrong, and this empowerment may not have been possible without her flattery to the mafia-esque right-wing and their American bosses.

It wasn't Kim alone, of course, who created the changes desperately needed for women. A small corps of women who came with and after her fought fiercely, enduring misunderstanding, abuse, and sometimes condemnation from the men and women who preferred women's servitude. But had it not been for Kim, Korean women may not have been able to achieve such fast and substantial progress. The generation that followed her was able to bridge much of not only the gender gap but also the gulf between rich and poor. They could extrapolate from their experience as the second sex to defend the workers' rights against the capitalists, to protest against dictatorship, and to endorse freedom against all forms of oppression. Ewha students eventually went on a social crusade in an effort to extend Kim's democracy into democracy for all Koreans.

In November 1973, the whole university—including its eight thousand students, professors, and chancellor—launched a massive, unified protest against Park Chung Hee, who finally succeeded in changing the constitution to make his presidency permanent. Ok-Gill Kim, the woman chosen to succeed Helen Kim, personally protected the student protest organizers, inviting them to stay in her campus residence while they were hounded by the police. She and her faculty stood in the front row, forming a human barricade against the police for the thousands of students marching out of the campus. Finally, in December, Ewha confronted the Park regime by demanding they release all student protestors in prison and grant freedom of speech to the press. Ewha continued to be a mecca for the student protest until the rise of a civilian government in 1992. Even in 1980, the year Chun Doo Hwan, Park's self-appointed successor, declared martial law, Ewha students refused to be cowed by the threat of torture and imprisonment, making their campus into the headquarters for the national assembly of the student movement. Its faculty, too, remained one of the most vocal groups of resistance against Chun's tyranny, while equally dedicated to solving gender-related problems in the country.

Naturally, until the 1973 protest, I found myself half a step removed from the women's movement in South Korea—and from the idea of Ewha as a pioneering institution for women's education. Until they started to be heard as a voice for the people of Korea, not just for a small minority of privileged women, it was difficult for me to acknowledge their legitimacy. Feminists in South Korea until then were perceived as a band of leisure women whose concerns were detached from the most urgent priorities of their country, and whose interests were elegantly confined to harmless matters such as cultivating good taste in music and art. For decades, Ewha was indeed a center for the kinds of feminine refinement that had nothing to do with any awareness of the larger world. With very few bookstores, the campus was surrounded with files of clothing shops, restaurants, record stores, and coffee houses where students gathered to discover the most recent fashion in *Vogue* and to boast their knowledge of the number one songs on the American billboards over rare brands of coffee and expensive delicacies.

While not every Ewha student enjoyed these frivolities, the more serious-minded feminists were eclipsed by the overall impression generated by Ewha and its women's movement. Men's false propaganda, too, reinforced the trivialities of these women's pursuits. The word "feminism" came to carry the disturbing connotation of an inconsequential endeavor, brushed off as a luxury the country couldn't afford to take seriously.

Given that there were just as many men who were uninterested in the nation's top priority—fighting dictatorship—the charges against the feminists were far from fair. Neither I nor any other woman who wasn't striving to help other women had the right to criticize the women's movement, whose members were at least engaged in the struggle to generate more equality, if only for their own elite group. My personal crusade was to lessen the inequality within my own family.

My eyes and ears were wide open. I felt grateful to those recognized feminists who worked to engender justice for women and democracy for the whole country. They were risking not only their jobs but also their physical safety to stand up to the dictators and to keep gender-specific issues visible. In this way, the two most important tasks for Korean men and women—the fight for democracy and women's equality in the country—came together. By making their voices heard, they eventually managed to broaden their campaign base to encompass the problems facing the whole country. Thanks to them, Korean women today are blessed with opportunities that were merely dreams to their mothers. To give just a couple examples, the parliament now has set up quotas for women, while the president's cabinet, including the head of the Justice Department, boasts several women in key policy-making positions. This, of course, is the result of the steadily increasing participation of women in all professional walks, of the ever-growing numbers of women who are making their names in traditionally male-dominated arenas—such as big corporations, small businesses, medicine, law, information technology, and public administration.

Since I left the country for New York in January 1980, I have done nothing to earn a place in the history of the aforementioned achievements. As a solitary academic, I have done little more than keep myself informed, and as a Korean who has lived more than half of her life in another country, I hardly have the right to brag about the long road my people have traveled in such a short time. But in my heart, I feel entitled to share with the world how talented my people in Korea are at making changes!

Under the Gun

IN FIFTH GRADE, I BURIED MY NOSE IN BOOKS, HOPING THE SMALL letters would make me smarter. I worked my eyes to death, and every night a headache made it hard for me to fall asleep. Putting pressure on my temples to reduce the ache, I spread my hands on my eyelids, and to block out the dim city lights of Taegu filtering in through the gray curtains, I pulled the quilt over my head. As usual, however, my performance in school wasn't good. No matter how hard I worked, I seemed good only at drawing pictures of a faerie queen and a blue dragon in the air.

When autumn came, my eyesight didn't come back. I couldn't read anything on the board in school, and sitting in the third row in class, I had to squint to decipher what the teacher wrote. Panic came naturally since doing worse was not an option. Moreover, I had heard people say how ugly girls with "four eyes" were. I was already homely enough without glasses to make my brothers suspect I had been a cruel warrior in my previous life. To read the small letters in books, I had to lower my face until it almost touched the desk. My neck and shoulders ached from the pressure and my head ached from fatigue.

At first, I didn't tell Mother, afraid she would confirm that glasses would make me look uglier. I was also fearful she might tell me how foolish I was to work so hard as to ruin my eyes and still achieve only mediocre results. But in the early autumn of fifth grade, I received a severe scolding from my teacher, who thought I had not been paying attention at all. I had flunked one test after another in all subjects, and he warned me that such negligence would make me stay two years in the same class.

"I can't see anything on the board," I said in a faint voice, as if it were my fault.

He was surprised. "Do you need glasses?" Upon my nod, he said, "Ask your parents to get you some. If you sit that close to the board and can't see anything, you have pretty bad vision."

When I came home, I showed my report card to Mother and repeated to her what the teacher had told me. Without responding to my request for glasses, she scolded me, "How can you present grades like these? You are a shame to the family." As one of those millions of Korean mothers whose worth as human beings was determined by their children's academic performance, Mother was reacting as any mother would have. But I was too young to understand her frustration and just hated her at that moment.

"What did she do this time?" Big Brother appeared, slamming the sliding door of his room. Less Big Brother followed him out, grabbing one end of the door.

Mother's low, husky voice made her despair clear. "Her report card is full of red marks. If she doesn't do better, she won't make it to the sixth grade next year."

"She won't be able to enter the best junior high." Big Brother was grave. "She's going to be the first person in this family who doesn't go to a first-rate school. We can't let it happen."

"How do you mold a mind that useless, though?" Less Big Brother sneered.

"She knows how lonely she'll be if she doesn't improve," Big Brother replied. "She'll find a solution for herself."

That evening, I skipped dinner. I didn't think I deserved to eat unless my test scores were perfect. I had to excel, with or without glasses.

I had never excelled at memorization. Later in my life, I would learn that there are disciplines that reward reasoning over data retention, and I would finally find my niche. But in fifth grade, nothing mattered but memorizing all the data. This was the style of educa-

My parents pushed us endlessly to achieve in school. This photo was taken at Big Brother's graduation from the Master's program in economics at Seoul National University—the most elite department at the most elite university in Korea. From Left to Right: Mother, Big Brother, Father, Big Sister, and Less Big Brother.

tion in Korea at that time. Desperate to cope and compete with the West and Japan, Koreans built an educational system designed around absorbing information, a system of methods that tested one's ability to memorize, regurgitate, and apply facts. Science and technology took the primary place in the national curriculum, while subjects necessary to develop the economy such as math, accounting, and economics took precedence over every other field. Learning materials by heart was the top priority, and everything else had to be postponed.

Even in languages and literature, which suited me far better than the rest of the subjects, the pedagogy emphasized understanding literal meanings rather than examining subsurface implications. English had to be learned to absorb information from the West, to pick up the tools necessary to help the nation to rise in the world. It wasn't taught to instill deeper understandings about human beings and their environments. As a child who wished to talk to the characters I met in books, I always wanted to interpret rather than translate, to imagine ways of improving the plot rather than find words to fill in the blanks. Creativity cannot be tested in any educational system, and imaginative children who don't do well in standardized exams tend to be misunderstood anywhere. But I suffered more than many such children in other countries because the pressure for excellence under standardized curricula was that much greater in Korea.

I was being tortured by the very educational system that in the end worked to make my country the seventh largest economy in the world just forty-five years after the Korean War. I was held back by the very methods that enabled Koreans to achieve in half a century what the West achieved in over two centuries. Memorizing, which I loathed, helped the young population not only to absorb but also apply maximum information within a limited amount of time, raising the nation's industrial productivity to a globally competent level in a remarkably short period. By 2000, South Korea managed to reach a semi-post-industrial state of existence, boasting highly advanced technology with exports ranging from simple machinery to sophisticated, enduring electronics. The solid economy helped democracy take root, bringing an elected civilian government less than fifty years after Syngman Rhee's 1945 inauguration. The memorized information eventually became an intellectual foundation for a range of fields unrelated to industrialization, opening doors for young men and women with creative talents. It succeeded in raising the overall consciousness of the people, building groundwork for cultural richness. In just half a century, Korea surpassed its own expectations in a number of areas. Its movies became as exciting as Hollywood movies, its music and fine arts as moving as those from the West, and its literature as rich and diverse as any in Japan and Western Europe. The educational style that I hated so much as a child was what created South Korea of today.

Even now, exams measuring one's ability to memorize remain the only means of evaluating one's academic qualifications in Korea. After six years of backbreaking work in secondary school, teenagers must prove they deserve to go to college with just a couple of eight-hour exam days. If they fail, they must wait for another whole year to try again. To go to graduate school, too, college students have to pass one-day exams. No matter how excellent they were in all the years prior to the exams, they are automatically excluded if they have the bad luck of not doing well on that one day.

It is still difficult for South Korea to encourage creativity. South Koreans know that to be able to nurture creative talents, a nation must have plenty of natural resources the leeway to experiment and cut loss. Living creatively, they say, requires adopting what works well and throwing out what doesn't. It is possible only when one can afford to waste what isn't used well.

They maintain the American educational system can afford to encourage long-term experimental thoughts and ideas because in the end it can afford to throw out what doesn't work. "If we tried the American way," they say, "we'd go bankrupt in a day." Although Korea years ago cancelled exams for secondary school admission, exams are still in place for admission to college and graduate school. When I was in grade school, it wasn't terribly unusual to see some eleven- and twelve-year-old children coping with a suicidal depression because they couldn't move on to the next level. Nowadays, one sees teenagers and young adults in despair because they can't go to college.

On my next test, I shocked myself by doing well. I somehow—inexplicably—succeeded in memorizing what was required of me. Under the gun, I pushed the memorization button in my brain until it squeaked in pain, until it somehow turned itself on with mysterious, dazzling brightness. Only two weeks after giving me the frightening news, my teacher began to fill his reports with praise. I was astonished rather than flattered, puzzled by how I couldn't read a thing on the board, yet could answer correctly all the questions on the tests. I seemed to be an academic stunt girl.

My mother and brothers had given me at once a disease and a medicine, and for this I was proud and grateful. My family was looking out for me, seeing far into my distant future. In Korea, academic excellence was the single most important factor determining one's social status; education, as the only hope for the country's progress, was valued more highly than anything else, including money. Money comes and goes, Koreans say, but what's in your head stays. If we give education to our children, they'll give it to their children, and it'll be passed on like that for as long as they're alive. But money won't be passed on like that. Every child wishes to enter a good school, and every mother and father aspires to send their children to renowned schools with track records in producing distinguished talents.

My parents zealously pushed their children to join the ranks of these achievers, to earn the guaranteed security granted to those standing on the leading edge of the nation's development. As the training started in childhood, the whole family was involved in the process. Without being asked, Big Brother and Less Big Brother joined to help Mother and Father. Together, they were carving out the goal of my life, which was to receive the best possible education within my reach and to use the privilege of such education as a socially useful individual. Father's Confucian manner of communication, stern and commanding and at times harsh, was handed down to my Mother and brothers. They were telling me that the *joy* of achieving, the intense exhilaration that arrives after creating a miracle, was going to be my life. It wasn't going to be *happiness*, a sense of satisfaction that could be gained without a dear price.

My grades would seesaw for all of secondary school—abysmal to excellent and back to abysmal. As much as my low grades angered and frustrated me, they had far less impact on my self-image than my family's reaction. They saw my grades as proof of my low intelligence, as a mark of ineptitude. I was proud of my imagination and my way with words. I could bring my family to the brink of madness with my tongue and I could paint in my mind vivid fantasy stories. I kept going back and forth between who I thought I was—a smart, articulate, suffering spirit—and who my family seemed to think I was—a dumb, inarticulate little brat who didn't know her place. I was at war with myself and everyone else a hundred times a day. Most of the time, my self-contempt was intermixed with my self-confidence, and going up and down the roller coaster of these two loud, opposite voices became my daily routine.

Before I started going to school, my stories were a source of entertainment for my family. When I said, "The tree is weeping. It must be sad," they would laugh, fascinated by the way I interpreted the power of the wind. As report cards flushed out everything but a child's ability to follow fixed rules, my family did the same, losing the good humor they had enjoyed over my charmingly odd comments. Yet it now occurs to me that their appreciation of my imagination, though short-lived, somehow encouraged me. I wonder if I would be writing books today if my ability to see a weeping tree had been entirely crushed.

In 1967, however, I was only an eleven-year-old child without an adult's insights. Blindly devoted to achieving excellence, I drove myself to a breaking point. As the winter break returned, I was so depressed I couldn't go back to books for two months on end. My eyes failed me again, and every day I fought an earthquake in my head. I needed glasses, and once again I confronted Mother in vain. Her face turned blank, and wearing that plastic mask with only one expression, she walked away into the kitchen without a word. At least she could have told me that it wasn't a lack of love that made her indifferent—it was poverty that made her incapable of providing anything but the essentials for the family's survival. But as I would find out as an adult, such an explanation was beyond her capacity. All her life, she had been told to practice the Confucian way, to believe that soft, affectionate talk would spoil a child.

"A worthless chick can demand so much," was Grandmother's unsurprising position. "We just don't have the money for her glasses. We have to buy winter underwear for the boys now and that'll leave us with less than nothing."

The summer before sixth grade, my report card was filled with red marks again. Panicking, Father ordered Big Brother to supervise my homework, Less Big Brother to teach me math, and Mother to pour a bucket of cold water on my face if I didn't get up before dawn to read. That I had stopped eating again failed to catch their attention; they saw nothing but the red marks on my report card. To be perfect, I had to be as light as a feather with a mind as steely as that of a brilliant blue dragon.

I was lost in despair until September came back to bring an even keel. One day my family gathered in front of the persimmon tree in the backyard of our house. Heavy with the fruit ready to fall, the tree was waiting for us to pick from it, and we were eager to get started. While Big Brother and Less Big Brother climbed up the tree to shake it, Big Sister and I gathered the fallen persimmons in a bucket, and Mother and Grandmother took them to a water pump to wash. Little Sister, too, carried a few in her hands, hopping back and forth between the tree and the pump a hundred times. Eventually, we had all the fruit on the ground. After washing them clean, Mother and Grandmother put them in a giant pot of salt water, which was then wrapped in black cloth. They told the boys to bring the pot inside and set it in a corner, where the persimmons stayed for several weeks to turn sweet and crisp with none of the tart taste.

Since persimmons didn't cost a cent, even Grandmother didn't grumble when I grabbed as many as I could and clutched them to my chest. I was driven to out-eat my brothers to avenge myself for how cruel they had been all summer. Practically living beside the pot, I was amazed at how many persimmons my stomach could digest in one evening. Imagining that each one I ate was a smack in Big Brother's face and that each stone I threw out in the trashcan was one of Less Big Brother's teeth, I gorged myself until it was difficult to stand up and walk from one room to another. That I was hurting myself to get even with them didn't occur to me until I woke up one night from a tearing abdominal pain, a severe case of obstruction. When Mother put me in a taxi and hammered her fist on the doctor's door, at an hour when even stray dogs found corners to hide in, I felt afraid. Standing alone with her on the deadly quiet street, I suddenly figured that my evil thoughts about my brothers had caught up with me and landed me in the hands of a doctor.

But when we left the doctor's office, I felt happy. I was holding Mother's hand, occupying her attention all by myself. This monopoly of her care, so rare and precious, was a treat.

"Why did you eat so many?" she stopped walking to ask. "Didn't I tell you to stop after two of them because persimmons can make you obstructed?"

"I wanted to eat the most," I answered, tilting my face up to look at her in the eye.

Mother broke into a peal of laughter. I had never heard her sound so exuberant before. "It's my fault," she said. "I ate too much kimchi while I was pregnant with you. All that spice and garlic got into your system and made you into a child who goes overboard with everything she does."

I could tell she was proud of me. She was watching herself—a part she never showed anyone—in the convex mirror that was me, and until I could fulfill this partial reflection, neither one of us would know how close we were.

I finally passed the entrance exams for junior high. During that cold January, relatives came to our house to celebrate, bundled up to show only their eyes.

"How does it feel to win such an awesome competition?" one of them exclaimed. "It's not just the best school in Taegu—it's one of the best in the nation!"

"A girl from K High School is so smart, I hear," another one chimed in. "Even her great-grandchildren are guaranteed a high IQ. If there were a way I could give a fraction of your gift to my girls, I'd pay with everything I have."

"But you don't want her aggressive personality," Mother interjected. "It's the most ferocious and intractable one that has ever been born from a woman's stomach." Her face, however, belied her voice. I detected a secret approval and pride in her eyes and in the set of her mouth, slanted down in an effort to hide a broad smile.

"Since she's got all the characteristics of a strong man, she's going to raise a bunch of tough boys who will cut trees down and pave roads bare-handed," another relative remarked.

"Before she has those boys, she's got to find a man to take her in. She's not going to find one if she doesn't tone her hot temperament down," Grandmother cut in. "No man likes a woman rougher than he, not to mention a girl smarter." But her critical voice, just like Mother's, revealed tremendous pride.

"Anyway, she brought all of us honor. For that alone, she deserves to be treated like a boy for a while."

In bed that night, I played the adults' conversation over in my mind, word by word. Everything I accomplished seemed to be for everyone but myself. In order to be respected by my family and relatives, I would have to be as smart and strong as any of the boys in my range of competition. But to raise the toughest boys in history, which was the most glorious thing a woman could do for herself and her family, I would have to find the bravest man in the world, and to find him, I would have to be the kindest, most subservient of women.

"If I have children, I will have to prefer boys to girls," I spoke to myself in the dark. "No, I will never marry. I would rather not have children than prefer boys to girls. I will never have a family." I ground my teeth and fell asleep to the echoing words of my relatives.

Thanks to their praise, I finally got glasses. For a while, my parents were convinced I was as good as a boy, worth the burden of borrowing a small fortune from a relative. They took me to an optometrist in downtown Taegu, to learn for the first time how bad my eyesight was.

"What made you wait this long?" the optometrist wondered. "In my twenty years as an optometrist, I've never seen parents who let their children's eyes get this bad."

"We didn't know," Father answered. "When she cried because she couldn't see anything, we thought she had a headache."

"Ha!" the optometrist cried in disbelief.

When I came home with my glasses on, the first thing I saw was Big Brother's mocking face.

"Hey, you know what?" he shouted. "You look like Okhee, your neighbor." He crossed his eyes, narrowing them to slits, and opened his mouth wide and long to look like an idiot.

Okhee was a girl who lived only a few doors away from my family. She always appeared with her mouth agape and her eyes blank, walking along the block with one shoulder drooping, carrying a bag full of books that never seemed to teach her anything. Her mouth was said to be so wide open that the boys in the neighborhood could push their fists in and out of it.

"You look like a purple yam," I retaliated, dashing to my room.

"Why the hell does she take a joke so seriously?" Big Brother asked Mother. "She's breathing like a dog in July. She's so angry."

"Because she's insecure." Mother was nonchalant. I wished she would defend me for once.

Although I resented Big Brother's joke, I believed him. I thought I looked like Okhee with my glasses on, so I rarely wore them except when I had to read small letters. I knew what I was missing, because when I wore glasses the darkness lifted and the outlines of objects rose sharply and clearly. It was as if the clouds had cleared up to show the bluest sky at noon. But I was a girl and looking like a geek was a crime. I chose to live with the same old darkness for a while longer.

Dead Man Speaks

BY THE TIME I STARTED TO ATTEND K GIRLS' JUNIOR HIGH, I WORE glasses all the time. I was the one born to *know*, and to *know*, I had to *see*. My desire to know was so overwhelming that I wished I could see what was happening around me when I was asleep. But it wasn't until I witnessed a shaman's exorcism for Grandmother that I had the experience of seeing the invisible. My eyes finally met ghosts.

Summoned by the shaman, the unseen spirits were hovering over Grandmother's face, dancing with shapeless bodies and crying and laughing in unheard voices. The shaman talked to them in a trance, her eyes barely open and her mouth moving without a sound. She was twisting her legs and arms in the motions of the spirits, gyrating her torso in a wide circle to follow their frantic gestures. Contorted with their pain and woe, the shaman's face was lifted toward the sky as if to look for an answer.

Her wardrobe was of dazzling bright colors, designed to counter the sadness a shaman was supposed to express through her body. Flowing down to her calves in a radiant purple, the long, wide, buttonless coat seemed capacious enough to conceal wild physical movements. The white folded collars attached on top stood for the pure mental state one enters after cleansing the dirt in one's soul. The purple and the white created an ensemble of rapture and peace, the two antithetical feelings one reaches at the end of an eternal road. But one could arrive at such a spiritual land only after a long pilgrimage of frustrated passions and unrealized dreams, and her shirt under the coat, red like fresh blood, symbolized this essential journey. Because she was covered by the half-sleeved coat, only parts of this red were visible on her arms. Perhaps the bright purple of the coat covered most of the red to emphasize the eventual joys that come from suffering, to envision the final laughter born of tears. Her broad sash, used to belt the coat, was also blood red. It represented a passion denied, and the failures that make one bleed during one's trek toward success.

My grandmother was my family's loudest advocate for the Confucian patriarchy that had ruined her back and her health and had left her a de facto slave to an unfaithful husband.

"I meant no harm, no grief, no lament, no sorrow, and no breakup!" she suddenly bellowed. "Blame me, blame me. I was the culprit and I still am!" She lowered her face, looking down on Grandmother who was sitting mute on the floor in the living room. "I did nothing for the son I gave you. You had to break your back to raise him. See what you've done for our son all by yourself. Shame on me and the gods praise you!" The contrition in her face and voice was so moving that I almost thought the shaman herself was apologizing to Grandmother.

"Who's talking to Grandmother?" I whispered to Mother.

"Your late grandfather," Mother whispered back.

"Grandfather?" I nearly cried in surprise. I had never heard anything positive about him from Grandmother. I wanted to know why he was begging her for forgiveness. "What happened?" I asked.

"Sshh," Mother hushed me. Talking in the middle of an exorcism would irritate the gods.

"I had no choice," the shaman kept on. "I was doomed at birth, doomed at life, and doomed at death. I didn't mean to steal your husband away. My fate did." She swung her arms in the air in a chaotic fashion, wailing in the soft, plaintive voice of an elderly woman.

Grandmother was sitting like a statue, her eyes fixed on the floor and her hands folded on her lap. Even her usual bitter expression was gone, her face impassive. I was dying to know who this new female ghost was. I could only guess that Grandfather had left Grandmother for her a long time ago. Only later did I learn that she was Grandfather's second wife, called his Small Wife and the Small Mother of his children.

"My children! Oh, my children!" The shaman broke into a loud sob. She continued to speak in the Small Mother's voice, "I want to see them one more time. Dead and gone, they are drifting here and there, nowhere between this and the other world." A smile of hope shined through her tears. "Oh, but I have one here in this world! He's a good boy, a good, good boy!"

"Who is this boy?" I couldn't resist asking, but Mother pressed her finger to her lips.

"Why, he lives in shame!" The shaman went back to sobbing, pounding her fist on her chest. "Why? He wishes he were dead just like his brother and sister." Her arms shook, making the wide sleeves dance.

For a moment, Grandmother's lips trembled slightly, but the blank expression came back to her face.

"He wants to see you, you, his Big Mother, but he can't." The shaman squatted down on the floor, facing Grandmother. "I, his Small Mother, his real mother, brought the curse upon him. I provoked the gods."

"Doesn't she know Grandmother will be buried beside Grandfather?" Big Sister murmured, sitting beside me. "She doesn't have a grave. Her son doesn't have a last name. She brought it upon herself."

"Sshh," Mother hushed.

"Big Mother, Big Mother," the spirit-bringer resumed in a new voice, a young woman's voice, while walking away from Grandmother, her purple coat fluttering. "Forgive me, forgive Small Mother, my mother, and forgive my living brother and my dead brother, your Small Sons. I didn't mean to kill myself. I didn't know I would have to roam around nowhere and everywhere, forever stuck in between this and the other world. I am trapped in the place for those who commit suicide." She stood still, her face lowered, her legs and arms together with a maiden's plaintive shyness. "Oh, but have mercy on me. The gods don't know how I suffered before I left this world. I still suffer, for I can't go to the other world." She closed her eyes, clasped her hands in prayer to the gods, bowed deeply three times, and walked back toward Grandmother.

But she had to stop as Little Sister sprang up from Mother's lap to grab an apple on the ceremonial table and Mother ran after her, gasping, "Aigoo!"

"No trouble, no trouble at all!" The shaman, restored to her own body, burst out laughing, holding Little Sister by the arm. "The gods enjoy mischievous little ones. Let her have what she wants." She picked up a piece of fried beef on the table and handed it to Little Sister. With an apple in one hand and the fried beef in the other, Little Sister smiled, looking at Mother for approval, and Mother laughed as everyone else did. Even Grandmother chuckled.

"Look at your little offspring," the shaman spoke to Grandfather's ghost, still holding Little Sister by the arm. "Your last one, your precious, precious little one. If you want to make it up to your Big Wife, follow this little one around and keep her from all harm." She picked up Little Sister and plopped her down on Grandmother's lap.

There was another round of hearty laughter as Grandmother put her arms around her little one and yelled at her husband's ghost: "A womanizer can't give his habit away to a dog! You can't! But you can make it up to your grandchildren! Guide them well, help them to succeed!"

There was nothing funny about her grief and anger, but we laughed because it was all too familiar to us. I laughed out of joy, watching her holding Little Sister on her lap with an affection she had never shown before. Her amused eyes were following the fried beef and apple as they disappeared into the tiny mouth. I felt certain that by now she had completely forgotten that she had called her a worthless chick. Little Sister was her flesh and blood, the last child of her only son whom she had had raised alone and with nothing.

"Look how special your grandchildren are," the shaman spoke to Grandfather's ghost cheerfully. "How striking they are! Look at the youngest one especially and the peculiar way she eats her apple!" She pointed her finger at Little Sister, who was making a thin circle around the middle of her apple like a ring. She always sank her teeth into the center of her apple first before eating other parts of it.

"Even when she's hungry, she doesn't forget to show off her artistic talent." The spirit woman turned to Grandmother. "Yes, he was a worthless womanizer, but look at what he gave your little ones. He gave them his gift, his flair, his delicious touch of deviancy, his passion for beauty, and his love for creation. Wide, wide roads with no stop signs are waiting for your grandchildren." She raised her voice and addressed Grandfather, "You see what you left to be with that Small Wife of yours! You left a jewel. You left this woman, this woman who made you flourish with a hoard of smart, healthy, pretty, and handsome offspring."

"Ah, but have mercy on me," Grandfather pleaded. "I would have given my life to my second Small Son had I been able to. How I wished I could pour my breath into his body when he was dying from encephalitis! He was only seven, dying when his life hadn't begun. I saw his mother, my Small Wife, cry until her eyes bled with red tears."

The shaman lifted her face toward the sky to push down

Grandfather's tears gathering in her eyes. I had never seen a man cry, but I saw Grandfather cry through a shaman; perhaps when men wept as ghosts, they didn't have to feel shame.

"Show your big heart, woman, to the people who buried their children," she spoke to Grandmother. "Stretch your loving hands toward your husband and his Small Wife, your hands that'll never lay your children in the ground before you die."

Grandfather's Small Wife had three children with him, one of whom died as a little boy and another as a young woman. His first Small Son—my illegitimate uncle—was alive and well somewhere in Korea, but his second Small Son, as Grandfather's ghost had lamented, died from encephalitis at seven. His Small Daughter committed suicide for a reason I couldn't figure out.

"Big Mother, Big Mother," the shaman resumed in a little boy's voice, standing up and sitting down alternately, her red skirt sweeping the floor. "I know you wanted to adopt me, me, your enemy's son. My mother, my Small Mother, stole your husband away from you, but oh, generous, loving Big Mother, you cared for me. You let me eat with you, let me sleep with your children, and took me to markets with you. You bought me fruits and candies, packed my books, sent me to school, held my hand when it was cold, and fanned me to sleep when it was hot." Sitting down in front of Grandmother and holding her hands, the shaman pleaded for the boy. "For my sake, Big Mother, please forgive my mother. She loved me as you loved me. I love her as I love you."

A flash of tender sorrow flitted across Grandmother's face, but passed as quickly as it came. Still holding her hands, the shaman continued, "If you forgive everyone who hurt you, gracious woman, the gods will reward you. They will give your offspring long, prosperous, and healthy lives."

To force Grandmother to look at her in the eye, she tilted her face downward and almost touched Grandmother's nose with her own. A funny sight, it brought a wave of laughter in the living room, cracking open a sunny spot in Grandmother's cloudy face.

"You want your girls in here," the negotiator said, pointing her finger respectively at me, Big Sister, and Little Sister on Grandmother's lap, "and your boys out there to achieve every prize and fortune they wish for, don't you? Especially for the boys who aren't here now, you want to forgive. You want to give them good wives with plenty of sons. You want to forgive everyone who hurt you, don't you?"

The shaman's differentiation between the boys and girls made me notice, for the first time since the exorcism had started, that none of the men in the family were present. Only women, including some from the neighborhood who had dropped in out of curiosity, were at the scene. Why only the girls? Girls who were called "strangers of the house" or "outsiders" because they would be given away to their husbands' families?

"Where are Father and Brothers?" I asked Mother.

"Men don't take part in things like this," Mother replied, frowning at me to be silent.

"You forgive, then?" The shaman wouldn't relent. "You are nodding, aren't you?" She kept looking at Grandmother's impassive face, and as the old woman nodded ever so slightly, she cried ecstatically, "This generous woman has finally forgiven all! Gods of the universe, watch her and reward her offspring!" She turned to the audience, "Applaud, applaud!"

Everyone clapped thunderously, laughing. I clapped until my palms felt sore.

"Take this little one out of the house," the shaman ordered the woman from next door, picking up Little Sister from Grandmother's lap. "Take her to your house and let her stay with your little ones. Lock the gate until my knife dance is over."

"You want to play with my girls, don't you?" the neighbor coaxed Little Sister, who didn't want to leave. "*The Three Vampires* is coming on TV in a moment—on our color TV! If you miss it this time, we won't let you in again."

Mother gave the woman three large apples, one for Little Sister and two for her little girls. "Follow her," she said to Little Sister. "She has your apple and the color TV you like so much. Be a good girl."

As a faint smile appeared on Little Sister's face, the woman took her hand and left the house. When the neighbor came back in a few minutes, the shaman ordered everyone, "Go down to the front yard and leave the door of the living room wide open. Stay as far away as you can from the old woman. You don't want to be touched by my knife."

She took a butcher's knife out of her large pouch and held it vertically, standing in front of Grandmother. It was one of those knives used by merchants at a market to butcher chickens for their customers. Razor sharp and polished until it shone blue in the sun, it made a chill like the February wind run down my spine.

"You, evil spirits in here and out there, in this and the other world, and inside and outside this woman's mind and body!" the shaman bellowed. "You, evil spirits, listen to the gods, get away from her!"

The knife danced wildly but purposefully. Was this chaos the pattern of the evil spirits? Did evil ghosts have no logic? Could anyone get caught in their random trails?

"Try to hamper her, to enter her, to stop her, to make her hate and to be cursed by the gods. They will look out for her, make her forgive, bless her heart, and reward her offspring!" she roared. "Take her and be damned!"

Maneuvering like a boxer, she leaped about the living room, following the rectangular edges with her back to the walls. There was a horrific beauty in the hair-raising precision with which the shaman wielded the butcher's knife. The living room was being cleansed of everything that could curse Grandmother to be angry and bitter.

"Get out, get out," the exorcist kept on, "or taste this blade, this blade sharper than the needle of a syringe. Fly away, fly far, far away."

Completing her galloping dance, she came back to the center and lunged toward Grandmother. The blade halted a fraction of an inch from Grandmother's nose, ready to behead her with one strike. But there was not a shred of fear in Grandmother's emotionless face. It was I who had to struggle not to scream. Terror made me sweat in the freezing February wind, forcing me to cover my face with my hands. I could understand why the shaman had sent Little Sister away.

But something in me pried my eyes open. They were going to *see* the evil ghosts being exorcised. I blinked my eyes, registering every bustle of the skirt and every flap of the coat. The red and the purple in the costume whirled, the snow white of her collar standing out against the determination in her face.

"Try to enter her and be cursed," she warned the evil spirits again, the tip of the blade poised at Grandmother's forehead. "Tempt her and be cut in a million pieces by the gods' weapon." She slowly lifted the knife above Grandmother's head, making wide circles several times, repeating, "Leave now and be saved. Leave now." For a moment, she was silent, moving the knife rapidly up and down over Grandmother's unmoving torso. Nobody uttered a sound. We were all mesmerized by her movements.

Before she spoke again, a picture came into my mind. The knife wielded by the shaman looked eerily familiar; I knew I had seen it before. It was the blade I had imagined throwing, in my furious fantasy, at Grandmother on the day of Little Sister's birth, when she had said, "Your mother had a worthless pussy."

"The gods will let you go," the shaman sang, "free as the wind, random as the air. Farewell, farewell!"

A shriek tore out of her throat, the sound of shearing metal. It was the cry of one particularly tenacious spirit refusing to leave Grandmother.

"You, the carrier of remorse," the shaman regained her own voice. "You're the only one still here. Everyone else has left. Leave quickly, now, or the gods' blade will cut you in pieces."

Another metallic cry soared in the air, and the shaman stabbed it, bringing the knife down vertically until it almost touched the floor.

"Come on in and eat," she commanded the audience in the yard after a deep, slow breath. Her voice was hoarse, her face wet with sweat. Her appearance had taken on the peaceful stillness of a tree after a raging wind.

Little Sister was fetched back from the neighbor's house and the feast started in the living room as all the women were seated around the lacquered ceremonial table. It was burdened with various items of fancy food, little lumps of choice ground beef held by short, thin wooden sticks, huge, salted croakers steamed slowly and thoroughly on a low fire, and a dried octopus soaked for hours in water to be boiled in graduating temperatures. There were bowls of soup, patiently simmered with blended pieces of radish, clam, mussel, and squid. Beside them were scores of little rice cakes delicately cut in various shapes. The large, square chunks of pork, from which the fat was drained by repeated boiling, were deliciously matched with spinach, bracken, bean sprouts, and bellflower roots, boiled slightly and then toasted in oil and soy sauce. These greens were to be mixed with perfectly steamed rice in a huge metal bowl and then doled out in a dozen or so small porcelain bowls. There were whole stalks of deep-fried green onions and squarely cut malted rice; the dark red of the dried jujubes were striking against the yellowish white of the peeled, raw chestnuts. The trays of whole pears and apples and persimmons, behind which the cooked items were arranged in double lines, tempted my eyes, too, with their seductively contrasting colors.

I thought I was going to have the rare privilege of sharing some of the painstakingly prepared beef and croakers, but Mother picked most of them up from the table and put them in an icebox for the Three Men of the Family. All that was left for the women who had honored the exorcism by waiting patiently on a freezing February day were the greens to go with the rice and the soup, some of the apples and jujubes, and a large lump of white rice cake cut into square pieces. Even the pears and persimmons were hidden away in the icebox because they were more expensive than the other fruits available in winter. I felt my appetite dwindle to the size of a pea.

Shakespeare on a Grass Roof

AFTER THE EXORCISM, NOTHING SEEMED TO HAVE CHANGED. As March came with a mellow spring breeze, Grandmother was still bitter. She lashed out as if everything she saw and heard provoked hate and disgust.

"You know what," she would instruct her grandchildren. "An impious daughter-in-law is the root of all evil. She'll devour her husband and his children, and sever the ties between him and his parents. Your relative, Dukhee, has an evil daughter-in-law like that. You watch if there is one like that in your own family."

Whenever Father wanted to go out with Mother, Grandfather sabotaged them with a disdainful harrumph. "Hmm," she would mutter, showing her back to them. "Before I feel sorry for Jongdae, I should feel sorry for myself. His only son squanders all his money on his wife and treats his mother like gravel under his feet, but my only son does even worse. He lavishes money on his wife when he ought to be saving every nickel and dime for his children." Feeling sorry for his wife but unable to say anything, Father would leave alone quietly, closing the gate behind him with as little sound as possible. Mother would return to her room and lie down with a deep sigh. To make her feel better, I would sit beside her, massaging her legs, and she would murmur, "You're the only one who tries to understand me. You deserve the best. Why are we giving you so little?"

"What's wrong with Grandmother?" I would inquire in an attempt to help her to vent her anger and frustration. "What happened?"

But there was no hate in in her voice, only compassion and forgiveness. "She's had a sad, sad life. She doesn't know what she's doing."

"Tell me about her life." Massaging Mother's legs, I realized how thin she was, lying on the floor like a long, brittle wooden stick, and I could feel the physical consequences of the hard, poor life she had to endure. Her shins seemed as narrow as the back of the shaman's knife, and her stomach and breasts as flat as roads ground down by fast cars. Such sparse flesh over such small bones reminded me of my anorexia and my own gaunt little body, and I thought I was witnessing my nightmares in her emaciation. Touching her soft muscles, I was seized by a desire to forgive her for all her harshness.

I wanted to forgive her for one night in particular. As a child, I kept a large pouch filled with coins and little bills I had accumulated. I used to take it out of the closet to open it and show off its contents to guests, soliciting them to make the pouch heavier by adding a few more. I didn't have to say anything, since showing the contents of my savings was enough. But upon discovering the pouch empty one day, I let out a scream. I found out that Mother had emptied it. To save and fill the pouch, I had sacrificed candies and cookies, for which every child has an irresistible appetite. Now, everything I had gathered was gone. I hated Mother. I wanted to get even, and when an opportunity came I took it. I bought cookies and ice cream with the money she had given me for notebooks and drawing paper. But because I had never told her how I felt about the empty pouch, she didn't know I was retaliating. Hard pressed for the money to buy food, she had stolen a child's coins and forgot. To her, I seemed a willful child who enjoyed spiting her mother. She interrogated me about the whereabouts of the dimes, and when I confessed, she slapped me in the face, accusing me of having treated myself to luxuries while she was starved of bread. Her face that night was terrifying.

Years later, I realized the connection between my empty pouch and Grandmother's exorcism. Mother had borrowed a fortune to hire the shaman and prepare the feast. As the daughter-in-law of a wealthy, powerful family would, she fulfilled her filial duty toward her mother-in-law by granting her wishes for a grand ritual, but as the wife of an underpaid high school teacher, she couldn't handle the expenses. To pay back the money she had borrowed from a friend, she had to scrape pennies together. She had to hurt her child by stealing her coins.

"Your grandmother," Mother began, "was buried alive by her mother-in-law, a truly evil woman. Your great-grandmother was the root of all the tragedy that fell upon every relation who came after her."

Stories about my great-grandmother's reign of terror reached far beyond her village. Great-Grandmother trained her daughter-in-law (Grandmother) to be her son's hands and feet and to be a machine catering to the needs of her in-laws. Under her iron hand, Grandmother had to be a mindless dog content with the crumbs of food thrown at her by her in-laws, a domestic slave bound to her husband's family. This institution of slavery was extremely effective and productive, especially for ambitious parents with bright sons and little financial means. Poor but with high hopes, my great-grandparents recruited a daughter-in-law who would not only serve their smart son's every whim but obviate their need for expensive servants. Hearing about a seventeen-year-old maiden wanted by nobody because of her plain, masculine face, they sent a matchmaker to her village. In a few days, they obtained approval from her parents, who were tired of having to feed a "leftover daughter" and were grateful enough to say yes. My great-grandparents reckoned their daughter-in-law would be too thankful to harbor any complaint about her backbreaking work.

They also predicted she would be able to produce a male child for their son and their glorious ancestors. According to the physiognomist they consulted, their future daughter-in-law had facial features forecasting a male child; she had that "son look" in her brows, which were separated from each other by a wide margin, and in her aquiline nose, which appeared in a man's face more often than in a woman's. The young bride exuded a willful aura commendable in a man, but condemnable in a woman. The physiognomist assured them that the very look that made her unattractive to men would bring them what they wanted the most—a bright, healthy, and handsome grandson. On top of the "son look," she had an excellent constitution that would endure endless labor, and, when necessary, abuse. She had all the right qualities to be the daughter-in-law of a poor family of noble heritage. When she married my grandfather in 1918, she was fit to be a perfect "kitchen dog."

To me, Grandmother's face seemed rather feminine. It was true she had a prominent, aquiline nose and a wide space between the brows, but these features made her appear to be a highly cerebral woman with wit and imagination. I even thought there was a sexually provocative air about her, enhanced by these unusual assets; I was proud that she had managed to preserve its vestige despite her hardships. Against the soot from the primitive wood stoves in her kitchen, where she spent nearly her entire life, I could picture a beautiful face. In the privacy of the kitchen, I imagined, she could be who she believed she was, her eyes twinkling with the desire to see what they had never seen, her mouth opening to say things she wasn't allowed to say. She was an attractive country woman whose down home wisdom could undo a sophisticated urban intellect. Grandmother was once a loving, smart woman whose marrow of life was drained out before she had a chance to be loved back.

To justify the way they treated Grandmother, my great-grandparents needed to believe that drudgery was her fate. They had to reinforce the Confucian way of thinking—whatever happened to a woman was her fate. As an adult, I could see how such distorted reasoning could lull a person's guilt—and the country's sexist ideology—into a peaceful sleep. I lived under the same roof with Grandmother and detested her myself to the degree that I more than once wished she would be struck dead. To absolve myself of this horrible thought, I elected to believe that she was an ugly person who deserved my secret curse. Only when I grew old enough, I could entertain my vision of her as a young woman, warm and radiantly beautiful.

"Why were my great-grandparents so poor?" I interrupted Mother. "Why did they have to make a slave out of their daughter-in law? Weren't they a noble family with plenty of money and lots of servants?"

"Their ancestors were noble and wealthy for many generations." Mother, too, frowned. "But your great-grandfather couldn't sustain the status he inherited."

"Why not?"

"He was trained all his life to become a government bureaucrat. But when he was ready to take the exam, the whole Confucian system of government was changed into a Western style. He lost everything he had worked for, and he never recovered from it."

In my history class, I had learned that by the last decade of the nineteenth century, Korea started to abolish the Confucian bureaucracy that had been the founding principle of the country for five centuries. But the habit of worshipping book knowledge—the core of Confucian ideology—lingered on to govern the Korean mind.

"Is that why he never did anything else except read those stupid Confucian books?" I was contemptuous. "Is that why he did nothing to fix the leaking roof of his house and sat—just sat—at his desk, watching the water soak into his precious books?"

Mother laughed. "He knew no other way of making a living except through books. It was deeply ingrained in him that commerce or physical labor was degrading for a scholar. So he wrote family histories for rich merchants and fell back on the land he had inherited from his ancestors."

But writing family histories for rich merchants was far from sufficient to provide for his wife and son. He found himself selling the land bit by bit to buy food—and books that he cherished as an escape from the reality of his failure. Increasingly irritated, his wife, who simply could not give up the dream of being an important man's wife, pinned all her hopes on her son—my bright, handsome, and healthy grandfather, who could memorize a book at one reading.

"But wasn't he adopted because she couldn't have children?"

"Yes, he was. She adopted him the day he was born."

"Tell me how he was adopted."

"Your great-grandfather had three brothers, one of whom was an extremely kind man. He felt bad that he had two sons while his oldest brother, the one to inherit the family name, had no children at all. So he promised, when his wife was pregnant with their third child, that he would give him the baby if it was a boy."

*My father, seated at center, with his half-siblings, Small
Mother's children. To the left is my Aunt Haeok, to the right,
Uncle Youngsan. Behind them is Father's young male cousin.*

"And Great-Grandmother loved her adopted son so."

"Yes, she did. Although she was horrible to her daughter-in-law, she was an angel to her son, her adopted son who she believed was meant to make her the proudest mother in the whole world."

"What happened?"

"I think it was because she was so cruel to her daughter-in-law that things didn't turn out as she planned. It was retribution."

What Mother called retribution was Grandfather's affair, which led to a thirty-year common-law marriage and three illegitimate children. It was a fatal union from the start, a secret matrimony between a lonely man far away from his wife and a woman desperate to escape the future facing her. An illegitimate daughter herself, Grandfather's Small Wife knew that if she married a man who had been born out of wedlock like she had, her children, too, would be permanently without a last name, repeating her curse.

In Korea, there was a form called a "household registration," which a man obtained upon marrying. In this form, he listed his name on top and added the names of his wife and children in the following columns. Then, he took it to his county registrar's office and had it kept there until his children married, at which point their names would have to be taken out. Unlike a birth certificate, its Western counterpart, a household registration could not be issued unless one had a father or a husband who could claim one as a dependent. In a family system founded on household registration, a single, unmarried mother could not give her children legal identities until she married a man, and children raised by a bastard mother alone could not obtain legal status until they found a male citizen willing to act as their legal sire. Nor could a man register his children born out of wedlock. They were considered fatherless and treated as outcasts under the laws of the very country that not only tolerated but encouraged married men to accumulate concubines.

Before she met him, Yunkyong, my Grandfather's Small Wife, promised herself she would marry a man with a legitimate lineage and deliver her children from the shame of her birth. She dreamed of loving and being loved by a promising young man with the courage to accept her as a spouse. Deep down, she knew the man of her dreams would probably not marry her, but she refused to deny herself the hope, no matter how unrealistic. And a miracle indeed came to her. She saw her prince in the handsome, courteous, well-educated young man who showed up as a new English teacher in her high school. He had just been transferred from a small school in a rural town and was full of the enthusiasm and vitality of a young educator, the kind of energy that made teenage girls' hearts throb. When he quoted lines from Shakespeare and Milton, he reminded them of Prince Hamlet and they all became Ophelias in love.

"You'd better tell me how she got his attention," I asked.

"She was a clever romance-monger," Mother described. "She would copy lines from Shaaiks—"

"Shakespeare."

"From the famous poet, anyhow," Mother went on, unembarrassed by her bad English accent, "on pink papers with flower patterns, and she would add her own lines, such as 'If you want to know who I am, please open the next envelope coming. I am your Cordelia and your Portia,' and leave them on his desk while he was away for lunch."

After three months of secret communication, Grandfather finally agreed to meet her at a place she designated in her letter. It was a small, cozy bookstore in downtown Seoul, with coffee tables and wooden chairs along a side wall. As she always had, she handed him a note, and this time he didn't look puzzled. He just blushed, flattered but self-conscious.

"Are you aware that I am married?" He tried to be firm without hurting her.

"The rumor is true then." She sounded disappointed, but far from surprised.

"What rumor?"

"That you are married to an illiterate woman handpicked for you by your parents." Her impetuous words were a challenge to him. "That you are just like all these traditional men. With all your sophisticated Western education and revolutionary ideas, you remain no different from all the other tradition-bound, hypocritical cowards. You quote Shakespeare from the grass roof of a traditional Korean house. You preach democracy, but you don't practice it. You don't have the courage to be heard at an amphitheatre. I am ashamed of you."

Grandfather was shocked and humiliated. Nobody, not even his best friends, had ever charged him with cowardice; none of them had ever provoked him to look into himself so mercilessly. By confronting him, she was inviting him to join her in abjuring the old and embracing the new. Grandfather and the sassy young girl named Yunkyong fell in love. Beautiful as it was, their affair clawed apart the earth upon which Grandfather's family was built, destroying everyone in their lives and uprooting those who came after them, one by one.

The first casualty was my illiterate grandmother, who lost her husband to a Western-educated, bright, and much younger student. My father and his sister were robbed of their father as children, fed by a jobless single mother and grandparents who had nothing except some old-fashioned Confucian books, a house with a leaking roof, and land they were too proud to plow.

"But it was that evil great-grandmother of ours," I cut in, "that caused all that grief for everyone. Didn't she separate Grandfather from Grandmother by force?"

"Yes, she did. When your grandfather was transferred to a school in Seoul, she didn't want to let your grandmother go with him."

"Why?"

"Because once your grandmother was gone, she was afraid she would have to do all the housework herself. She wanted to live like a noble lady."

"Didn't Grandmother have every right to follow her husband?"

"That's what we believe now. But back then, my dear child," Mother explained, "most married women were chattel of their husbands' families. If your grandmother had said no to her mother-in-law and gone with her husband, she would have been condemned as a 'whore' who knew only her man and neglected all duties of a good daughter-in-law. In 1929, the Yi Dynasty had only just legally ended."

"What about Grandfather? Why didn't he do anything to take his wife with him?" I was hot with fury.

"He couldn't, for the same reason your Grandmother couldn't. He couldn't take the risk of being called a wimp controlled by his wife. He couldn't betray his parents."

"But he shouldn't have picked another woman. Just because he was far away from his wife, he had no right to betray the marriage. He was irresponsible!"

"He was! Everyone, including your father, sees it. Not every man with a Western education abandoned his traditional wife for a 'new woman.' Most of them remained faithful to their marriage oaths because they didn't want to bring grief to their wives and children."

"Grandfather put Father through a miserable childhood by abandoning him."

"Yes, your father grew up without a father. He was forced to support himself from grade school through college, torn between filial loyalty and contempt for his father. He felt so sorry for his mother he even contemplated dropping out of high school to work as a grocery clerk, so he could hire a village woman to help your grandmother out with some of the backbreaking domestic chores."

"Tell me what Great-Grandfather did. Didn't he say anything?"

"He was a henpecked husband," Mother said with a guffaw. I couldn't tell whether she was contemptuous or sympathetic. "All he knew how to do was to read books in his room. Despite the Confucian scriptures telling him that men were number one and women number ten, he couldn't control his tyrannical wife."

"Big Sister told me he was probably impotent," I whispered. I was being impish, exhilarated by the chance to denigrate the stupid old man. "Maybe that's why he couldn't put her under his thumb."

Mother burst out laughing. "When did Big Sister tell you that?"

"Right after we had that exorcism."

"Did she explain to you what impotence means?"

"Yeah, an impotent man can't get it up."

She let out an explosive laugh again. "He was more likely sterile than impotent."

"What's sterile?"

"A sterile man can get it up, but he can't have children because his stuff doesn't have the thing that makes babies. But," she conjectured, "this was about the turn of the century. It was impossible to find out medically whether a man was sterile or not. Your big sister might be right. He might have been impotent. But," she paused, "they lived in a small village, where everyone would have known it if he was impotent."

Thus, Grandmother remained with her in-laws. Not knowing she was being permanently torn away from her husband, she only hoped that he would keep his promise and come back one day to take her to Seoul. It seemed sufficient to her then that she was the wife of a brilliant young scholar. All else was the price she had to pay as a woman married to such a man. Surely, her self-sacrifice for him would not go unnoticed by the gods.

But the gods played a joke on Grandmother. After separating her from her husband, they let her witness the births of his three illegitimate children. Because Grandfather could not obtain a divorce from her, his personal commitment to Yunkyong could never be legalized, and the three children he had with her were officially declared bastards by his parents and society, permanently excluded from household registration. Out of guilt, Grandfather devoted all his attention to the three cursed children, ignoring the two from his legal wife. He gave Grandmother his leftovers, which consisted of sporadic visits and a few dollars every now and then. She was what Koreans called a "widow with a living husband."

Great-Grandmother would proclaim, "He's not going to walk out on his good old wife, not before I walk into my grave." She refused to grant her son and his unloved wife a divorce because she wanted to keep her daughter-in-law by her side. But she was also being faithful to the five-thousand-year-old Korean belief that a man can, married or not, have as many women as he can afford, but should not abandon his number one wife under any circumstances. This mindset kept forsaken first wives from starving on the streets, but it was a cage that locked them up with no hope of spreading their wings. With no possibility of a divorce or financial independence, they were left to pine away for however long they lived.

Grandmother's parents-in-law had by now lost everything they owned except the outdated Confucian scripts and the notorious leaking roof of their house; they couldn't help her raise her two children. People in Grandmother's village, who knew all the details of her tribulations, weren't surprised when they saw her toting buckets of water from the river to peddle to her neighbors. To be able to carry as much water as possible in one trip, she made a wooden pole with loose metal chains for four full buckets. With this device, all she had to carry was a pole on her back, and even though it nearly broke her back, it saved her time. Each day, she took short intervals from her housework to make several trips back and forth between the river and her neighbors' houses. Although they had their own wells, they wanted to help her and volunteered to pay little bills for her water. It saved them the labor of pulling up the bucket from the well, they said.

The water-carrying business made it difficult for her to stand up without a groan, but the children had to be fed. She ignored the fact that she was showing signs of a serious, permanent medical condition. The pain in her back, she thought, was from having to cook in the kitchen with no sink or running water, and the ache in her legs was from having to stand all day to clean and wash. It didn't occur to her that at the age of thirty she was already suffering from early symptoms of spinal disc degeneration, and that she would be a cripple at the age of fifty, almost paralyzed from the waist down. All that she could think of was how delicious a few minutes of afternoon nap would be. Although it was a crime for a daughter-in-law to lie down during the day, she was certain a short break would increase her energy. She decided to emulate a horse and slept in the kitchen, standing up. Grandmother was a virtuous daughter-in-law who never lay down except when she went to bed at night.

Grandmother could persevere because she had one blessing: she had her children, and they were beautiful, smart, and healthy. Of the two, her son became her shining hope. From the age of six, he was intelligent enough to put himself through school and to bring home, each year, the adult pig awarded to the top student. Because he had a stipend from the local educators to go to school, he could give his mother all the money he earned by tutoring his classmates after school and she could save most of it for his future. Feeding the pig he won and watching her secret pouch in the closet grow bulkier with the little bills he handed her, Grandmother realized she had something to live for. She envisioned him going to college and having a prestigious job, marrying a nice lady from a good home. Although her life as a wife was lost, her future as a mother and a grandmother was still ahead, and she felt alive. Just picturing a happy old age with grandchildren climbing all over her and a peaceful death in a son's arms, she could keep going. So deserving was the boy that even her mother-in-law, who had never before taken one step into the poorly equipped kitchen, would squat down in front of the wooden fire to make rice cakes for him when he brought prizes home from school.

His sister, too, was pretty and smart, but Grandmother didn't pin the same hope on her since she was a girl to be given away to a stranger's family someday. As soon as she graduated from grade school and entered puberty, she, just like all the girls in her village, would be paired with a suitable young man with a decent job. Luckily, she didn't have that masculine look in her face, which cursed her mother, but she did have that "son look" that would bless her with plenty of male children. The broad space between her brows, her straight, thin nose, and her wide forehead exposed by thick, braided hair were signs of a rich motherhood. All she needed was an obedient mind and good housekeeping skills.

"But I heard she wanted to go to high school so badly," I interrupted, "and that she carried her backpack for a year, to a tree out in the woods, pretending it was an outdoor school."

Mother nodded. "When she was sixteen, she finally realized she wasn't going any further than she had, so she began to fantasize. She constructed an imaginary classroom in an alcove in the bush and pretended she was reading famous English books."

"She was smart."

"She was. As soon as she finished washing dishes after breakfast, she ran out of the house." Mother gazed in the air wistfully, looking herself like a dreamy teenager whose eyes were traveling far beyond the thatched roofs and dirt alleys in her village. "She ran toward the low hills across the rice fields to a grove of pines near the river to the East Sea, and she sat reading and reading and reading."

"Tell me how she got her books."

"She saved the change she made from doing house chores for some of her neighbors, and she offered them to her friends who came home from school at the end of the semester. She traded what was in her piggy bank for the books they didn't need any longer."

I had heard about my aunt many times before, but relished hearing it all again. After all, she was a dreamy, English-reading romantic, just like I was. "Tell me how she once lost her track of time, went home late, and got whipped by Grandmother."

Mother smiled. "She was reading a British novel called *Wuthering Heights* and thought she was the heroine waiting for Hee—what's his name?"

"Heasclip," I said. I meant to say Heathcliff, but back then I was unable to pronounce th and f sounds, neither of which exists in Korean.

"Your aunt was waiting for a passionate, handsome, intelligent young man to sweep her off of her feet, but she saw nothing but piles of dirty dishes and mountains of clothes to wash. So she started to seek him in the books she read and found him in Heasclip one day." I could almost see my young aunt in Mother. The two women probably shared the same dream. "She fell in love with the passion she read in *Wuthering Heights*, that awesome, everlasting love between Hea—sclip and Caa—what's her name?"

"Caserine," I pronounced. "And one day, the wind blew in the pine woods, making eerie sounds, and she thought she was in the windy hills in England, where Heasclip and Caserine wandered around as children."

"Yes, she got carried away. She started to run around in the woods, thinking she was holding Heasclip's hands, laughing and crying and screaming."

"And a neighbor heard her when he was passing by the woods."

"Yes! He thought your aunt was going crazy and ran to Grandmother's house to tell her." Mother laughed.

"And Grandmother ran with him to the woods to grab her by the neck and bring her back to the house." I laughed, too. "When they came home, Grandmother picked a branch off of a tree and beat her with it until she exhausted herself."

There was nothing funny about the story, however. A year after her imaginary affair with Heathcliff, my aunt was married off to a man from another village, and at the age of seventeen she was pregnant with her first child. Thanks to her "son look," she had a boy and received hearty congratulations from her family and relatives, but her dream of being swept off her feet by a Heathcliff died. Routines full of crying babies and a dull husband who made little money marked the end of her affair with books.

Meanwhile, her brilliant brother—Father—graduated from high school with honors, becoming one of the few in the country to pass the Japanese Law Preliminaries and the first from his village to enter Seoul National University. On the day he left for Seoul, his mother watched him walk away to the bus stop across the rice fields, feeling her heart pounding with pride and worries. Though overwhelmingly happy, she was afraid the gods might be jealous of him because he was so exceedingly handsome and bright.

"You never told me about Father's college life."

"I don't know anything about it. He never told me."

There was that indifferent tone Mother exercised whenever my questions about his college life came up. I had asked her repeatedly, but she had always cut it short with a curt answer, claiming ignorance. My determination to find out became a secret obsession.

"Life is an endless jigsaw puzzle," Mother would warn me. "There are millions of pieces missing from zillions of puzzles, child.

If you try to find the right piece for every empty puzzle, you'll end up at an insane asylum. Be careful."

But I never gave up searching for the missing pieces. Once, I spent half a day looking for the mate of a white cotton sock I was about to wash. So absorbed in finding it, I didn't know that I had run back and forth between the water pump and the house about nine times in a row, and I was unaware that Mother had been observing me.

"My child," she admonished, "I can see pain written all over your life. If you don't learn how to stop, you're going to end up cutting your own throat."

"Where is my sock?" I cried, burnt out, but still far from ready to give up. "Why that one? Why?"

"Why?" Mother struggled not to laugh. "It could have been any of those socks, dear. You could have lost all of them and asked why." She paused. "You know what happened? A rat took your sock."

"I'll kill the rat!" I shouted, starting to smile. Whenever she needed an answer for my unanswerable questions, she resorted to the rat to make me relax. Rats were all over our house, stealing the rice we kept in straw sacks and soap bars on the cement drain under the water pump. They sometimes snatched salted raw fish from the cupboards in the kitchen, and it broke Mother's heart. It not only cost her a small fortune but also reminded her of the humiliating fact that we didn't own a refrigerator. But Mother had the strength to turn her hardships into a family joke. Whenever her children lost something, she would say, "Rats took it," and a ripple of laughter would lift our spirits above the metal roof of the small, crowded house. "Rats took it" was an official answer for anything that disappeared mysteriously from our house. But rats weren't what took Father's college years.

"You said Father loved his bastard siblings," I continued.

"Yes, he even brought one of them, the youngest one, to his home during the summer to meet your grandmother."

Although Yunkyong had given birth to Myongsan, she was only his "small mother." And although Myongsan was a symbol of Grandmother's husband's infidelity and her own lack of power, Grandmother was expected to love him as if he were her own—and, being a good Confucian wife, she did.

"Grandmother wanted to adopt him because he looked so much like Father."

"And because Yunkyong and Grandfather didn't have enough money to raise three children in Seoul."

Herself impoverished, Grandmother offered to adopt Myongsan, who looked like a carbon copy of her own son. Myongsan reminded her of the light that her son brought to her life. While Father was away in college in Seoul, she was certain the boy's company would make her winter nights shorter and her summer days cooler, and make her feel that her life wasn't all dishes and laundry. That he came from the woman who took her husband away was eclipsed by her desire for a youngster who could give her a chance to be a good mother all over again.

But Yunkyong turned down her offer. She was fierce about raising her children in Seoul, where they at least could keep their birth private and go to good schools to have steady jobs someday. They knew from the time they could utter one-syllable words that they were outcasts without household registration. They saw the noose of social stigma around their mother's neck. Once a budding, talented young girl whose beauty was compared to a transparent pink marble, she was now a huge raisin with nothing but wrinkles and loose pores, withering physically and emotionally. Her children were doomed to repeat her curse; all that mattered was that she diminish their shame. She believed only a good education would make their background less glaring, and for this she could live on one meal a day for a dozen years.

"But Myongsan died from encephalitis, didn't he?"

"Yes, it was during one of those excruciatingly hot summers in the thirties," Mother said. "Encephalitis was killing children like flies. He died in a few days, before he had a chance to say good-bye to his family and his kind Big Mother, your Grandmother."

When Yunkyong sank into a bottomless depression, even Grandmother shed tears for her. They were both mothers who loved the same boy, and this she was able to communicate to her husband's common-law wife through her son, who wrote her a letter of condolences for his illiterate mother.

It would be a mistake to believe that Grandmother took a liking to the other woman or that she absolved her husband, but the compassion she felt for both when the boy died was genuine. She learned in the end how to hate the tragedy itself, to resent the norms that separated her from her husband. Blaming her fate, she told herself, "I'm a woman and that's why I'm stuck with this life." But all she could show was the bitterness directed at Grandfather and his small wife, the hate I thought I saw in her thin, shrewd eyes. Grandmother, I believe, ultimately tried to go beyond the feelings of love and hate to cope with the situation, but equipped with nothing but a knifelike tongue, she didn't know what to say. She probably hated her husband because she loved him, and she perhaps cursed Yunkyong because she sympathized with her. I think, for this reason, her voice would sometimes blur into momentary resignation during her tirades.

Perhaps Grandmother wished she could put an end to the gods' cruel jokes on Yunkyong, as they apparently weren't satisfied with taking just one of her children away. They wanted one more, and this time it was her daughter, Haeok. To be more accurate, the gods didn't take her; she went to them, uninvited.

"What drove her to commit suicide?"

"When she graduated from grade school, she wanted to go on to high school. But her parents didn't have enough money for a girl, since they had to save for the boy's college education. After Myongsan's death, his older brother—your Uncle Youngsan—went to a private university in Seoul, which cost them dearly, and they had to sacrifice Haeok's education."

With little education and no job, Haeok couldn't find an escape from the path predetermined for her, which was either to become someone's mistress or to be damned as an old maid. As she entered her wistful teens and started to dream of a life better than her mother's, she realized neither of these options was possible. She was a young woman who felt for Ophelia and secretly admired Lady Macbeth, who sought Byron in the dingy alleys on the outskirts of Seoul. For her, the road to becoming a mistress or an old maid could lead only to one thing—a glass coffin. She couldn't allow circumstance to break her as it did her mother.

"I heard Uncle Youngsan kept harassing her, telling her to die."

"He thought she was a nuisance. Her mind wasn't on the dishes she had to fix. It was on books, stylish clothes, smart words, and a fairy-tale romance. To him, she was a parasite living off of her parents."

"Didn't he try to marry her off, though?"

"Several times, but none of the suitors was any good, not to her anyway. The men her brother set her up with were brutes who wanted to take advantage of her weakness as an illegitimate child. The men she met through everyone else were bastard sons from poor families whom she could not bring herself to consider."

"Why was Uncle Youngsan so mean to her?"

"He needed someone to be mean to. Because society looked down upon him, he looked down upon himself and took it out on his little sister."

After numerous meetings with men introduced to her by her family and relatives, Haeok began to feel a strange peace of mind. She felt she could really die, as her brother frequently told her to, having paid her dues to her family by meeting all the marriage candidates. Her parents had nothing to give her, and she missed her little brother, Myongsan, who used to wrap his arms around her neck as a baby. In the worst case, she would see him again in the other world. In peace and tranquility, she stole a bill out of her older brother's pocket one night, bought potassium cyanide, and took it.

After her daughter's suicide, Yunkyong sank into another depression that turned her into an unfeeling stone. She didn't have to commit suicide and follow her son and daughter to the cemetery; she was in the grave of a living death already.

Her oldest son, however, pulled her out of this grave. When she saw him graduate from college and get a job as a journalist for a rep-

utable daily paper in Seoul, the air tasted crisp again and the mois-
ture came back to her dry mouth. Youngsan was to her as Father was
to Grandmother. Youngsan made enough money for himself and his
parents to lift them slowly from poverty. Although nobody admitted
it, the deaths of the other two children alleviated the sting of the
empty purse, and for the first time since that beautiful, fatal rendezvous at the bookstore, Yunkyong saw the clear blue sky beyond
the tree in the front yard of her house. In 1956, nearly three decades
after she met my grandfather, she finally felt happy. She didn't know
that this would last only a year.

"What did Uncle Youngsan do this time?" I asked.

"He fell in love with a woman, a secretary at the newspaper
where he was working. He wanted to marry her, but when she found
out he was an illegitimate son, she turned him down."

The hate he felt toward himself and his parents, which had begun
to die down after his sister's suicide, erupted again, and he couldn't
clamp it down. He began to come home drunk every night, yelling
and screaming at his parents, soiling his mother's handmade, freshly
washed quilts with his vomit. He let his anger out on them; he was
a bastard, and it was their fault. "Die, die!" he shouted. "I want to
see you die before I do!" He stopped giving them money. Although
his father's meager retirement was enough to survive off of,
Youngsan's tongue kept working like a blade.

"Grandmother Yunkyong and Grandfather started to tear each
other apart." Mother's eyes turned watery. "After they had endured
so many breaking points together, they fell apart."

When Grandfather first met Yunkyong, he was a married man a
dozen years older than his student-girlfriend, and he should have
known better than to plunge headlong into love. At the very least, he
should have been stronger and obtained a divorce, no matter how
difficult. Wasn't he, after all, a legitimate son from a reputable,
although poor, family? Did he not have the power to lift his loved ones
from the iron grip of their birth? All things considered, Yunkyong
endured more suffering than he. She was a woman with the courage

to dream. In the end, Yunkyong gave in to her son's anger.

"Go home and die there!" she yelled at Grandfather. "This is not your home. You belong to your wife and children. I am not your wife and he is not your child."

Grandfather began to dissolve. The hatred of his wife and son was enough to melt his bones, and he had no energy left. His blood pressure, which had always been high, soared even higher, resulting in a stroke. He turned into a vegetable, unable to get out of bed. He had to be fed and changed, and Yunkyong's loathing of him grew. In the haze of his fading mind, he looked back at the road he had traveled and he cried. He was ready to follow his daughter's path. He somehow crawled out of bed, checked into a shady inn, and took potassium cyanide. He was finally free of his curse.

"What happened to Uncle Youngsan and Grandmother Yunkyong?"

"They lived together for a few years until he met through a matchmaker a girl born out of wedlock and married her."

"Did Grandmother Yunkyong get along with her daughter-in-law?"

"She had to. She had no means to live alone."

Having killed Grandfather, mother and son reconciled. Guilt still haunted them, but it gradually dissipated into tiny drops of sadness nestled deep within them. It rarely rose to the surface. After driving Grandfather into a premature grave, they no longer had to deal with the man who had another family to whom they were inferior. The fact that Youngsan brought another "litter" of bastard children into this world seemed less tragic. While the initial joy of his marriage tapered off into the daily routines of life, he made it a habit to watch his children go to sleep every night. His heart pounded less bitterly now; the acuteness of his pain was diluted by tangible hopes and dreams.

Enough money for everyone in the house, above all, softened his sorrow. A talented writer, he was the chief editor of the section called "Culture and the World" at a respected national paper, and he imagined a future in which children would watch space shuttles instead of Vietnam-like wars on the evening news. He wrote about how the earth would look like a dot from the moon, and how insignificant the arbitrary distinctions between human beings would be in such a small place. Carrying a lunch pail to work to save money, he looked forward to depositing half of his paycheck in the trust account for his children's college education. How relieved he was to realize each month that he didn't have to starve himself, as his parents had, to send his children to school! Their lives were no longer restricted by centuries-old mores. The government had lifted at the turn of the century all the official and unofficial barriers against illegitimate children, which had been kept for over half a millennium, and people's attitudes, too, changed considerably.

As his country turned the corner into the seventies, he began to dream again.

"But we've never seen our cousins," I said sadly.

"No. There is one thing your Uncle Youngsan cannot deal with, and that is facing his legitimate brother, your father, and his family. He doesn't want to be reminded of his life's lost opportunities. He and his wife and children are living in Seoul now, and it'd take them four hours by train to get to Taegu. But they won't come to see us."

"Can I write him a letter?"

"Ha!" Mother's tone turned sarcastic. "Your father sent him a hundred letters over the past thirty years, but he never got a reply. Your Uncle Youngsan has done all that writing about world peace, but he can't resolve his own internal war."

Nobody in my family ever met him except Father, who used to visit Grandfather and his illegitimate siblings while he was a college student in Seoul. Still, Uncle Youngsan seemed like a survivor to me. Gazing at the stars at night, I prayed that I would someday see his children standing beside me, talking about how small the earth would look from the moon.

Love in a
Dust Storm

DURING MY ENTIRE CHILDHOOD, MY MOTHER SEEMED LIKE A SAINT.
She lived above natural feelings, celebrated the good she salvaged
out of the wreckage of her family, and seemed immune to misery.
Despite the grueling daily routines, she somehow sustained compassion.
She didn't retaliate against those who hurt her without provocation and
could grow roses in a cement dumpster full of plastic trash. At twelve
going on thirteen, though, I never imagined I would covet that ability. I
only saw what she did in the kitchen.

The truth was, Mother was no saint by nature. She had simply
made her choice between the two impossible roles open to Korean
women of her age and situation: a saint or a bad woman. In a poor
household torn by hardship, someone had to become an incinerator
into which the family could dump their pain and anger without fear of
retaliation. The other role, that of a bad woman who fought her venomous mother-in-law, was beneath her. It was degrading to punish her
children for nagging at her or to fight her husband for venting his rage
upon her. The grief and frustration haunting her family weren't going
to end in the near future. She understood the circular nature of oppression, and by playing a saint she tried to put an end to this circle.

Mother played her role for so long that it indeed became part of
her personality. She *was* a saint more often than not. When Grandmother complained about her frequent nightmares about her late
husband, Mother was genuinely moved, and went to the lengths she

Here I am as a baby, strapped on my mother's back.

did to host the expensive exorcism. Nobody could tell whether Grandmother stopped dreaming of Grandfather after the exorcism, but she no longer talked about her nightmares. The old woman appeared to have gained some ability to clamp down her destructive attitude, thanks to her daughter-in-law.

But there was a secret self in Mother, one that appeared in flashes when she was sorely tried. In a moment her face would turn from nurturing to frighteningly cold, an iceberg chiseled into an egg shape. Her eyes would turn icy, her mouth draw a thin line of disapproval, and her chin thrust out in silent protest. Whenever this happened, I would steal fearful glances at her, trying to stay out of her way. But she would only ever allow her true feelings to come through for a moment at a time, before the martyr's calm returned, her cheeks lovely and plump, her eyes twinkling.

Mother wasn't beautiful in a conventional sense. Her nose was on the flat, short side and her brow flew up in a straight, steep line with no curve. But she had a peculiarly charming aura. With her glasses on, she could pass for the chancellor of a university, I thought, or a gifted feminine scholar. Her skin, silky smooth and elastic, gave her a virginal look. Even after she had five children, it was almost as soft and milky as it had been during her youth. Mother was nearly as tall as Father, but with narrow shoulders and a slender waist she looked a lot more petite than women of her height; her girlish physique contributed to her youthfulness. I saw in her face a scholar's rigor, a fighter's anger, a conqueror's pride, and a martyr's surrender, all at once, and I was amazed by this spectrum. Mother was a warrior and a slave, a leader and an obedient follower. I most admired the grace she exercised toward her enemies, the strength of character it required, and the wisdom with which she applied it. It was a means of conquering without fighting.

As I admired Mother, however, I felt an intense sadness. Her sainthood was a choice without a choice, an enforced martyrdom and self-erasure. Her life mirrored the lives of so many other women, and I would work as hard to escape that life as she worked to maintain it. Between playing a saint and playing a bad woman, I had to find a happy medium.

As it is human nature to remember the bad more than the good, I remember the times when Mother's saintly face disappeared. When I was twelve and half, I saw the other face. I had not washed the dishes she had left in the sink, so when she dragged her heavy feet back from the market with groceries, she saw the pile waiting for her.

"Once you die, you'll be able to sit on your ass in heaven and read!" she screamed. "But until then, you've got to do your job! You've got to know your place in this house, which is the kitchen!" She snatched the book from my hand and threw it to the floor. It was *Jane Eyre*, one of several books Big Sister had borrowed from a local library. Big Sister was an avid reader, and at nineteen knew by heart all the English classics available in translation. She passed her book recommendations and her love for reverie on to me. I pretended to understand, too proud to admit that I was still a child. Just like our great-grandfather who read Confucian scripts under a leaking roof, we read advanced Western novels in a house heated by coal briquette, convinced of our superior intellect.

Mother, however, was unimpressed. "Your mother doesn't have the energy to stand, and you are reading some fancy book about a foreign woman who marries a rich man!" Mother shouted. "You're not some privileged foreign woman! You're just a little nobody born to serve people! Who's going to marry such a conceited, self-involved bitch?"

I was silent, cringing, my hands on my head.

"You know nothing but books," she warned. "Didn't I tell you what happened to your Aunt Haeok who read all those English books and ended up dead?" Mother's rage had turned to misery, and she wiped her tears with her skirt. "Even for me, an ignorant house-wife with no time for books, life is hard enough. I want to kill myself sometimes. Last night, I took thirty-five sleeping pills to die."

Overcome by shock and guilt, I suppressed a gasp. Mother was in too dark a place to realize I was only a child or to consider the weight her confession put on me. With nobody to listen to her, she would have talked to the persimmon tree in the backyard, to any walking creature on the street. I stayed by Mother's side more than any of her other children, and Mother was used to unburdening on me; I, too, was accustomed to listening. I had not expected, however, a confession about a suicide attempt.

"Thirty-five sleeping pills," she almost whispered. "But I just woke up this morning, feeling sick. The pills were no good because I bought them last summer and kept them in the closet for a year. Besides, I drank a bottle of wine before I took them. I thought alcohol would get them into my system faster, but I guess it washed them out, and I woke up."

Her face was as pallid as it was after she gave birth to Little Sister, when she had lost so much blood I had feared for her life. But this time her face terrified me. It petrified me in the pit of my stom-ach. Without a word, I leaped to my feet and darted out of the liv-ing room. I couldn't care less where I was going; I just wanted to go away from the house as far as my feet could carry me. I wasn't old enough to process Mother's pain. I could only think about myself, a child whose mother told her she wanted to die.

I wanted a *home*, a home with no ghosts and no stories about people who committed suicide or wished to die. I wanted a home where I wouldn't be scolded for reading a "fancy book." Yes, I had to fly away to America. America was a country much kinder to women, a place where women could be brave and desirable at the same time. Wasn't I destined to go to that big, beautiful country?

All the way home, I rolled my tongue—"buttering it up," as Koreans say—to try to master difficult English sounds: distinguishing an R from an L, the th sound, and an F in the middle of a word. The phonemes that didn't exist in Korean made English a nightmare for most Koreans, so for a week I rolled my "buttered up" tongue. While going to school and coming back home, on sidewalks and beside traffic lights, walking to a store to run an errand for Mother, and washing socks near the pump, I muttered to myself.

"Th-ea-ter, Ca-th-e-rine, th-ou-ght, th-ir-teen," I repeated, dividing the syllables to give myself a long pause after each agonizing th sound. Fumbling for a sentence with as many th words as I could think of, I would chant until my tongue was sore. I simply had to go to America. If the Three Men of the Family were right—if America had the power to ruin the lives of women who drank its water—it was a country I felt I had to explore. A forbidden fruit was that much more attractive to me.

In junior high, I did poorly in every subject, even English. I rarely paid attention to the grammar in class. I spent all my time instead wondering about things like why Judy from the grammar exercises said "Thank you" to her mother whenever she was paid for running an errand for her family. I wondered why she was paid at all. Being praised, let alone being paid, for serving one's family struck me as selfish and unnatural.

I tried to memorize theorems of algebra and rules of geometry, but my eyes kept wandering off to distant places, my ears listening to faraway drums. Folding cotton baby diapers in home economics, I asked myself why people made babies, why they wanted to expose them to all that pain and suffering. Life, as everyone seemed to agree, was full of sadness, and to me, it seemed particularly nightmarish. Gazing at the pictures of diapers in the home economics text, I found myself dead set against having children.

Mother's confession about her suicide attempt came back to me again and again as I stared at the blackboard. It also made me hyper aware of the mini-dramas that happened every day in my house, and I started to see the episodes stacking against Mother's psychological well-being. One morning not long after her confession, Father was bitching as usual about Mother's tardiness. With a husband, a mother-in-law, and five children to feed at six in the morning, Mother was a machine and a model of efficiency, but Father worked himself into a violent rage over his un-ironed shirt.

"I'll iron it for you," Grandmother offered, gloating over Mother's failure. Her osteoporosis had caused spinal degeneration, and she could no longer stand up without holding onto someone else. But whenever she saw a chance to turn her son against her daughter-in-law, she maximized it. She crawled to the closet, took the iron out, well aware of the effect such a sight would have on him.

"You let my mother do the ironing for you!" Father bellowed at Mother. His anger made my hair stand up. He knew perfectly well she never let the old woman do anything that required her to crawl or stand up.

"The youngest one kept crying all morning," Mother replied calmly, biting her tongue. "I got delayed trying to feed her."

"You stupid, sluggish bitch! Don't you give me any back talk!"

He picked up a beer bottle lying beside him and smashed it, with all his might, on the wall right above Mother's head. I screamed as the glass fragments rained down on her shoulders, and then I ran out of the house, tears flooding my face. I heard Mother weeping behind me, but I couldn't stop running. I was afraid she might die of grief.

I was late for school that morning, and endured a sharp scolding from my teacher. All day long, I pretended to follow her instructions, staring blankly at the books and the board. But my hand took no notes, my ears heard no sounds. I asked myself why Mother's devotion to the family came back to her as a boomerang. At forty-four, she was suffering from problems that ordinarily struck women in their sixties: pain in her back, weakening bones in her legs. She couldn't walk longer than ten minutes without plopping down on a sidewalk bench. It was easy to see that she would be a dysfunctional old woman just like Grandmother. A permanently disabled life was what awaited women, I thought.

Coming home from school, however, I hit upon an entirely different question. I wondered where the beer bottle had come from. Father didn't drink, nobody else in the family drank, and as far as I could remember, there never were any alcoholic beverages kept in the house. Women weren't supposed to drink at all, and I was certain none of the women in the family brought it in. It had to have been Big Brother: I had once overheard him talking Less Big Brother into sharing a bottle of beer that he had snuck into the house. Student body president, valedictorian, and somewhat of a straight arrow, Big Brother rarely violated rules. But he was still a teenager, and couldn't entirely resist peer pressure.

"Nothing is as good as the taste of cold beer at the end of a hot day," he whispered to Less Big Brother, taking him to the outhouse. I pressed my ears against the wall and overheard them gulping. While listening to their giggles, I felt fresh envy. They were best friends, but I had no friend in the family. Little Sister was too young, and Big Sister was too old.

I had a golden chance to get even with my brothers. Father was stricter than Confucius when it came to rules for minors. One word from me would be enough to inflame him, and I would have the glee of watching them get whipped by Father. But I said nothing. They called me ugly and stupid, but they were still my beloveds, and I wanted to protect them. If I promised them not to snitch, they might even let me have a sip of their secret beer. So when I got home that day, I had something to smile about. I told Big Brother what I wanted, and, surprised at my cleverness, he promised me a sip from the next bottle he was planning to sneak in.

Puzzled by our high humor, Father looked at us and laughed. He clearly had no memory of what he had done that morning. Mother managed to make a faint smile, too, and we were back to the normal routine. But smiles were scarce in our family. We either frowned or laughed explosively, seldom hitting the middle. Always in need of escaping something, we involved ourselves in high-pitched brawls and raucous reconciliation. Being locked in a tiger's stomach together divided us deeply, but it united us as well.

As summer wore on, I got restless again. Nurturing a taste for danger, I invited two of the neighborhood girls to our house and talked them into walking with me on the raised edge of the rooftop of our two-story house. Because the edge was barely wide enough for my two feet, I had always wanted to experience the sensation of running on it, to feel the fear of being close to death. That's not quite how I sold it to the other girls, though. "Look," I coaxed. "You can see the whole city from here." Stepping on the edge, I pointed at the tower of a radio station on top of a hill. "Once you get on, you won't be scared anymore." I started to walk, my arms spread horizontally, my toes turned out. I sang and laughed, fluttering my arms like a bird. Fearfully but eagerly, the two girls joined me, taking little slow steps at first, and after a few paces they managed to spread their arms and giggle awkwardly. When they picked up my song, I quickened my pace. Soon, the three of us were walking in a circle like a group of acrobats, having a good time.

"Look at the kids over there!" I heard a woman scream from below. "Somebody's got to get them off!"

"Hey, girls, get down! Get down!" another woman yelled. "If you don't want to break your back, get off!" A throng of women gathered in front of the house, and ripples of shouts and shrieks echoed over the block. The two girls' mothers ran out, livid with fear, and rushed into my front yard to climb up the stairs. But drugged by the danger, we continued our acrobatics, walking faster and faster.

"They must be possessed," Mother gasped, climbing up the stairs with the two other mothers. "Grab them by the arms and pull them to the ground."

Hearing their footsteps, we quickened our pace, singing in higher pitches. Until they yanked us down from the edge, we had no idea how scared they were.

"When your father comes home tonight, he'll spank you until you lose your mind," one of the mothers shrilled at her daughter, hitting her on the head with her fist. The other mother followed suit. In a moment, they both had their daughters by the arms, dragging them down the stairs.

"I told you not to go on the rooftop!" Mother shouted, slapping me in the face. "Why do you always go against everyone? What has gotten into you?"

I admitted I had done something extremely dangerous, but I could not understand Father's reaction that night. He threw me on the floor and hit me in the face and stomach over and over again, accusing me of having tried to harm him deliberately.

"You did it on purpose, didn't you?" he shouted, his eyes twitching and his lips trembling. "You did it to ruin me, to discredit me, didn't you?" I just sat on the floor like a sack of wheat being kicked around and picked up. "Did I survive all the fear and humiliation to provide for a wicked child like this?" he raved on, this time to Mother.

Sitting at a corner, Mother was silent. She never interrupted to defend me from any of the Three Men of the Family; her job was to warn me, when the punishment was over, not to provoke the gods again.

"Every day at work I am persecuted and hounded, followed and threatened!" he screamed. "Why should I be troubled at home by my own child?"

I couldn't tell whether he wanted me to agree with him or not. Either way, he was going to kill me, and I was going to die quietly. He would see he couldn't break me.

I was so overwhelmed by hate I wanted to kill him. A month after the beating, I took a kitchen knife and snuck into his room as noiselessly as a cat. Father, reading at his desk, didn't sense my presence behind him. So engrossed in Park Chung Hee's conspiracy, he couldn't even tell his life was in danger in his own house. "Good," I thought, "he will die in the middle of his favorite hobby." But a powerful hand seized mine and twisted my arm, wrenching the knife away. I looked back and saw Mother's fierce face staring at me.

"Get up!" Mother shook my shoulder. "You're going to be late for school."

It was only when she woke me up that I realized it had been a dream. Mother sided with Father even in my dreams. What was it that made her defend the man who treated her like a slave to be kicked around? I was twenty years away from understanding why. Father was being chased by the ones who could put him right back to a torture chamber. He was torturing me the same way he had been tortured by them.

Trapped in my house and bored, I started a solitary crusade against the rats that stole rice and bits of fish from my family. The rats mated in the dark of the outhouse beside my bedroom, making a shrill sound like porcelain shattering. It was the ugliest, most repulsive noise I had ever heard, and with my hands over my ears, I tossed in bed.

I cut a sturdy branch off of the persimmon tree in the back of the house and trimmed the lean end for a club. With my club and a butcher knife, I watched the rats rushing into holes in the wall. I imagined the rats were the late Syngman Rhee, the current dictator Park Chung Hee, the Yankee bastards who set them up, and the fellows who built the Ulsan Pollution Center. The rats were the herds of brainless people who celebrated the supposed economic progress of these industrial complexes, who believed government propaganda. But rats are fast, and my club could hardly end our infestation.

I finally convinced Mother to get a cat, although it took some work. Koreans have all sorts of myths about the supposed wickedness of cats, and when I was young, few people liked them. Once Mother conceded, I was so infatuated with the cat that I insisted on sleeping with her beside me. My family thought I was slightly demented. Because cats are aloof and often disobedient, people projected into them the qualities they deemed as being treacherous in any living creatures; they believed cats were cunning in a mysterious way and were capable of the most relentless, secretive vengeance. How unfair it was of them, I thought, to blame the lovely felines! Because cats were smart, they knew how to be willful and independent, to use human beings for their own good. They were clever enough to "betray" people and make them mad.

I became an avid fan of cats after reading a legend. It was about a particularly venomous cat, about a female one that seemed to be an incarnation of the craftiest, most spiteful characteristics that were ever imagined by the Koreans about the feline species. This cat came back to the living from the dead to revenge herself on her former owner who had abused and then killed her, to destroy his family in a most prolonged, aggravating manner. She entered the body of his seven-year-old son, to make him shrill and meow in her voice, to make him climb up the walls and hang upside down the ceiling of the grass-roof house. The boy had a fever, too, hallucinating while asleep and unable to eat anything. Finally, a shaman was called in to exorcise the cat's ghost, to ask her to forgive the boy's father and to accept his apology. "You shouldn't be so selfish," the shaman admonished him after the cat had returned to the dead. "You hated the cat because she had her own mind. She didn't come with a wagging tale when you called her name. You were being a typical human being. Human beings are so self-centered that they do not like any creature that doesn't blindly follow them." How I admired the legendary cat!

Cats were my favorite animal because a lot of people disliked them. Because most people wanted them purely for the purpose of removing rats and mice, I wanted mine for the sake of love. Because most people kept them outdoors, I wanted to keep mine indoors.

"She belongs outdoors!" Big Brother yelled. "She's an animal!"

But I snuck her in to my room as often as I could and held her on my lap. Wrapping her front paws around my neck, she switched her tail, clinging to me like a baby, and I thought she was the prettiest thing I had ever seen. She was brave, too, and a heartless killer. She would catch a rat, chew it up, and swallow everything but the tail, which she let hang from her mouth, and I would cheer and clap my hands. But less than two months after I adopted her, she left. The consensus in my family was that she'd left me because she didn't like me.

"She's probably dead by now," Mother tried to console me. "Or she's a fat, ugly cat with a horde of kittens. It's nothing to be so sad about."

After the cat disappeared, I was very depressed. I had been abandoned by my only friend. I stopped eating and talking. To coax me into eating, Mother promised to open a can of shredded peaches on condition that I have three meals a day on time. Canned peaches were a luxury item available only in foreign markets. "Get that stupid cat out of your mind," she said. "She left you."

"Why would she want to leave me?"

"You suffocated her. You loved her too much. You go too far even with loving."

After several nights of hard thinking, I decided that I preferred my cat dead than alive with a bunch of kittens. If she had left me for a male cat, she deserved to be fat and ugly with no control over her body. Mother was right; I always went too far, even with loving.

But knowing myself didn't help me figure out division and multiplication. My grades were terrible; I couldn't memorize; I'd never marry well. The pressure was intense even when I was more than five years away from college.

To Seoul

O N THE DAY FATHER ANNOUNCED HIS DECISION TO MOVE THE WHOLE family to Seoul, I was as worried as I was excited. Competition for colleges in Seoul was much keener than it was in Taegu, and I knew I would look only worse in my report cards. But Seoul was everybody's dream city; it was the capital of the nation and the center of all activities. "You should be glad," Father said, "because you'll attend good schools and reap the benefits of being taught by the best teachers." As the third largest metropolis in Korea, Taegu had everything one needed for a comfortable lifestyle, but it didn't offer Seoul's educational opportunities. All the prestigious schools, both secondary and higher, were in Seoul, so it was no wonder parents in the country sold their houses and farmlands, even going bankrupt, in order to send their children to top colleges and universities in Seoul. My hungry, driven parents were determined to put their children through some of the most highly rated schools in the nation by whatever means necessary. They knew we needed no more than a Taegu college diploma for a trouble-free, middle-class life, but they expected more from their children. They wanted preeminence.

In January of 1969, we moved to Seoul. To have enough time to buy a house and help the children settle in time for the new semester, Father left a month ahead of everyone else, while Mother stayed behind for two weeks to clean the old house in Taegu and put it up for sale. Grandmother had to stay in a relative's house until Father could bring her back to Seoul. Hence, we children traveled alone. Big Sister had already graduated from a two-year college and was teaching at an elementary school in a small town near Taegu and wouldn't be coming with us, so Big Brother was captain of the team. Bundled up from top to toe against the knifelike wind of February, the four of us—Big Brother, Less Big Brother, Little Sister, and myself—boarded the train in a line, plopping down on our seats one by one like a bunch of tumblers. In 1969, the heating and cooling systems in public transportation were patchy at best, and we would be on the train for four hours. Bundled into six layers of ragged cotton clothing, we had a hard time standing straight and sitting comfortably, so we laughed and walked sideways to avoid falling down. Little Sister struggled especially hard, tumbling down on her back like a fat bowling pin. I had to be careful, too, wrapped in folds of worn underwear thicker than my arms. Luckily, we had nothing to carry but a shoulder bag Mother had packed for each of us. Mother had shipped all of our belongings and furniture to Seoul on a small truck. It didn't cost us much to move everything we owned because we owned very little: four chests of drawers for eight people, and a small desk for each of the four children.

On the train, the four of us busily planned our future in Seoul. From our carriage window, we saw something bright in the frozen, gray sky—something to celebrate while our own planet was so barren. We saw hope in the air, hope as visible as a star, as Big Brother started to talk about his visions. Promising each of his siblings a handsome chunk of his earnings, he declared his plan to revolutionize Korea's economic system. He was a born idealist, determined to end the exploitation of workers by capitalists, to play a leading role in maximizing the national wealth of Korea, and to return part of his earnings to his country by supporting artists and writers who would democratize the feudal culture. Following him, Less Big Brother proudly confessed his passion for politics; he wished to be a George Washington of Korea, a great leader heading the birth of a new country. His new party would consist of brilliant dissidents and clever tacticians who would place his Korea on top of the globe.

Less Big Brother turned to me suddenly. "What do you want to do?"

Caught off guard, I heard myself improvising, "I want to be the best in English in Korea."

"That's a great plan," Big Brother said. "You could become a reporter for *The New York Times* office in Korea."

"Even for a man, writing for *The New York Times* is the highest honor," Less Big Brother added. "For a woman—"

"You have to be better than the best man at your job," Big Brother interrupted. "That's the only way a woman can get ahead."

They were asking me to be exceptional. I felt my desire to please them, to make them proud, stirring once again in my chest.

"What do you want to be when you grow up?" Big Brother asked Little Sister.

Even at seven, Little Sister meditated before she spoke. "I want to be an inventor," she pronounced.

"Excellent!" Big Brother said. "If there's one thing this country can't do without, it's inventions—of all kinds. Our children will be in their prime in the twenty-first century, and in the twenty-first century, scientific and technological inventors will rule the world. I'm proud of you."

"If you can figure out how to manufacture a flying saucer, you'll be the world's top scientist," Less Big Brother suggested.

"You always come up with something ludicrous," Big Brother snapped. "We don't even know if flying saucers exist. She'd better go for something realistic, like an electronic plane to take us to New York in an hour and a half." He looked at Little Sister and cooed, "Are you going to invent a plane like that?"

"I am," she replied confidently. She was a dreamer like the rest of us.

On the train to Seoul, I discovered something new: my brothers understood my dream. This came to me as a revelation. That they, too, had dreams gave me hope, and that they, too, had suffered as dreamers suffer brightened up my dark mood.

Big Brother went from the top of his high school to one of the most elite university programs in the country. He was a freshman in economics, one of only fifty, at Seoul National University, and its graduates were famous for their contributions to the economic and social progress of their country. He was adored by his peers and teachers; everyone knew him for his rigor and compassion. Although his authoritarian behavior as the almighty oldest son prevented me from clearly seeing the gentleman in him, I could see the enormous impact he had on others. He awakened me, as he awakened his friends, to the concept of a *country*, to the idea of serving one's people, and to the truth that there was something bigger—much bigger—than me in my life. How I wished I could possess his magnificent, commanding eyes! I dug a furrow between my brows, putting pressure on them to make my eyes look slanted.

But he noticed my scowl and scolded me. "What are you doing? What's that face for? A woman should always smile."

I don't want to be a woman! I wanted to bark at him. *I want to be somebody!*

But I was his sister, and for this reason alone, I was expected to adopt excellence as my guiding principle. Just like Less Big Brother, who, after years of poor performance in school, suddenly picked up the highest grades and entered the best high school to prove he was Big Brother's brother, I was to be nothing but the best to show that I was his sister.

I knew how much pressure Big Brother was under. He worked until he nearly ruined his health. Two years earlier, he had spent six months in bed with tuberculosis, and he still hadn't recovered entirely. In terms of the competition and required test scores, being admitted into the economics department at Seoul National University was harder than being admitted to Harvard, and for the oldest son of a poor family with no extracurricular help, it was an achievement indeed. I knew that he gave up everything he liked to do in order to be a son faithful to Father's expectations. He threw out not only playing guitar, painting, and reading for pleasure, but also sports, his social life, and dating.

Always, and with a sense of destiny, he set himself on fulfilling his role as the oldest son, while his little brother put his self-interest above all else. Big Brother was a second father to his little siblings, stuck with the duty of disciplining Less Big Brother, who habitually played truant from school and failed to make passing grades. As the "brat" picked up the habit of smoking and drinking at just fourteen, mixing with fallen young men and women, Big Brother would go to his teachers to apologize on his behalf, promising in vain to steer the delinquent in the right direction. "He's incredibly knowledgeable and bright," the older one would plead. "He just doesn't want to make the effort. Do you know that he's only fifteen and can explain Kafka to me? Can you give him one more chance, so that he can bring his talents to fruition?" It was in fact Big Brother who got Less Big Brother through the exams for the second best high school in Korea, who pushed him—over and over again—to show the best of himself.

Less Big Brother was handsome. His face was unusual in its combination of ideal opposites; it exuded a sophisticated mind and a simple, down-to-earth sensuality, a mental furnace boiling with wild ideas and meticulous logic. Almost a carbon copy of Father's, it was pale but radiant with energy, with striking features and flawless symmetry. His smoldering eyes cast an air of seductive glamour into the distinguished features.

In the end, nobody, not even Big Brother, could prevent Less Big Brother from rotting in the cesspool of his own promise. Bereft of discipline, he was unable to channel any of the clashing creative thoughts in his head into an organized expression, so he just sank into a swamp of chaotic feelings. He was only a teenager, but he was an expert in sophistry. He already knew how to represent himself as a genius misunderstood by the world, how to call his laziness a thinking rebel's rejection of mundane routines, and how to squeeze money out of his family.

The train slowed down to come to a jolting stop at Seoul Station. We picked up our bags and rushed out to the platform, spotting

Me (left) at twelve.

Father on the stairs leading to the ticketing boxes. Standing straight, away from the rails, holding his fedora above the crowd, he stood out like an alabaster statue.

"Father!" we all cried, running toward him like a brood of chickens. "Father!"

"Don't hurry!" he cried back. "You may fall down!" As if to prove him right, Little Sister plopped down on the platform, unable to stand the weight of the heavy clothing under her coat. Big Brother picked her up on his back, giving Less Big Brother his suitcase.

"Hold on to your brother!" Father shouted to Little Sister, and then to Big Brother, "Slow down!" Watching his children climb up the stairs, he seemed utterly satisfied. The breath from his mouth, easily visible in the February air, reminded me of the smoke from the train that had carried us to Seoul. At forty-nine, Father was of medium height, with a complexion of light yellow plaster, broad shoulders, and sturdy legs. He had a firm, tightly closed mouth and a prominent, round chin, giving him the austere but compassionate air of a middle-aged family man. At thirteen, I was captivated by his face. I could sense he had once been a romantic youth; from what Mother told me, I knew he still had a streak of his old dreaminess.

"He thought about becoming an actor before he got married," she said to me once. "He was so very handsome that everyone encouraged him. But coming from a strict Confucian family, he talked himself out of it." She smoothed out some crumpled tickets she had removed from his pockets. "Whenever I wash his pants, I check his pockets to see if there are little bills he forgot to take out. But I only see tickets for Hollywood movies he's gone to see all by himself. I guess he likes to think he's one of those handsome actors on the screen. What's the name of the actor he adores, Paul Noo—?"

"Paul Newman," I pronounced, "the good-looking fellow with steamy eyes!"

"I bet he thinks he is Paul Newman sometimes. He probably thinks if he had blue eyes, he would look just like him." She laughed.

Boy, how could Father be that stuck up? I wondered. I never saw him looking at Mother as the famous actor looked at his female co-stars. It was impossible for me to picture him gazing at any woman with anything but the most efficient, professional attitude in his eyes.

"I'll show you something." Mother took a box out of his desk drawer. "Here are some pictures he's proud of. He got them taken when he was at Peabody College in Nashville." She handed them to me, with her finger on one of them. "As I told you, he was invited—and paid in full, including his room and board and expenses—to study in America by the U.S. secretary of state, and he chose Peabody College because it was one of the best for education, the subject he was interested in at that time."

With his face tilted slightly to one side, Father wore a broad, impish smile, making long, thin puckers around his eyes that almost reached his hairline. It was the face of a man enjoying himself heartily, or of a naughty little boy pulling a prank to spice up the dull lives of the adults around him. The face of the beaming young man in the picture was so different from the face I knew; I could only

Father with his students at George Peabody College in America.

imagine the tangled circumstances that had changed Father. The picture aroused my curiosity about America even further.

"Your father isn't like other men," Mother told me when I was thirteen. "He doesn't care for women, not even for rich, pretty ones. There was this woman who had a crush on him, but he didn't give her a look. Not because she wasn't attractive, but because he looked at women as if they were stones. He was a stone himself." Every time I heard this story, it struck me. For a man of Father's age and with his smashing looks, not taking up a chance to womanize was very unusual. In his culture, a man who rejected such an easy opportunity was branded either a eunuch or a saint. Although polygamy had been legally repealed at the end of the Yi Dynasty, the custom of having as many wives as one could afford lingered on. As part of the Confucian heritage, extramarital affairs were accepted as a rite of passage for men. They were grudgingly tolerated by women and secretly recommended by other men, viewed as proof of manhood. In being so faithful to his oath of matrimony, Father was half a century ahead of his time.

"This woman coveted Father, who was a frequent customer at the fancy teahouse she owned," Mother went on. "Nobody knew how many times she asked him out, but everyone knew how many times he had said no. She finally persuaded a friend of his, Kosan, to call him late one night and ask him to come over to a hotel room where she had checked herself in for the night. Father rushed to the hotel, believing Kosan's lie that he had a personal emergency. When he saw the teahouse owner instead of his friend, he shouted, 'What are you doing, woman? Can't you find better things to do? Get dressed and go home. If you got drunk and lay down on a street in broad daylight, it wouldn't be as wasteful as this.' He slammed the door and walked to the elevator."

"Who told you the story?" I asked.

"Kosan did," she said. "I believe him. I know your father."

The following Sunday, Kosan found himself speaking for all the gentlemen at the table, who were of one mind in wondering about Father: "He won't do anything to hurt his children. They are his life, and he knows they'll be devastated if they find out he has another woman." As they packed Father's empty seat with the secondhand books they had brought to exchange, they wrote off his absence with their dime-store psychology. They couldn't have guessed that Father was being faithful to Mother because he was being faithful to himself.

"In any case, he's not a man," the men in the teahouse decided. "We know that much."

"Is Father not a man?" I interrupted Mother, wide-eyed.

Mother gave me an amused look. "My dear child, you take things too seriously. They were joking."

I didn't believe they had been joking, but I bit my tongue. "But . . . but . . . Does he love you? Is that why he turned down the woman who offered herself?" The possibility of him not loving her had always made me ache.

Mother stared at me. "You're only a kid. A kid isn't supposed to ask a question like that."

"But . . ." I persisted. I couldn't understand why my question upset her. I wanted to see Mother and Father holding hands and acting like a young couple in love. Because Grandmother eavesdropped on them out of jealousy, they couldn't talk freely even in the privacy of their own bedroom. But Father seemed hardly better than Grandmother, thinking of Mother as no more than a maid hired for the family.

More incredible to me was that Mother didn't seem to mind at all. To a woman like Mother, romance and love would be a luxury, and I had no right to make her long for something she didn't ask for. When I was growing up, most of my peers didn't question that a man showing romantic love for his wife was a wimp.

"He's a responsible father and he doesn't mess around on me," she replied sharply. "He is so devoted to his family that he doesn't have the time to go camping with his friends on weekends. He spends every penny he earns for your education, don't you see? He is a man among men."

"So he loves you, then," I said.

"He won't leave us, no matter what," she assured me. "If there is anything you can absolutely count on in this changing world, it's your Father's devotion."

I thought she was telling me the truth. In order not to repeat his father's mistake, he avoided women as the captain of a ship would avoid reefs. But I wasn't proud of Father; I was rather ashamed of him. He suppressed romantic joy, giving his wife nothing but orders. I decided that if I could speak English as fluently as one of those glamorous Hollywood actresses, a man wouldn't be able to brush me off the way Father brushed Mother off. Didn't Grandfather leave his good old wife for a young, English-speaking woman? Didn't Father sneak out on Mother to experience the vicarious hot love of the theater screens? There seemed only one way to be free from Grandmother's fate, and this was mastering the English language. I had to speak it as well as, if not better than, all those women Father secretly courted in those dark, empty halls.

Running to meet Father on the train platform in Seoul Station, I saw the face that his children had always loved. Now, I know that it was love—love that my family was unable to express except in the form of quarrels—governing our house. It was love in a dust storm. Blinded by the wind, we each made the mistake of believing the others were throwing dirt at us, and picked up the same dirt to hurt each other in return.

A Woman Who Flew
Down from the Moon

"WE'LL GET A TAXI HOME," FATHER ANNOUNCED. "IT'S A SPE-
CIAL day, and I'm afraid the bus will be too crowded for
us." With Big Brother and Less Big Brother at his side, he started
to walk ahead of me and Little Sister, and I followed him closely,
holding Little Sister's hand. She was a tiny seven-year-old, and I
remembered Mother telling me to keep her by my side all the way
to the new house.

"That six-story stone building you see on your right side is the Seoul
District Court," Father explained to the boys, lifting his index finger.

"In other words," Big Brother said, "it's the place where alley
thieves end up. Not any criminals who really deserve justice; they all
get tortured by the Korean CIA."

"Hush!" Father whispered. It was one of those years when
nobody dared make a negative comment about the government in a
public place unless he was ready to risk his job or even his life.

"Father," I interrupted, "can you and the boys walk a bit more
slowly?" I was out of breath trying to keep up. The plaza in front
of the train station was crowded with travelers who had just
arrived, and I was frantic, almost hauling Little Sister along with my
right hand.

Instead of looking back, Father kept talking to the boys, excited
to have them with him again. "That three-story tile-roof tower,

Seoul City Hall, 1966.

which is designed after a traditional Korean house, is called the South Gate. During the Yi Dynasty, travelers knew they were entering the capitol of the country from the South when they saw it."

"That is when men from the noble class walked for days all the way to Seoul to take the exam to become government bureaucrats," Less Big Brother said knowledgeably. "Those who failed lived the rest of their lives like social derelicts."

"Father," I called out again, this time in a louder voice. But he didn't look back.

"Not exactly," Big Brother corrected, playing the patient tutor. "Our great-great-grandfather failed the exam, but in his hometown he was a renowned scholar." This was the first I'd learned of a great-great-grandfather who had failed the exam for the government bureaucrats, but I wasn't interested. I was beginning to panic because it was getting dark and we still had one more crowded block to walk to the taxi depot.

"With no money?" Less Big Brother's voice was sharp.

"At that time, being poor was not a vice," Big Brother said. "Poverty was supposed to boost one's spiritual morale."

"Actually, your great-great-grandfather was glad to give up retaking the exam after he had failed once," Father explained. "He was a poor member of the old rich and couldn't come up with the money to travel to Seoul again. So he stayed at home, making a living by writing books for the nouveaux riches. He was an excellent calligrapher."

"How could he prepare his son, our great-grandfather, for the exam, then?" Less Big Brother's handsome face smoldered with sarcasm, but he wasn't going to contradict Father directly.

"Your great-grandfather told me his father saved a penny every day for twenty-eight years to prepare for his son's trip to Seoul," Father replied. "But by the time he was ready, the exam was abolished by the modernized government. Life isn't fair!"

"Father!" I pleaded, shouting. "I can't walk any longer. I'm afraid Little Sister is going to fall down!" At last, Father looked back at his daughters, but he went right back to talking to the boys. Luckily, we had arrived at the taxi depot. The sky was almost completely dark now and neon signs began to flicker on here and there. I was cold and hungry, and Little Sister was stomping her feet on the ground to fight off the cold.

"This country has to reduce economic inequities first and allow opportunities for more income and education to farmers and people in local cities," Big Brother said. Again, they were talking about how to bring justice to this unjust world, but I was thinking about a bowl of hot soup and a warm place to lie down. I felt sorry for Little Sister, whose tiny body was trembling in the icy February air. So when a taxi pulled in front of us, I jumped ahead, pulling Little Sister by the hand. Less Big Brother growled at me, "You're being rude. Don't you cut in front of your elders!" Father and Big Brother frowned at me. Hanging my head, I waited until they all got in and handed Little Sister over to Father through the front door of the taxi, and he spread his arms to receive her on his lap. I sat on the right edge of the backseat, feeling relaxed at last. The taxi began to wriggle out of the crowded depot, entering the congested traffic of K Plaza.

"The gray-blue building on the right side is the City Hall," Father explained as we went by, "and the beige one right next to it is the

Ministry of Education. The nine-story building on the left is the Korean Supreme Court. Right now, it's in the middle of a major renovation."

"On what," Less Big Brother quipped, "the inner workings of the legal system?"

Father turned his head sharply, and with a finger on his lips, stared at Less Big Brother. He looked at each one of us with a warning in his eyes. Anyone, including a taxi driver, could be an informant for the government.

"This is the Presidential House," he said, pointing at an estate with one-story houses and long, low stonewalls winding along the block on the left. "It's called the Green House, as you know. In America, it would be called the White House."

That evening, I was in a tiger's stomach. I was disappointed and angry that Father cared so little about seeing me and Little Sister. I was particularly sad that Big Sister wasn't there with us, and I was disturbed by how easily the men of the family seemed to have forgotten her.

Big Sister had the bad luck of being the "family capital," the name Koreans called oldest daughters who also happened to be the oldest children of their families. As the family capital, she was supposed to be a second mother, to help raise her little siblings through personal sacrifice, to cook and wash and clean to alleviate Mother's household chores, and eventually to contribute financially to the little ones' education by either giving up her own or devoting her earnings to the family. It was common in rural Korea to see ten-year-old girls changing their little brothers' and sisters' diapers, and nine-year-old girls carrying baskets of laundry for their parents and grandparents.

Being an obedient, filial child, Big Sister accepted this prescription without question. In contrast to me, she gladly took the few wizened grapes she was doled out, quietly joined the circle of the women who finished the leftovers on the dinner table, and silently followed Mother to the kitchen afterward. "At least," she said, faint laughter tempering her cynicism, "Father was refined enough not to choose a ridiculous name for me." Some parents would name their family capital things like "bringer of a son," "second to none of the boys," or "the same as a boy." Big Sister was named "refined one."

When it came time for us to relocate to Seoul for our education, Big Sister was left in a shady little town outside of Taegu, in a neighborhood frequented by hoodlums, drunks, and prostitutes. Since money had to be saved for the boys' prestigious private colleges, Father had sent her to a free, government-owned two-year college for elementary school teachers and got her a job at a grade school in the nearest town. He told her, "We're moving because the boys have to go to schools in Seoul. You, however, will relocate to K City and live there until I can get you transferred to a school in Seoul." Compared to most fathers with his income, who didn't even contemplate college education for their daughters, Father was enlightened. Big Sister knew it was poverty that made him resort to the traditional sexism—the custom of sacrificing the oldest girl for the other children—but this knowledge couldn't keep her from feeling abandoned.

The night before we moved to Seoul, Big Sister had sobbed in front of me. She told me she was chronically fatigued, ready to crash anywhere at any time. Commuting to K City six days a week, teaching eight hours a day, and grading at night, she felt the stress wearing down her frail constitution. "I have totally irregular periods," she confided to me. "This hard life screws up my cycle so badly that I bleed twice a month sometimes and don't bleed at all for half a year other times. I wish I had the money to go to a doctor, but I give a chunk of my salary to Mother for the other kids. We don't have enough. Father had to get a loan from a bank to buy our little house in Seoul and will have to put every penny of his earnings toward the interest for the next twenty years or so. As you'll see, it's just a hole in the wall, but since it's in Seoul, it cost us everything we have." She stopped to wipe her tears with her palm. "All the way to and from K City today, I had to stand on the bus because there was no seat. It was so damn crowded I barely found a spot on the top rail to hang onto. But even standing, I began to doze off. I was that tired. I'd give everything I have to be able to sleep just half an hour more a day."

I struggled for something to say. I was at a loss, the same way I was when Mother rambled on about her grief in front of me. I finally marshaled a cliché: "You may find a rich man to marry you. You are beautiful and smart. Cinderella was beautiful and smart and she found her prince."

"Girls with a two-year college education don't marry nearly as well as girls who have gone to four-year colleges. I'm afraid I'll be stuck with a man who's not my choice."

I knew she was right. In an arranged marriage, a diploma from a renowned four-year college was virtually the only key to open the door for an "elegant match."

"But you see it happening," I insisted. "You see pretty girls who never went to college marrying handsome, rich men who graduated from the most prestigious universities. It may happen to you."

Big Sister stared at me again. My naïveté seemed to amuse her. "It happens in love marriages, but rarely in arranged marriages. Don't you see this family will tear me apart if I go out with a man who's not chosen by Father? Do you think Grandmother, who says only whores get mixed up with men before they get married, would approve of a love match? If I choose someone before Father does, I'll never be forgiven." She paused. "I was smart enough to get into Ehwa University, at the very least. I am sure, because girls in my class who got far lower scores than I did entered that school. Now they are showing off their school insignia, swaggering through downtown Seoul. They're going to end up with the men women like me want."

I didn't relent. "But you're beautiful. People call you the Liz Taylor of Korea! You're smart, too. If you're careful with what little money you make and manage to buy some pretty clothes, you'll be an instant head-turner."

She let out a subdued laugh. "You guessed I've been keeping a back pouch?" A "back pouch" meant the secret purse a wife kept from her husband for her personal use.

"I had a feeling," I replied. "I saw your imported lipsticks and the blush. I wondered how you could afford them."

Big Sister shook her head. "As you know, I never had a winter coat when I was in high school. When it was ten degrees, I walked to school six days a week, twenty minutes each way, with no coat. Father couldn't afford to buy me a coat because of the boys' tuition. Every day, on my way to school, I ground my teeth. I promised myself a thousand times that when I got a job and made my own money, no matter how little, I would get myself a nice, warm coat and a pair of leather boots with cotton lining inside. Now that I make a little, I stash a few coins a week. You've seen my black wool coat and my rayon scarf? Thanks to them, I don't feel like a knife is cutting my ears apart anymore when I walk to a bus station in winter." She lifted her chin. "Yes, I scrape every penny of my salary to support my family. I help Father pay the boys' tuition, too. But there is no way I will stop putting little bills in my back pouch."

Somehow, Big Sister managed to preserve a secret self, an independent spirit beneath the mask of the good daughter. I still wonder if anyone in the family ever noticed what I saw—the daggers shooting out of her eyes—and I prefer to think that Father and Mother saw them. Perhaps, they hesitated to acknowledge them because doing so would have made it difficult to keep her in the place of the "family capital."

"No way in hell I will ignore my back pouch!" I whispered back, and we giggled.

Until the faint rays of dawn landed on the windows of our old house in Taegu, I lay awake in bed, trying to sigh off my sadness for Big Sister. I used to envy her for her face—her magnificent aura, her geometrically perfect features. She had small, thin lips with vividly clear lines, oval cheeks, crescent-moon brows, and large, ebony eyes. Her nose was in flawless symmetry, its prominent bridge sloping gently into a pointed dune. I couldn't believe such a beautiful girl wouldn't be able to preserve her exuberant spirit.

That night, I made decisions about my own life. Number one: I would have a love marriage, not an arranged one; I would not marry a man picked by Father for reasons other than my own; I would not spend my life with a man who was Father's son-in-law, but not my husband; and I would not grow to love a man whose soul was not intimate with mine. Number two: I would rather be a free whore than a bound lady of virtue. If consorting with a man to whom I was not bound by holy matrimony made me a whore, I would gladly be a whore; even if it would make me a snake in my next life and be stoned to death by children, I would treasure the torturous death. Number three: I would wear a back pouch, no matter what.

In our new house in Seoul, I replayed my conversation with Big Sister over and over again. Having forgotten her in the excitement of moving to the new city, I felt guilty. I realized I was no different from the Three Men of the Family, who had neglected me and Little Sister when we arrived at Seoul Station. I wanted to celebrate my memories of Big Sister.

In the small room where two desks, one lamp, two chairs, and two quilts fought for space, I saw no way to escape Father's choosing of my husband. Big Sister, who was now living alone in a smaller room in K City with a few dishes and blankets, would be called to Seoul in two years to marry a man she had never met before. I, too, after sleeping beside Little Sister for another nine years, would follow Big Sister into mundane housewife's drudgery.

Although I was only thirteen, I knew our circumstances would not change; I was certain Father wouldn't land a better-paying job in the foreseeable future. I'd overheard him telling Mother how grateful she should be that he was even alive. "To get my family the things they want, I'd have to sell my soul to the devil," Father had said, as I pressed my ears to the door of their room. "I just cannot bring myself to serve in Park Chung Hee's regime."

"I haven't told you to," Mother said. I heard the emotion behind her words. "I just want you to know I am at a breaking point. It cuts my heart in two to see our children without warm winter boots. Our little one is getting bigger, but I can't even give her a pair of pants that fits. Is it so evil of me to wish my children to have what every child in this world deserves?"

He let out an explosive sigh. "But I can't do anything about it."

"Why not? Why not?" Mother was now sobbing.

"Don't you know I tried? Don't you remember the toy-making business my friends and I started?"

"Can't you try something else now? Just because you failed once—"

"I am the only one who came out of it unscathed. I had the smarts to pull out before they filed for bankruptcy, but the other fellows lost their lifetime savings after they had worked at it day and night for six months."

"If you were smart enough to pull out of it, you'll be smart enough to start something else," Mother pleaded.

"A high school teacher's salary is a pittance, I know. But if I hold onto it, we'll be able to eke out a living at least. If I quit and find myself bankrupt, who will feed our little ones?"

"But I can't bear to see our oldest daughter going to school without a coat in this weather," she wailed softly. Her children were doing their homework and they needed absolute quiet.

"So you're saying I should've joined Park's administration!"

"No, no, I am not saying that!" Mother protested. "Wasn't I the first one who said no to the idea of you working in Park's administration?"

"Yes, you did, and I'm grateful for it. But let's not talk about the past. Tell me what I should do to provide you and the girls with those coats and pants."

Mother drew a long, deep breath. She stood by her convictions that Father had done the right thing by turning down a job in Park's regime—he had been offered the position of chief organizer of North Kyongsang Province—but the lost opportunity was hard to forget. From that position, he would have been able to run for parliament, and his election would have been practically guaranteed. In South Korea, there were creative ways of "getting votes in," ranging from gerrymandering to rigging the polls. To maintain the facade of democracy, Park's government recruited candidates from all quarters, but its list of the preselected parliament members relied heavily on ghost ballots and fraudulent tabulation. Park's henchmen, entrenched in every corner of the country, worked sedulously to buy the loyalties of bright, prominent citizens—the kind of citizens with a high potential to turn into dissidents—and in nine cases out of ten, they won. With the promise of a national Pax Romana, they also succeeded in persuading people like Father to throw out their once-progressive ideas to work for the fascist government. Converting their prospective, present, and past enemies, and manipulating voters with parties, gifts, and personal visits, they essentially purchased their ballots for various prices. South Korea was less than forty years away from a nationalized electronic ballot-counting system, but to those who watched the fraud, it seemed the dark ages would never end.

For Park, who apparently received over a 90 percent approval rate from South Koreans, anything was possible. He was no better than Kim Il Sung, who received a 100 percent approval rate from North Koreans. The only difference was that in the Stalinist state of North Korea, there were no elections and no ballot boxes to be stuffed in the dark. Nobody saw the lights in an election office suddenly go off for several minutes while the votes were being counted, the way they might have in Seoul, since there were no votes to count.

But rigging elections through electricity failures was a lot of work. It was much easier to rely on charming, charismatic men, people with integrity and a good public image, to convince the masses to vote Park's way. It was highly likely that Father, once hired as the chief organizer of a designated province, would have been selected as one of these spokesmen, and eventually "elected" as a member of Park's parliament. Father would have certainly appealed to voters. He had been sent to America as a student by the U.S. secretary of state, and he spoke slow but correct English. He was knowledgeable on world affairs and contemporary politics. He was popular among his students and colleagues, and skilled in handling unruly masses. Park's henchmen saw an exuberant, competent, pleasant, and dazzlingly handsome man in Father. They saw the dandy hero Mother adored, not the brooding despot his daughters feared.

But Father slept on the job offer for only one night before the excitement was gone. Mother and I both knew Father's true calling was politics, but he wasn't the kind of man to fight for just any set of beliefs. He couldn't work for the same right-wing zealots who, wielding knives and baseball bats, had broken into the buildings where his progressive friends had met. He couldn't betray himself by serving them.

I knew all this and more from the many whisper-scream conversations he and Mother had behind the closed door of their bedroom during my childhood. I grew up with the ambient knowledge of what Father might have had, why he gave it up, and what giving it up had cost him. His rejection of that job offer, his decision to remain a poorly paid high school teacher, shadowed him the rest of his life.

I listened as Mother, in her frustration, spoke in Father's words: "They're all such hypocrites. Park himself was a socialist once. Everybody knows he sold the list of South Korean communists to Syngman Rhee's military. Now he is bent on exterminating all his former friends and their sympathizers. Those he can't kill and imprison, he bribes. You're one of them. And without those Yankee bastards behind him, he never would have been able to get away with all this."

"Of course the United States was behind Park's overthrow of the democratic government," Father said. "But what good does blaming the United States for everything do us?"

I was listening to one of Korea's big open secrets. Park was once a member of the South Korean communist underground party, as one of the secret liaison officers who infiltrated the ruling right-wing military. When he was arrested in 1948, he escaped a death sentence by turning over the names of all the communists planted inside the right-wing military with him. Park betrayed his comrades and started running errands for his erstwhile enemy. He enjoyed a rapid, brilliant rise in the South Korean army, and eventually rose to be its head, an ex-communist bent on smoking out the communists.

In 1961, it was with the United States' approval that Park led a coup d'état, installing an anticommunist regime so rigorous that McCarthy

Father with his high school students.

would have approved, and then stayed in power until his death. Koreans put it succinctly: "Park made a deal with 'big noses' to be the president." But only in whispers, of course. It didn't come out publicly until much later. In summer 1988, Father told me the following:

Kim Jong Pil, Park's buddy and partner in the coup d'état, later served as Park's prime minister and started the Korean Central Intelligence Agency. Kim testified in 1986 that a faction within the U.S. government—probably headed by a fellow named Peer de Silva, the director of the Korean office of the American CIA—had planned and succeeded to use the Korean military to demolish the democratically elected government. After Syngman Rhee's right-wing terrorist regime, which had been established and supported by the United States after World War II, was ousted by the people's protest, the Americans felt uneasy and wanted to handpick a man who would do their bidding to build a strong anticommunist, extreme right-wing base. They found him in Park, one of the most atrocious dictators the world has ever produced, and helped him to wrest power from a pro-

American, anticommunist administration chosen by the people. The Americans knew that the leaders of a moderate right wing could try to reconcile with the masses who were still leaning towards Socialism.

However well-supported Park might have been by the U.S. government, he could not retain even the loyalty of his most trusted henchmen. Reportedly, even his right arm, Kim Jong Pil, turned on him. Kim Hyung Wook, a former Central Intelligence officer, came forward to condemn Park because he saw his boss going too far. Another chief intelligence officer, a man named Kim Jae Kyu, shot Park to death in 1979, making international headlines with what appeared but was never proven to be a lone gunman's work.

After eighteen terrifying years under his iron fist, few Koreans mourned Park's sudden death. Everyone except his hard-core followers was rather relieved, glad to see so much blood saved, to shake off the yoke of constant fear. Had Park lived on, the list of those kidnapped, tortured, imprisoned, and assassinated would have only grown longer.

Here is just one example of the extent of Park's terror. In 1974, he fabricated an incident called the "People's Revolutionary Party Movement" and arrested twenty-three people on the common cover-all charge of national security violation. He accused them of association with North Korean reds, had them tortured to the point of false confession, and then sentenced eight of them to death, and the rest to fifteen years or life in prison. To keep them from talking, he had the eight death row inmates executed within twenty hours of sentencing.

One of the eight individuals executed was a friend of Father's, a construction company owner whose name was Do Ye Jong. He used to come to our house in Taegu to visit Father, to have long, whispered conversations with him over coffee Mother made for them. After he was executed, Father told his boys about him, and the boys were relieved Father wasn't implicated in the "conspiracy." Guilt by association was national law; anyone who was vaguely associated with a suspect could be arrested and tortured.

"Do you think the American people know what their government does?" Mother asked.

"Some know, but I'm afraid most of them don't have a clue. Their government doesn't tell them what it does overseas."

"What about your friends in America? Aren't they aware?"

"They are, but they go out of their way to find out. They know their media can't be trusted, so they read books and they travel." Father sighed. "When I was in America, I met so many good people. I can't believe such good people can have such bad governments." As a child eavesdropping, I didn't catch the irony in this statement; it didn't cross my mind that there were surely people on the other side of the world thinking the same thing about my country and my government.

"Why does that happen?"

"Those good people, those very people who were kind and compassionate to me, are devout anticommunists. They didn't even know what communism is about, but they condemned it, because their government told them to. Most Americans don't see how their government uses anticommunism as an excuse to crush democracy in other countries. As individuals, those Americans are nice and tolerant, but as a group, they can be cruel and ignorant. They're smart, but they're not trained to apply their smarts in political thinking. I told you about the librarian at Peabody College who never frowned at my poor English, who helped me find what I was looking for right away. But she thought America had saved South Korea from the commies."

Squatting down beside the door, I was seized by the conflicting images of good Americans and bad Americans. I couldn't make out any real humans.

Mother's voice rose from under the door. "If you ever get to go back there and see your old friends again, you must tell them about your life."

"If I don't, our children will. Our oldest son will certainly have an opportunity."

"Will we have the money to send him to America, though?"

"He'll find his way," Father assured her. "Schools in America will woo him. I can see the scholarships and honors. He'll be at a loss to choose. You watch!"

"He'll impress his American friends and teachers," Mother said excitedly. "He'll tell them about what their government did to you and your friends."

"He'll tell them how I hope that, someday, the gap between the American people and their government will be bridged. He'll tell them how they can be as good as a nation as they are as individuals."

"What about our second son? Do you think he'll make it, too?"

Father paused, and I could picture his frown. "He doesn't have much discipline."

"If only he had his younger sister's tenacity! She's not the brightest girl I've seen, but she works hard and she doesn't leave anything half done."

"I don't pin much hope on her. At her best, she's average. She makes the dumbest mistakes on the most obvious things." His laugh was jocular. With four bright children, he could afford to have one child turn out mediocre. "Remember the literature test about the faerie queen?"

Father was referring to the Korean literature test I had taken three years before, when I was nine. The fateful question, which everyone joked was the easiest one on the test, was: "Who does the faerie queen marry after she loses her winged garments?" The correct answer to the question, which even a Korean dog could bark out if asked, was: "She marries the woodcutter who steals her winged garments."

"Contentment is the secret to happiness," the teacher had lectured the day we third graders learned about the old myth. "The legend of the faerie queen and the woodcutter is a prime example. Who wants to tell the story for us?"

"I will!" A teacher's pet, a small boy with glasses who always sat in the first row, raised his hand. He recited eagerly, regurgitating the teacher's words like an audiotape. "The faerie queen lived on the moon, but she was bored. She wanted excitement. She traveled until coming upon Earth, the planet that seemed most wondrous to her. It had a brook with water so clear that the grains of the sands at the bottom could be counted, and the fields so lush green that she thought she could roll in them without getting dirty. But while she was taking a bath in the brook, the woodcutter living in the forest saw her and instantly fell in love. To keep her from leaving, he stole her winged garments and persuaded her to go to his hut, where she lived with him for nine years. They had a boy and a girl." The boy took a short, deep breath, preparing for the climax. "One day during the tenth year of their marriage, however, the faerie queen saw a sleeve sticking out of the crack under the wooden pillar of the hut. It was her stolen winged garments. She dragged them out and put them on. Picking the two children in her arms, she flew back to the moon, leaving her weeping husband alone."

"Tell us the ending," the teacher prompted.

"After he had cried himself to sleep for ninety-nine days, she flew back down to Earth to take him to the moon, to live happily ever after," the boy finished, beaming.

I believed the tale was sending a wrong message to women by promoting compromise and false contentment; one might go as far as to say it promoted acquiescence to rape and kidnapping. The beautiful faerie queen was my secret icon and alter ego. It had been my favorite pastime to imagine myself flying back and forth between Earth and the moon. I couldn't help but identify with her, and I believed the faerie queen ought to marry a faerie king—her equal— not an abusive, tricky woodcutter. What else could I have written in the test?

When I brought home my literature test with my answer to this oh-so-easy question marked wrong, my brothers went crazy. At nine, I almost understood why some people died of a broken heart; I felt too weak to contain the humiliation. Now, four years later, as my parents laughed about this recollection, I felt a stone of rage congealing in my stomach. *No, I won't lapse into tears; I won't miss a word of my parents' conversation.*

"What about our youngest one?" Mother said.

"She's too young yet. In a few years, we might be able to tell. But I'm pretty sure she's smarter than her older sister." Father chuckled.

There was a brief silence, during which I waited for them to compare Big Sister's quickness to my slowness, but they didn't even mention her name. If she didn't go astray and get pregnant out of wedlock, it was good enough for Father. There was nothing he esteemed more highly than a woman's moral and physical chastity, and yet he'd left Big Sister alone in a shady neighborhood.

Mother's thoughts must have shifted to her own absent siblings. "Do you think my brother and sister have children in North Korea? If they do, they must be at least as smart as ours." Sometimes, she would wallow in the idea that one of these days all of our families would rush toward each other over the demolished DMZ.

I had never met Mother's brother, whom we called Outside Uncle (once married, a daughter was considered an outsider to her birth family, so her brothers were called Outside Uncles by her children). Because of his association with the left before and after 1945, he could not live in South Korea without facing mortal danger. From 1947 through 1950, there was a massive search-and-destroy campaign in South Korea against lawyers, many of whom were known to have socialist sympathies. Outside Uncle was one of these lawyers, an active socialist with ties to the KPR, the Korean People's Republic, the grassroots socialist government that was declared immediately before General Hodge's landing in Korea. My uncle was a prime target of the Syngman Rhee regime, and was arrested for harboring "red thoughts" in 1947. His reputation as a scholar-lawyer was taken into account and he was released on probation, but he found himself living in a prison of fear, just like my father. At any moment he might have been framed as a conspirator against national security and sent back to prison. He was an object of constant suspicion, a marked person whose every word and action was being closely watched by Syngman Rhee's secret police. It seemed that fleeing was his only option.

*Outside Uncle, seated at left, was my mother's brother and
my father's good friend. He and his feminist sister disappeared
in North Korea before I had a chance to meet them.*

After the Korean War, which lasted from 1950 through 1953,
Rhee's anticommunist frenzy reached its peak. The war brought to
the surface the clashes between the two opposing ideologies—South
Korean capitalism and North Korean socialism/communism—and
the brutality escalated. Syngman Rhee in South Korea redoubled his
campaign to exterminate what remained of the left. Kim Il Sung, in
the North, was equally frantic to obliterate the remnants of the right.
Unaware of the purge in the North, Outside Uncle boarded a ship to
Japan with his sister, my socialist-feminist aunt, to seek refuge in

North Korea. They hoped, according to Mother, that the "wind of the blood" in the South would die down in a few years and that they would be able to return home. But for half a century, she heard nothing of or from them. Nobody knew whether they were alive or dead.

"They probably do have children, if they haven't been condemned to forced labor," Father said soothingly. What he didn't say was that Mother's siblings almost certainly had been called out for their beliefs, that there was a very small chance they hadn't been persecuted or killed. "If anyone could survive, your sister could. She was a remarkable woman."

"I just hope they are alive." I knew she fretted about her siblings' safety every day.

"If your brother has managed to keep his thoughts to himself, they might be okay. In North Korea, they can condemn you to a life in a gulag for what's in your mind."

"South Korea might be a political mess, but North Korea is hell. One slip of the tongue could get you into the coal mines," Mother said.

"They condemn you for what you think in South Korea, too," Father said softly. "Do you remember how they arrested my friend Chung Ho for harboring 'seditious thoughts?'"

I remembered Chung Ho, a tall, lanky middle-aged gentleman who used to visit Father on holidays and chat with him over a Go table. He was one of those few men with whom Father could talk freely about the forbidden subjects, and every now and then the two friends would close the door to engage in a long, confidential conversation. Chung Ho was taken to the basement of the Korean CIA one night, accused of being a threat to national security, and tortured until he lost consciousness. After the agents poured water over his face to wake him up and beat him up again, they released him, pushing his half-dead body in a wheelchair to his wife and two sons waiting outside. On condition that he promise not to instigate communist ideologies and pollute the young minds of Korea, he was allowed to receive treatments at a hospital and to go back to teaching at the university

*Outside Uncle's students took this picture for him as a
goodbye gift when he left for Japan.*

where he was a tenured professor. What remained in my memory,
however, was how, when the news of his arrest came, Father hid in
his room all day, fearing further persecution that might come from
being affiliated with him.

"They wanted to exact names from him, didn't they?" Mother
asked.

"They were planning to frame some of his students. None of his
friends were in danger, I learned later." Father sighed.

"On what grounds were they going to charge his students?"

"They had a discussion group every Wednesday, and during one
of their sessions, they read a book with a chapter on Marxism. A
copy of this book, unfortunately, was found in Chung Ho's home."

"Did he give out the students' names?"

"No, he didn't know who they were. The agents just heard about
the meeting."

"The pain could have forced him to give up random names, but
he didn't. He's a remarkable man."

"Yes, he is," Father affirmed.

"By the way, you burnt all your books on Marxism, didn't you?"

"I did." Father paused. "When we were in the movement, Chung

Ho and I shared one life, one death, and one love—our country. Once, we were chased into the dead end of a narrow alley. Before we jumped over the walls of the houses there, we shook hands and swore to each other, 'We will live and die together!'"

I could tell that Mother was dabbing her eyes on her sleeve.

"He won't die," Father said resolutely. "Park won't kill him for this. But until he gets out of the Presidential House, Chung Ho will live a life in death."

"I know that's why you don't want to serve in Park's administration."

"Serving his regime is just like serving in Kim Il Sung's army. Park is no different from Kim." With suppressed steam in his voice, he went on, "My friend Tae Hoon went to North Korea, Kim's promised socialist paradise. When he objected to the brutal dictatorship, Kim kicked him out. He forced him to come down to South Korea as a spy, and of course Tae Hoon was caught and arrested. He's on death row right now."

Mother was silent for a moment. "Sometimes, in my dreams, my brother shows up as a spy from North Korea."

"I have a feeling your brother's okay." I could hear Father trying to sound hopeful. "He survived the Japanese police. You know how cruel they were. Besides, he's too useful for Kim Il Sung to cast out. Such a brilliant man can't easily be harmed in any country."

Mother sobbed, "I wish I could see them just once before I die."

"If we had lots of money, I mean lots and lots, we could try to find out. But we'll have to move to America first and become American citizens. We can't try to contact them in this country. We may be killed."

"How long is this regime going to last?"

"I told you." Father sounded impatient. "It's not going to end before Park dies."

"If a miracle happens and he dies tomorrow from some mysterious accident, you might be able to serve in the new president's administration."

"If he dies tonight," Father retorted, "those Yankee bastards will set up another right-wing terrorist-style government tomorrow morning. But I think it will end sometime before we die." Father's prediction was familiar to me. "If I joined Park's regime, our children would live in splendor. For the next twenty years at least, this house would be packed with a mountain of gifts and bribes. But I would be a turncoat. You don't want that, do you?"

"No, I don't," Mother said in haste. "I want you to be who you are now."

Father said nothing. For a thirteen-year-old, their pain was too much. It had robbed them of time, and I didn't know how to handle it. I vaguely understood why my parents lived in a constant state of fear for their safety and sorrow for their loved ones, but I had a long way to travel before I had anything better than a one-dimensional understanding of their choices.

Eleven years later, in 1979, Park Chung Hee was shot to death by the chief of the Korean CIA—by his own dog, as Koreans liked to say. As Father predicted, Park didn't relinquish his power until death took him, until he had succeeded in changing everything about Korea except the rules of nature.

"It's retribution," Father told his children when Park was killed. "It is rumored that a few years ago, Park personally shot Kim Hyung Wook, his former intelligence chief, in the basement of the Presidential House. Tyranny devours tyrants and their errand boys alike. One must be absolutely heedful of one's political choices."

I knew I wouldn't trade the moral wisdom Father gave me for anything else in the world.

My Mother's Daughter

WHEN I WAS FOURTEEN, I DECIDED I WANTED TO BE A BOY. Pretending to be a boy, I thought, could prevent me from growing into a beautiful woman and getting distracted. If I were plain looking, I wouldn't attract men and be diverted from my goals. I knew by heart all the ancient rules of Korea condemning women of "loose conduct." Most Koreans criticized even a remarried widow, calling her a lecherous creature who forsook her children for her carnal urges. The Yi Dynasty's five-hundred-year-old law prohibiting widows' second marriages had been repealed at the dawn of the twentieth century, but its spirit lingered on as an unspoken cultural norm—even in 1968—and Korean widows lived without an accepted alternative to their widowhood. Women widowed in their twenties were faced with fifty or sixty lonely years.

Because I couldn't articulate my fears and unhappiness, depression became my only language and rebellion my only weapon. I was a nightmare to my family and friends, an archetypal teenager—belligerent, abrasive, and impudent. I took every chance I could to goad them, pulling mean tricks on classmates and teachers. One unfortunate target was the new, young bachelor teacher who taught Chinese literature and always carried a huge leather bag full of books. A short, stubby fellow with round, thick glasses that made him look like an insect, he was resigned to dating books instead of women. He reminded me of myself, and hence was unforgivable. I harassed and

Me in college.

belittled him, demoralized him in front of the class, asking him to write difficult classical Chinese characters I had randomly picked from a dictionary the night before. Nobody, perhaps not even a native speaker of Chinese, could have written all of them from memory, and the class laughed at him, watching him at a loss. I also impersonated him behind his back, grabbing the rims of my glasses with my thumbs and index fingers, imitating his penguin gait with my spider legs and stooping my bony back to look stocky. When he grabbed me one day by the throat and slapped me in the midst of my impersonation, I wasn't surprised at all. I was amazed that it had taken him a whole semester to bring himself to show his anger. Any fool would have exploded sooner, I thought.

"I don't know what your parents taught you, but I'll find out soon," he growled, pushing his face against mine. It was scarlet with anger. His beady eyes seemed ready to pop out and land on my face.

"Hey, Mr. Kim! If you hit her again, she wins," a teacher hollered, storming through the crowd of students in the hallway.

"Let us deal with her, please!" another teacher shouted.

But neither he nor I wanted the confrontation to stop. I went back to impersonating him and he raised his hand again to strike me.

"If you don't let go of her, you'll be expelled from school," a female teacher's voice hammered into my ears.

"Back off!" an old male teacher thundered.

I saw the teachers pulling him away from me and the students surrounding us in the hallway. All the classes in the building had stopped and everybody, teachers and students alike, had come out to watch the scene.

That evening, when Father came home, his eyes smoldered with rage. My principal had called Father at his school and asked him to come over for a confidential meeting. Surprisingly, Father didn't beat me. Everything about him, except his eyes, seemed dead from exhaustion. He collapsed on a chair.

"After you've eaten, you'll feel better," Mother soothed him, putting food on the table for dinner.

Father held his spoon and put it into his rice. But then he laid it back down on the table, his eyes fixed on the bowl, his fingers stuck at the end of the spoon. Everyone waited for him to explode. Even Little Sister kept glancing at him furtively.

"If you write a letter of apology to the teacher," he said calmly, "and deliver it to him personally by eight o'clock tomorrow morning, you won't be expelled."

For the remainder of my junior high years, I had no friends. I wanted no friends. I wanted nothing of myself and none of my family. All I wanted was to wallow in my pain, loneliness, misunderstanding, and depression. Naturally, red marks came back on my report cards. Although I left home at six-thirty every morning and came home at five-thirty every evening, I learned nothing. I failed to multiply a diameter by pi because I wondered why I should. Boredom pounded on me like a club. I was empty and immobile, a breathing automaton going back and forth between school and home.

The outhouse attached to our house in Seoul was smaller than the one we had had in Taegu, but it offered enough room for me to sit and be alone. In the rectangular space measuring twelve feet long and seven feet wide, we kept coal briquettes and sometimes boxes of poison that we unpacked to kill the rats and mice. The outhouse was located at the farthest right of the house, attached through a door to the room Little Sister and I shared. Using this door, I could go in and out without being seen by the rest of the family.

Just like our house in Taegu, our house in Seoul was built in the shape of the English letter L, the two legs connected by the kitchen. Every day, Mother—and now I—had to heat the floors of the rooms from the basement with charcoal briquettes, rushing from the basement to diffuse the horrible fumes we had breathed in, and ducking back in again and again over the course of the day. The house had no room for a dining area, so we ate our meals in the master bedroom. To get the food there from the kitchen, the women had to walk along a short, narrow hallway. By the time all the dishes were placed on the table, we were too exhausted to feel hungry.

Nevertheless, I thought I should be grateful. We had moved up, living in a clean, upwardly mobile middle-class neighborhood where people put every penny of their money into their children's education. Because Big Brother was an economics major at Seoul National University and Less Big Brother was attending one of the most competitive high schools in the nation, my family enjoyed a special standing in the neighborhood, respected and even admired by some. As usual, Mother ran out of money at the end of the month, and we wore rags under the well-ironed, tidy-looking school uniforms, but the appearance we tried to keep seemed less absurd now. It seemed less of a lie to me.

Six days a week—in secondary school, Saturday was a school day—I woke up at five-thirty in the morning, sat on a bus for an hour, and walked fifteen minutes from the bus stop to my school. In winter, it was so cold on the bus that I curled up my toes inside my shoes and covered my red nose with my gloved hands. Until the bus became warm enough, packed with sitting and standing passengers, I couldn't even doze off. Now, nearly thirty years have passed since this daily bus ride took me from one end of Seoul to another, and everyone owns a car. I laugh when I realize I've become one of those long-winded old women remembering "the good old days," how I used to wake up exactly at the moment I'd need to disembark, like an alarm clock wound up for the same time.

When I turned fourteen, reality was rushing in. I would have to face the entrance exam for high school and brace myself for the thirteen-hour-a-day work schedule. I applied myself to memorization, driving away my malaise. And I succeeded. In three months, my report card was transformed and my family showered me with attention. Mother gave me some of the same dishes she reserved for her boys, and my brothers blessed me with a few approving glances and words. Father's smile, too, so rarely cast at me, lightened the burden of my long days.

When I failed to enter the high school of my first choice, I cried all night long. Father didn't berate me, though. He said, "I've seen how well you can do in a short time. If you keep at it steadily, you'll go to a good college. College is your ultimate contest." Big Brother, too, supported me. "Work at your English especially," he advised. "Remember: in order for a woman to get somewhere, she must be better than men."

I appreciated his encouragement, but wondered about his intent. He'd recently spoken disparagingly of a female English professor of his. "She has a graduate degree from Princeton," he'd told us. "She's smart, but she's a bitch. She doesn't think much of men, and I heard her husband got fed up and divorced her because she kept ordering him around. She didn't treat him as a wife should treat a husband. A truly smart woman excels in her field and still makes her man feel superior."

Perhaps, I thought, Big Brother believed I was capable enough to be a truly smart woman. To maximize my chances of passing the exam of my second-choice high school, he tutored me in math for five hours every day for three weeks on end. It was tedious and exhausting, but he did it gladly, knowing as well as everyone else that if I failed the coming exams, I would have to wait one more year for another chance. Even when he had to repeat the same rule five times in a row, he refrained from raising his brows, always looking at me with an encouraging smile. It was probably the sense of urgency we both felt that made him so warm toward me, but whatever the reason was, I was grateful.

I used to watch Big Brother's back in his chair while we studied. There seemed to be an incredible number of solid bones and muscles—making an airtight shelter to protect his loved ones in all conditions. I felt I could hide behind him in a snowstorm and escape untouched by any rushing flakes. Although my back was also firm and strong, I couldn't show it off. According to Grandmother, only shameless whores took pleasure in revealing the contours of their bodies to men, and in her judgment, these women had no right to protest when accosted or even assaulted by lascivious men. To heed her injunction, I always wore a bra that bound my already flat chest. When I sat, I hunched my shoulders; when I stood, I bent my neck; and when I walked, I lowered my face and kept my eyes on the ground. I narrowed my overworked rabbit eyes behind thick, goofy glasses that covered half of my face.

I made it into my second-choice high school in Seoul. Yearning for greatness, I forgot my depression in the excitement of meeting new friends and teachers. I reveled in the newly found blue dragon in me—the power of intellect suggested by my modest academic achievements. But I had a new problem. Boys and girls of my age never received sex education. I had learned about the reproductive process in biology in junior high, and I was aware of the eggs in a woman's body, but I had never been told what the experience of menstruation might actually be like. Having imagined a thin stain of red in my underwear, I was shocked the first time I discovered nuggets of blood as big as my thumb clumping against my nylon slip and threatening to ooze through my skirt. I had to rush to the bathroom in the middle of a class to replace yet another napkin several times an hour, thrown into a constant panic that made me forget my splitting cramps. No standard female napkins could contain my blood, and I had to resort to gauze to be safe.

None of these fears and cramps, however, could make me to talk to Mother. Menstruation was a taboo subject, whispered about behind closed doors, and quietly accepted as a relief because it was a sign of a normal female body. A girl might secretly welcome the beginning of her adulthood to offset the shame and guilt that came with this new awareness of her sexuality and ability to procreate. In a family, nobody but the girl's mother knew when she started to menstruate, but among her peers, it was a topic of discussion mixed with a subtle, fearful rejoicing.

Like a typical teenage girl, I was overcome with a mixture of shame and pride. Although I never talked to Mother about it, not wanting to add to her burdens, I thought she would share the same ambivalence if she knew. I assumed my excessive bleeding would stop sooner or later. Certainly, it wasn't natural and it couldn't continue forever, I decided. Sleeping with a bucket of water and a washing sponge at my bedside, I just could wash the bloody spots off of my nightgown and the cotton quilt before anyone entered the room in the morning.

But the abnormal bleeding continued. For six months, I bled for half a month each time, with only two weeks of break in between the periods. Several times during the day, I had to lie down on the wooden floor in the back of the classroom, clutching my cramping waist with both hands. Finally, I broke down and told Mother.

"It's been like this for six months," I groaned. "If the blood doesn't stop, I'm afraid I'm going to die."

"You're not going to die," she said, imperturbable. "It's normal to feel bad during your period."

"It's not normal to bleed fifteen days out of every month, is it?" I wasn't angry. I was in too much pain to feel anything else.

"It's going to get better. When your periods start for the first time, they can be irregular."

"The cramps are killing me. I can't stand straight sometimes. I come home with a stooped back like an old woman."

Mother was interested in terminating the conversation. "I'll ask a doctor."

She never asked a doctor, and I never asked her to take me to one. There were too many things that were more important. Among them, Big Brother's poor health was the most alarming. The tuberculosis he had beaten three years before returned, and it weakened him. He couldn't get up on time for his morning classes at the university. He needed something to strengthen his constitution, as well as antibiotics to exterminate the bacteria permanently. Mother and Father took him to a doctor of Oriental medicine and came home with a package of ginseng and herbs.

Then, there was Father's high blood pressure. He had collapsed at work, and was on constant alert for the slightest signs of abnormality in his body. He had symptoms of severe anxiety, including shortness of breath, excessive sweating, panic attacks, and headaches. He couldn't relax. "His father almost died from hypertension several times," Mother recalled. "Grandmother believes he committed suicide to put an end to his remorse. But your father and I think he probably had severe panic attacks that increased his blood pressure and in the end caused his fatal depression." The whole family feared for Father's life. If something happened to him, we knew we would be reduced to autumn leaves scattered on the ground.

As if to complete the circle of illness among the Three Men of the Family, Less Big Brother also contracted tuberculosis. He had always been thin, but now he trudged along on legs shaped like two long birch stalks.

I felt guilty. I had no right to complain when the men in the family were suffering and all the women in the house were making sacrifices for them. Even Mother, who had more right than anyone else in the world to feel pain, was a rock. Around this time, she put it all in perspective for me by sharing a secret: two years after Little Sister was born, she had had an abortion, and the lack of rest nearly made her faint for several months.

"Nobody in the family, not even your father, knows," she whispered. "You are the first and last to hear about this." I had pushed her for the truth after visiting a friend's house, where I had been offered a free fortune reading by her family astrologist. He had told me that there was another child, younger than Little Sister, in my family who had been artificially removed.

"Why did you get an abortion?" I probed.

There was a flinch in her eyes, but she said flatly, "We couldn't afford to feed another mouth."

"I heard it hurts terribly," I pursued. I wanted her to talk.

"I'm still paying for it." Sadness began to eclipse the austere monotone in her voice. "I feel guilty, but the damage in my body is harder to bear since I chose to have it done to me." To avoid the taboo word, she referred to the abortion as "it."

"I thought you've been hurting because giving birth to Little Sister was hard."

"If I had been able to take good care of myself after having her, I'd be in much better shape. A woman needs a break for twenty-one days after childbirth. But Grandmother only let me rest for a week. When she had your father and his sister, her mother-in-law only let her stay in bed for five days each time. Your great-grandmother never had children. She didn't know what it was like to have a baby."

"But Grandmother had no right to drag you out of bed."

"She didn't drag me out of bed. I got out because I couldn't bear to see her resent me so much."

"She was evil to you!"

"She was just repeating what her mother-in-law did to her, my dear."

Mother might have been understanding, but I was livid that no one had protected her. "What about Father? How come he didn't know? Didn't he notice something unusual about you?" I wasn't afraid of the unspeakable word. "You had an abortion, for God's sake."

"Don't you drag your father into this!" she snapped. "I never told him. Besides, he had his own health problems. You don't know what he went through. You will never know. Go do your homework now." She turned her back on me and walked into the kitchen.

How could she protect him at such great expense to herself? That night, I couldn't sleep; I was filled with such contempt for Mother. I disrespected her for worshipping a man who could only show his "love"—if any—through abuse.

Nor could I bring myself to understand why she defended her wicked mother-in-law. At fifteen, I was still too young to see how far ahead in the future Mother was looking. By keeping her vow of silence, she was preparing for her coming relationship with her own daughter-in-law, shaping her own style of conduct with Big Brother's wife and his children. She wanted to put an end to the vicious circle of war between a man's wife and mother, to protect her grandchildren from being pulled in two different directions, and most of all to shield another innocent young woman from the same nightmares she suffered for half of her life.

When I was fifteen, something else happened to reinforce my decision to be strong. Coming back from the bookstore one night with a new schoolbook, I opened the door to be greeted by Big Brother, who struck me across the face.

"I told you to help Mom wash the dishes. Where did you go after dinner?" Big Brother asked, breathing hard. I had collapsed on the floor from the shock of the blow, and was biting my tongue. Towering over me, he looked like a Brobdingnagian giant from Jonathan Swift's *Gulliver's Travels*. Nothing in his demeanor hinted he had any regrets about having raised his hand against me.

"I went to a bookstore to buy an English textbook," I explained with militant composure. Big Brother had no clue about my bleeding or fatigue, and surely had no idea how much energy it took me to draw myself back up to my feet. "My teacher said he'll downgrade us if we don't bring it tomorrow with the meanings of all the new words written down."

"Why didn't you buy it at a bookstore near your school before coming home?" he growled.

"I didn't have the money. I had to get it from Mother."

"You could have washed the dishes first and then gone to get the book. You just wanted to avoid stepping into the kitchen," he accused.

"I was afraid the bookstore might be closed."

"We don't have that many dishes tonight. Father's still at work, your less big brother is at a party, and your little sister is at her friends house. Only my friend Chaeyoon, Mother, Grandmother, and I dined at home." He turned back to look at his friend, who was fumbling with poker cards in his room. "If you had washed those few dishes fast, you would have made it to the bookstore on time."

I stared at him stupidly, trying to figure out how to escape. "I have to find the new words in the dictionary tonight, and I have other homework."

"Before you find new English words, you'd better understand old Korean words. Look at Mother." He pointed to the kitchen, where Mother was washing dishes. Her back was turned toward me, but from her silence, I could tell she condoned his violence. "She's not feeling well tonight. When you are at home, she shouldn't have to do anything. You are young and healthy."

As much as I wished to help Mother, I couldn't. When I had returned from school, it was already past six, and I had to walk twenty minutes to the bookstore and another twenty to come back. I had hours of homework for three different classes. But I couldn't explain this to Big Brother, afraid that it would sound like an excuse. *You are young and healthy, too!* I was shouting inwardly, my tongue locked in fear.

"If I ever see you mimicking any of the English phrases in that damn book, I'll split your skull in two." With this ultimatum, he strode off to his room and resumed playing cards with his friend. He encouraged me to excel in English, but whenever he saw me choosing English over housework, he couldn't stand the sight. I had to study English only during the spare time in between the chores, and I had to be good.

I'll practice English until all the bones in my body crumble and fall. I am stronger than you; I will last longer than you, I thought. I sat up until three o'clock in the morning, memorizing all the new words in that "damn book." Reciting the same sentences and spelling the same idioms nine or ten times each, I was grateful I was finally reaching adulthood—acquiring the self-crucifying strength that seemed necessary for my survival in the family. But as the days wore on, my body couldn't persist with only three hours of sleep and I had to relapse to the old habit of going to bed at midnight.

That week, Mother started to boil the herbal medicine she had gotten from a doctor to wring juice twice every day for Big Brother, so that he could drink it before breakfast and dinner. It was obvious she had forgotten my menstrual problems, as preoccupied as she was with eradicating Big Brother's lingering tuberculosis. I avoided looking at the pot with the boiling juice, wherever it was. When it was on the stove, I turned my eyes to the sink; when it was on a table to be cooled down, I fixed my gaze on my rice bowl; and when it was on the floor, waiting to have its contents disposed, I lifted my face toward the windows. It was an object that proved my invisibility, and I didn't want to see it.

"It's bitter as hell, but it'll make you strong," Father told Big Brother, who frowned as he tossed a candy into his mouth to cut the taste.

I bet I can drink it without a candy, I thought, seized by jealousy. But how could I have dreamed of competing with Big Brother? How could I have dared to expect to be treated equally to the pillar of my family and the idol of his friends? He was in pain, too, I reasoned. It was hideously arrogant of me to wish to receive the same respect. I knew Father pinned his every hope and dream on his oldest son. Burdened with carrying the whole family out of the tiger's stomach, Big Brother always suffered spells of anxiety and fatigue. At one moment, I wanted to pick up a baseball bat and break Big Brother's skull, and at another, I completely adored him; on one day, I would imagine polishing a knife to cut the Three Men of the Family in pieces, and on another, I would be overwhelmed with gratitude for what they taught me.

The same old guilt toward Mother haunted me as well. Going through a difficult menopause, she hardly had an adequate diet, let alone medical treatment. Often, she replaced lunch with a few pieces of kimchi and a glass of water, afraid that she might not have enough for the family's dinner. *I eat more than she does, and I don't have nearly the same strength she has*, I berated myself. *To support the family, she sacrifices everything she has. She doesn't see herself. How can she see me?* I couldn't stand myself. To others, I might have seemed like a jovial sixteen-year-old who often made her friends laugh until their bellies hurt, but my soul was intent on destroying itself.

I did one thing to help myself. After learning about a medicine in a woman's magazine, I had the courage to obtain it at a drugstore and the smarts to figure out the rather complicated instructions on my own. They were hormone pills that I took at gradually increasing doses over a certain period of time on an intermittent basis. In six miraculous months, my excessive bleeding came to an end, reduced to four days a month from two weeks. My energy came back, and the daily routines of an overworked high school student were no longer beyond my tolerance. I felt as light as a bird, and I was proud of having cured myself of a disease. I began to eat again, with a monstrous appetite to make up for all the food I had missed.

Mother had her own moment of courage around this time. She succeeded in dismantling Grandmother's dinner table DMZ. One night, there was a loud bang on the dinner table—the sound of the revolution that I was to celebrate for the rest of my life—as Mother dropped the eight bowls of steamed rice on the same spot. Without consulting Grandmother, Mother carried equal portions of rice over to the table on the same plate, proclaiming, "We're not going to serve anyone first or last. We're going to serve everyone at the same time." She placed the bowls on the table one by one with a defiant rap, meeting Grandmother's protest with a charged, unflinching stare. The rest of the family, even Father, joined to support Mother.

I had a chance to see the warrior in Mother, the brave woman flouting the rules of our matriarch. Once again, I wished to be my mother's daughter.

None of my beloved family, of course, had had a change of mind regarding the second-class citizenship of women. But in being so firmly united against the DMZ on the dinner table, they managed to give me hope. My family's unconditional love for each other was strengthened by the sudden coup. They were declaring that even if men and women were unequal, there were perhaps other, more subtle and less dehumanizing ways of segregating them. They demonstrated to me the seeds of change.

In high school, I began to make friends. I learned that I wasn't the only one waking up in a puddle of blood in the night and that some girls had it worse than I did. Sharing my horror stories with other girls my age helped me in ways nothing else could. As I was to find out years later from medical sources, it isn't uncommon for girls during menarche to bleed severely for a prolonged period of time because their hormones are still struggling to achieve balanced circulation.

One of my classmates, with whom I occasionally shared a donut or cookie after school, confided to me one day that she had been bleeding for two months in a row and was at a loss as to what to do. She couldn't bring herself to talk to her mother about it because her family couldn't afford to take her to a doctor. They were spending every penny they had on her older brother, who was expected to enter Seoul National University, go to law school, and become a judge; he was the one who had to deliver the whole family from poverty. Nothing, including his little sister's health, could jeopardize his chances.

As I was telling her about the pills I had bought at the drugstore near my home, another girl, whose cute face and petite figure gave her the nickname China Doll, confessed to me about her monthly nightmares. Because sanitary pads were inadequate to absorb all the blood, she, too, resorted to thick gauze, and had to wash it at night when her family was asleep. Unable to dry it in the sun, she wrapped it in a towel, wrung it repeatedly, and wore it wet. In January and February, the water was so cold that she made fists to keep her fingers from freezing and pounded on the wet gauze to get the blood out.

At the end of the day, when we said good-bye to one another, we laughed despite our shared miseries. We promised each other not to let the dreadful blood get us down. If we could stand losing that much blood every month, there was nothing we couldn't handle. We were winners, brave and strong.

I knew now that my family was just like most other Korean families, and that I was better off than most girls my age in Korea. I had reason to be grateful, being more privileged than Mother, Grandmother, and Big Sister. But I also knew that finding satisfaction in comparing one's blessings to others' misfortunes was hardly different from lowering one's standards; it was a way of justifying complacency and resignation. To vent my frustration, I held my classmates' sleeves and burnt their ears with my tirades, pointing out the worst aspects of everything I saw. Once, walking to catch a bus home with my friends, I spotted a half-eaten apple covered with ants on a sidewalk.

"That's a mirror of life," I shrilled. "Millions of people tearing at a rotten piece of apple! The few rich throw a tiny piece to the poor multitude, and the poor multitude attacks it like hungry ants . . ."

My friends stared at me. "We were talking about getting an ice cream cone. You ruined my appetite," one of them growled.

"Oh, well," I stammered, but improvised with a social instinct nobody had taught me. "As an apology, I'll tell you a story," I offered. "You know Yi Sung Kae, the founder of the Yi Dynasty? One day, he suggested to his mentor and best friend Muhak, a Buddhist monk, that they play a game of jokes. He started by saying, 'You look like a pig,' to which Muhak responded, 'To a pig, everyone looks like a pig.'"

The girls burst out laughing, puzzled but entertained by me. I knew they could tell something in me didn't quite fit, and they were right.

Less Big Brother had told me about the king and the monk. "You can be a Muhak if you work at it," he encouraged me. But then, he would come home at midnight and order me to cook dinner for him just to make me mad.

One night, I screamed at him, "I can't! I'm studying! Can't you feed yourself?"

"Before I beat you to pieces, you'd better do it. I'm starving."

"I have to get up at six in the morning. Don't you know my college entrance exam is coming up?"

"I know lots of girls who do all the housework for their families and make good grades. If you were smart, you could do it, too," he snorted.

My tongue froze, as it frequently did in the presence of my brothers. But I detested Less Big Brother more often than Big Brother. Big Brother was equally self-serving, but at least he was hardworking. While attending college, he tutored a high school student to support himself and worked at a bank during the summer to help Mother and Father. Although he made good grades at Seoul National University, he never flaunted any of his accomplishments. But Less Big Brother was arrogant. Whenever he saw me read the same page twice, he reminded me of how it took him only three months to prepare for the entrance exam for Yonsei University, the second best university in the country.

"You will fail because you're overconfident and I will thrive because I understand my limitations and have the discipline to overcome them," I spat.

Mother came out of her room in a nightgown. "He's your brother. Girls cook dinner for their brothers."

"I'm not like most girls," I said stubbornly.

Less Big Brother sneered. "You're not even smart. A dumb girl who doesn't like to do housework is just like a dog that doesn't want to be a dog."

"A guy who drags his sister out of her room at midnight to fix dinner is just like a man who beats his dog because he had a bad

*Less Big Brother, right, sits proudly with Big Brother, Mother,
and Father at the time he entered college.*

day." The more I talked, the more retaliatory my words became.

I regretted my inability to practice Father's advice: A woman must train herself to maneuver her loved ones to the best of her ability, to conceal her voice and inveigle others to speak for her. An unwise woman, who speaks for herself directly because she doesn't know how to use her wiles, invites trouble not only for herself but also for everyone involved. Father said that a woman who practices the four virtues—maneuvering, concealment, patience, and sacrifice—empowers everyone in her life, including her husband, her children, and herself. A woman standing up to a man is doomed to bring bad luck to those around her. But Father's catechism couldn't help me to win the fight with Less Big Brother.

"I am teaching you how to survive. You ought to thank me," he thundered.

"If you change your mind now and cook him dinner, he'll leave you alone," Mother entreated.

"He can feed himself."

Less Big Brother grabbed my ponytail. "You really want me to show you what happens to a woman who denies her duties, don't you?"

"You have no right." It was the line Katharine Hepburn used in one of her movies.

"I'll show you." He started to pound my head on the kitchen wall. I screamed, but more from fear than from pain; I was afraid that I would have a concussion and suffer brain damage, that it would hurt my chances of entering a decent university.

"If you beg him to forgive you, he'll let you go," Mother pleaded again.

"I was wrong, and you were right," I heard myself say. To avoid a concussion, I was ready to say anything.

Upon hearing my apology, he was appeased and let me go back to my room. Mother went into the kitchen to serve him, and he didn't insist on my cooking anymore.

Until late that night, I cried. Everyone else in the family except Little Sister, who took the trouble of coming out of her room to sit with me, pretended to be asleep while Less Big Brother beat me. Little Sister was different from Big Sister, who sided with the Three Men of the Family to make a good impression on them. When I was fifteen and a half, Big Sister moved to Seoul to live with the rest of the family after two years alone in K City. She was thankful that Father had made it possible for her to get a job at a school in Seoul, proud that her little brothers had made it into the most prestigious schools in Korea. She felt she was from a good family, so to speak, owing to the men. Since a large part of a woman's worth on the marriage market was determined by the achievement of her male siblings, she didn't mind them receiving preferential treatment. Her resentment was now replaced with gratitude.

Increasingly, I became aware that Big Sister was "normal" and that I was not. All the girls in my class agreed it was their duty to be subservient to their brothers. As their mothers served their fathers, they served their brothers, and as they served their brothers, they would serve their husbands and sons in the future, they said. To

Big Sister and Less Big Brother as adolescents.

emphasize the point, one of the girls, a university chancellor's daughter, talked about the practices at her home. She told me that her
mother didn't cook at all when the men in her family were absent;
she would just put the leftovers on the table. Chiming in with her,
another girl confessed that her mother, one of those few prominent
female lawyers in the country, boiled instant noodles for herself and
her daughter, while spending hours in the kitchen to produce far
more elaborate dishes when her husband and son were around.
Listening to these girls, I was struck by the fact that most families in
Korea had a DMZ on the dinner table. I felt hopeless, learning that
well-educated women who espoused progressive ideas still perpetuated medieval values in their own houses.

I was the one with an impossible dream. My brothers were more
enlightened than most men of their generation. They were the men-
tors who brought me the names of Susan B. Anthony, Eleanor
Roosevelt, Harriet Beecher Stowe, Simone de Beauvoir, and many
more women whose voices suggested a new direction for the world.
Handing me his college English book one night, Big Brother turned

the pages to point at an article on Margaret Mead and her legacy. After explaining that she was a famous anthropologist who became a role model for countless women, he added that despite three different marriages, she never changed her last name. She was a woman who showed new possibilities for other women and represented what I should aspire to become. My brothers were the ones who gave me the weapon with which I could criticize them.

Thanks to my brothers, I was capable of feeling repulsed by the dance teacher in my high school who one day lectured on the female virtues: "A woman should choose where she sleeps very carefully, but she shouldn't be picky about what she eats at all. When she is selective about the bed she sleeps on, she guards her chastity, her most sacred property, and when she puts into her mouth anything that her chopsticks can pick up, she practices her humility, her most virtuous asset." Thankful for the wisdom she imparted, the girls in the class talked about her advice for several days. How glad they were to have a woman teacher who could give them such invaluable tips! The dance teacher and my classmates made my protests for equality a joke; they readily volunteered to be inferior, to subjugate themselves and other women to men.

Perfection was my best way out of the trap of becoming like my countrywomen, docile and unquestioning. I slept no more than five hours a day and utilized every waking second to cram myself with information. While standing on a bus, I read; walking out of a class, I memorized names in biology books; going to the restroom, I recited math formulas; walking home, I rehearsed English words. I washed dishes as fast as I could, sometimes soaping up two bowls at once. I was constantly tired. Sometimes I hit my head with a spatula to stay awake or pinched my arm to reenergize myself. I knew my intelligence level would not go up just because I worked hard. But my goal was to move the gods, so that they would make my paper wings flutter. I was convinced of the truth of the Korean saying: "When a woman is bent on unraveling the knot in her heart, she can cover the sky in July with snow."

Aunt Minsoon,
the Comfort Woman

To remind myself that I had no right to feel hopeless about my life, I would ask Mother to tell me about the Korean comfort women. Most of them had been my age, fifteen, or younger when they were "recruited." Compared to the hell they had lived through, the worst passage in the average person's life looked like a picnic gone bad. The story of Minsoon, a surviving comfort woman from Mother's village, was another one that I made Mother tell and retell. I wanted a story that would make mine look pale by comparison.

"Sometimes, conquerors use local women to keep their soldiers satisfied," Mother would begin. "Americans at least didn't instruct their soldiers to rape women of the countries they conquered, but the Japanese did. They not only condoned sexual violence, but also organized it. 'Comfort Women' is the name the Japanese government used for the girls they gathered for sexual slavery from 1932 through 1945. We don't know exactly how many girls they drafted, somewhere between a hundred thousand and two hundred thousand. Most of them were Korean, some Chinese and Filipino, some from other countries around Asia.

"Do you know these women were classified as 'cargo' by the Japanese naval forces that shipped them? This meant that if they were lost, no records of them would be found. Dogs and cats would

A Korean country village, 1966.

have been classified as 'animals' at least, but the girls were regarded as less than animals."

"Why did the girls go if they knew they were going to be sexual slaves?"

"They didn't know. The Japanese government tricked, kidnapped, and lied to them. Some of them were told that they would work as domestics or in factories or as nurses at a hospital; others were kidnapped from their front yards. When they were taken to their 'work' and raped by thirty to forty soldiers every day, they realized what they had been brought for. Some had to take in a hundred soldiers a day."

"A hundred—"

"To numb their pain, the Japanese gave them opium and the painkiller called '606 shots.' Some girls got pregnant, but didn't know they were. So they kept getting the shots and suffered massive hemorrhages. Most of them were only twelve, thirteen, or fourteen years old, and knew nothing of sex or pregnancy. They had no idea what was happening to their bodies."

"They were children."

"Yes, they were."

"How do you know all these details?"

"Please don't tell anyone," she said furtively. "We'll get into trouble, as will the lady who told me about her experience as a Comfort Woman. It's one of those things our government wants to hide."

"You know her personally?'

"Her name is Minsoon. You met her a few years ago." Mother wiped away unobtrusive tears as she talked. "She was the one living at the far side of my village, renting a tiny shack on the other side of the bamboo forest. It was a spot the villagers feared as being haunted, and some said they saw a ghost of a woman there. But my mother and I used to visit her when I was a teenager. She was only three years older than I, but her life had taken such a different path. We knew how much she needed human contact."

I could remember the face of the shunned woman. Only four feet nine with about seventy pounds on her bones, Aunt Minsoon exuded a commanding aura, a look of genuine dignity. I clearly recalled the eyes shimmering with quiet determination and the mouth ready with cautious but eloquent words. It was not the face I would have imagined on a woman who had been raped by a hundred men in a single day. Aunt Minsoon was fearless and focused. No wonder she lived alone.

Aunt Minsoon was one of those few women lucky and strong enough to outlive the unspeakable and return home. It is impossible to obtain accurate statistics regarding how many of the Comfort Women were still alive at the end of World War II and how many came back home, but one may guess that three-quarters probably died during the war. Fewer than the surviving quarter came back home, a large number of them stranded in China or other countries in the Pacific—Burma, Malaysia, the Philippines. Minsoon was one of this small minority. She was barely seventeen in 1945, the year she returned to Korea, but in a period of a few years, she managed to nurture herself back to health and start a new life.

"What did Aunt Minsoon tell you?" I asked.

"So many terrible things. At fourteen, she was approached by a recruiter, who told her that she could go work at a factory. Her family was dirt poor, so to reduce the number of the mouths her parents had to feed, she agreed to go."

Minsoon was taken to a desolate, windy battlefield in Manchuria, where the army barracks were divided into little cubicles the size of a bed. Called a "Comfort Station," each of these cubicles functioned as a room, though barely big enough for one person to lie down. Between the barracks and the outside hung an army blanket to serve as the door, and in front of this makeshift door, soldiers stood in line, waiting for their turn as they would to use an outhouse. Sometimes, one of them would storm in before the previous one was done, and often those waiting outside would yell to those inside, "Hurry, hurry! Why is it taking so long?" Most people wouldn't say that in front of an outhouse, of course. Neither would an outhouse smell as foul as the rotting uteruses of these girls, who, after being taken to a doctor's office more than twice, didn't come back at all.

Although there were twenty girls who had been brought to the same barracks as Minsoon, only seven of them were still breathing when the Japanese surrendered, and among these seven, Minsoon was the only one who could return home, since she was the only one who could walk. The rest were unable to move, with uteruses swollen like mountains and filled with bloody gangrene, and she wondered what would happen to them. She had a good idea, however, having witnessed a series of mass burials in the battlefields. Every once in a while, the Japanese would drive in a truck loaded with dead soldiers, dig a huge grave, drag the sick girls out of the cubicles, drop them into the bottom of the grave, and then pile the dead soldiers on top to bury them together. To this day, Minsoon feels certain that the other six girls were buried alive by the Japanese, who were on their way out of the Manchurian fields as quickly and efficiently as they could evacuate.

As if being gang-raped around the clock weren't enough, Minsoon and the girls had to endure random violence from the soldiers, who victimized whomever happened to fall in their sight to vent their wartime hate and frustration. They beat the girls for watching the moon and being sentimental, for crying and getting sick; they beat them for talking and dreaming of going home, for being silent, for looking at them in the eye and keeping their heads up. The soldiers kicked the girls for any reason at all: for walking out of the barracks, for bumping into a soldier when obeying the order to cover their eyes in the barracks, even for talking to themselves to overcome their loneliness. Dogs would have been treated better.

When the war ended in 1945, Minsoon's trials weren't over. After walking all the way to Seoul from Manchuria in the crowd of Koreans who had been drafted by the Japanese for forced labor, she found a job as a maid at a restaurant, where she saved enough money to buy a train ticket to her hometown. There, she lived alone for a few years until a man in the village, my maternal grandfather, offered her a chance to build a new life by loaning her the money to go to a doctor in a city nearby. Although it took her years to get her health back, a surgery saved her life by taking out the gangrene in her uterus and half of her rotten intestines. According to Mother, who went to see her often in her little shack after the surgery, Minsoon looked so smart and dignified that she couldn't believe she had just escaped a near-death experience.

"Not surprisingly, the first thing she did when she could stand on her own two legs was to pay your grandfather back," Mother said. "But later, he offered to loan all of it back to her, so that she could own a little restaurant she was renting in town and be completely self-sufficient."

"She paid it back, too, I'm sure."

"Yes, including the interest your grandfather didn't ask for. She came to our house on the same day every month with the paper money neatly folded in an envelope."

"Why was Grandfather so nice to her?" I asked, pretending not to have heard the story before.

"Grandfather loaned money to everyone who wanted it from

him," Mother answered. "But she was his favorite because she was proof of what he always liked to say: 'Adversity creates character.'"

"How did she open a restaurant?"

"Well, she sold noodles in a town nearby on market days, but it was barely enough to cover the rent. So my father helped her with groceries for several years until he could loan her the money to open a little restaurant of her own. Because she didn't like to go to the village, where she was afraid people might point their fingers at her, my mother and I took the groceries to her shack."

"What was she like?"

"She was nice when she knew you appreciated her strength and nasty when she thought you pitied or looked down upon her. My mother and I were the only people she didn't hesitate to see."

My mother's father, who lent Aunt Minsoon
the money to open her own noodle shop.

"Did the villagers really talk badly of her?"

"She certainly had reasons to feel they didn't perceive her as a human being."

"Why?" I was furious.

"When the surviving Comfort Women came back, they found themselves living in exile in their own country. Nobody welcomed poor, uneducated women who had been raped by dozens of soldiers a day for several years. And the women themselves were ashamed of their past, being sexually used in a country where virginity is the most important qualification in an unmarried woman's life."

"What about their families?"

"Some rejoined their families, but emotionally, they were totally alone. A few did get married, but they couldn't stay married. Their bodies were too destroyed to bear children and their minds too damaged to engage in normal sexual activities. How could they even look at a man in the eye after experiencing what they had been through?"

"What about Aunt Minsoon's family?"

"Both of her parents passed away while she was in Manchuria, and she had two brothers and one sister who moved away. She saw them every now and then, but they couldn't afford to help her. They were struggling to eke out a living."

"But they didn't shun her?"

"No, they've been good to her. She's lucky, compared to the girls whose families turned them out. One of the girls she knew was married to a widower by her parents who wished to be rid of her, and gave birth to a deaf and mute child. She didn't know she had contracted syphilis while she was a comfort woman."

"Aunt Minsoon had no reasons to get married."

"No, she could support herself, so there was no reason for her to chance an unhappy marriage. Nor did she want to take the risk of having disabled children. She was independent. She worked hard and made enough money off of the little restaurant to move to Seoul eventually. We're still in touch."

"Most of the former Comfort Women lived by themselves, then?"

"Yes, they are still pariahs in their own country."

"It's not their fault!" I protested.

"Of course not. But is there anything that's not a woman's fault in this country?"

I wasn't satisfied with her answer. I asked, "Why is her story a secret?"

"As I told you, we're not supposed to know that the Comfort Women existed." Mother's voice sank into a whisper. "Our government doesn't want us to know."

Now, nearly four decades after the first time I heard of the Comfort Women, I can offer several different reasons for the government's silence. One is Korea's economic dependence on Japan after World War II. In need of Japan's investments, Korea was in no position to bring up anything that might jeopardize the status quo. Up until the nineties, when South Korea rose to be a competitive global economic player, strict secrecy governed all the information concerning the negative components of the Japan-Korea relationship. Behind this, of course, was the South Korean right-wing dictators' close alliance with the remnants of the Japanese colonialists, the hegemony of the pro-Japanese power set up and perpetuated by the Americans. Hence, the truth of the Comfort Women was systematically suppressed, along with anything that might turn the Koreans against the Japanese.

America, too, not only condoned but also encouraged Japan to hide its war crimes. As the only state with a thriving capitalist infrastructure in Asia, Japan was the only reliable player that could balance the rising threat of communism in the region. Exposing its criminal history would have weakened this security blanket and made the United States look like a bad country championing an evil people. National guilt also became a motivating factor. Having dropped atomic bombs over Hiroshima and Nagasaki, the Americans felt they owed the Japanese. Shielding them from all sorts of blame, including their crimes against humanity, the Americans helped the Japanese to reconstruct their economy and allowed them to continue their predatory economic presence in Korea. The Americans were no different from the Japanese in their treatment of women; to both, the price of women was cheaper than anything else. Of course, an oppressive psychological burden of stigma and shame prevented Comfort Women from going public with their stories, but had it not been for these complicated political and economic circumstances, they would have been encouraged to tell the truth decades sooner.

It wasn't until the nineties, nearly half a century after the end of World War II, that the former Comfort Women in Korea started to be heard in their own country. By then, South Korea had stopped providing labor for Japan. It had turned a landmark corner toward democracy by ousting the military dictatorship and by entrenching a civilian administration that couldn't be crushed by another coup d'état. While a series of sweeping reforms was being enforced in all areas of the country, the people's attention naturally turned to the various matters that had been ignored by the growth-oriented former regimes, such as building infrastructures and balancing the distribution of wealth. As the women's movement, too, started to gain momentum, it brought the surviving Comfort Women to the spotlight of the national media, encouraging them to organize and protest.

Thanks to the breakdown of the Cold War, Americans played a role in airing the truth. They no longer needed Japan as the buffer against communism in Asia, and, incensed by Japan's uncompromising trade policies, they found themselves in a mood to welcome news that would make Japan look bad. Starting in the nineties, Americans were more inclined to recognize the postwar conflicts between Asian nations. Although still far from widely known, the horrific story of the Comfort Women is familiar to some internationally minded Americans, many of whom, for several years now, have maintained a close working relationship with the survivors and their supporters across the Pacific. In July 2007, 168 members of the American Congress signed a resolution asking the Japanese government to issue an official apology to its victims. Six months after being initiated by Michael Honda, a California congressman of Japanese descent, it was passed by unanimous votes. Regrettably, the resolution possesses no binding power, but as a historical vindication for the women and as a global reminder for the Japanese government, it could very well be an effective step toward a long overdue apology. In cooperation with their American partners, a number of Japanese women and men, too, are actively involved in putting pressure on their own government to respond to the surviving women.

Most Koreans are afraid that the Japanese government is stalling deliberately until all of the surviving Comfort Women have died. To this day, Japan refuses to offer an apology, and some flatly deny that the sexual slavery ever existed. A little over ten years after my conversation with Mother, when she predicted that the Japanese government would someday launch a national campaign to deny their historical crimes, I came to see how spot-on she had been. Many Japanese history textbooks provide no or only a passing record of Japanese atrocities in Korea and other Asian countries, eliminating their activities before, during, and after World War II. There is one textbook that briefly describes the "comfort facilities" without an explanation of the activities that took place there, and another that acknowledges the women's forced labor. The successful obliteration of Comfort Women from Japanese history textbooks, which took place over a period of twenty years or so, is a frightening example of how history can disappear. Destroying history is also a terrifying way of dehumanizing the ordinary Japanese who had been dragged into the war by the imperial government. I have heard that many of the Japanese soldiers who had been brainwashed to take part in the inhumanity of the war suffered pain and psychological trauma for many years. Most likely, few of them recovered completely before they died.

It has been over three and a half decades since Mother told me about Minsoon for the first time. In their capacity to prove the undefeatable human spirit, the Comfort Women in Korea indeed are without match. In their everlasting fight for justice, these women speak no words against the Japanese people, but firmly unite their voices for a righteous condemnation of the Japanese government. Now, I can tell their stories with pride and gratitude for their courage, and celebrate how we—the women of Korea who beat the unthinkable—came out of the tiger's stomach.

Minsoon, whom we now call Grandmother Minsoon, is still alive and still actively working to bring the Japanese government to justice. She made the promise to herself and everyone else that she would fight until her very last breath, and has proven to be every bit as good as her word. She is no longer able to participate in the annual peaceful protest that in January 2009 marked its seventeenth year. Since 1992, dozens of the surviving Comfort Women have gathered every Wednesday in front of the Japanese embassy in Seoul to ask for Japan's apology, walking in a circle with pickets in their hands. During these past seventeen years, not one weekly protest has been cancelled due to snow, rain, or heat. There have been over 850 protests so far, and there will be more as long as the survivors continue to gather. Among the 234 former Comfort Women registered by the Korean government, there are now only 94 still living, all of whom are between the ages of seventy-five and ninety-two. They wish to see the final resolution—the Japanese government's apology—before they die, to finish the fight in their generation.

These women know that the Japanese government is waiting for them to die, but they also know that it is a foolish decision because it will only draw more finger-pointing in the court of international opinion. Grandmother Minsoon certainly knows this. When other protesters come to see her, she offers them tea and fruit and coaches them, "Lift your arm ninety degrees when you march. It'll give you a nice shoulder exercise. If you lift it only by forty-five degrees, it won't be nearly as energizing."

Now living in Seoul, Grandmother Minsoon visits Mother every now and then. When I happen to be there, I quietly excuse myself to go out for a walk, so I can laugh at the old women's amazing ability to repeat the same old stories to each other. After exchanging brief notes about their health, they immediately plunge into their usual business—establishing the true history in the place of the false one manufactured by the Japanese government. They set up a court of law in the living room and start recounting all the intimate details of the destruction that the Japanese brought upon the Koreans during the thirty-six years of their occupation of the peninsula. I've learned by heart every word and sentence of the familiar conversation: "A nation trying to distort history is bringing a curse upon itself. Japan will pay for it one way or another"; or "Liars will eventually find themselves powerless against the truth." Having grown up under the Japanese occupation, both women can tell younger women about the horrors of life under one of the most atrocious systems of colonialism in human history.

During the Japanese occupation of the Korean peninsula from 1910 to 1945, the worst aspects of colonialism—exploitation and abject racism—constituted the bulk of relations between Japan and Korea. Of course, the exploitation and racism ran only in one direction, from conqueror to conquered, and they affected Koreans living in Japan as well. Mother once told me about the great Kanto Earthquake of 1923, which rocked the whole of Honshu, the main island of Japan, leveled Tokyo, and destroyed many large cities in several prefectures. By 1923, many Koreans had emigrated to Japan. Mother said, "Perhaps, out of their desire to pin the blame on someone for all the devastation, the Japanese spread the rumor that the Koreans in Japan put poison into wells to kill them. They charged Koreans with causing a natural disaster!" A race riot took place, and six thousand Koreans were slaughtered.

This racism and exploitation—the dehumanization of colonialism—provided the backbone of Japan's guilt-free occupation; for three and a half decades, Japan wrung Korea dry for the resources to finance their campaign to take over all of Asia. "During World War II, the Japanese ransacked every house in our country to take away what they needed in the war," Mother told me. "They took our grains, wood, cloth, and metal. My parents used to dig a hole in the ground at two o'clock in the morning to hide the few grains and the little logs of wood we needed for winter. In the pitch black of the night, we were afraid that the Japanese would come to raid the house, beat us, and snatch away what little we were putting away to survive."

"Weren't they predatory before World War II?" I asked.

"They were. For thirty-six years, they refused to treat Koreans as human beings. We didn't hate them as individuals. We just hated the government, the ones who made the decision to destroy our country. But eventually, they turned so bad that it became nearly impossible for us to retain the friendly feeling we had managed to keep in our hearts for the Japanese civilians we came in contact with personally. When they started to rob us of our *culture*, we found our hearts turning cold. We were only human." She paused, the corner of her mouth curving up in bitter anger. "In the waning years of World War II, they forced us to change our names into Japanese, to speak Japanese in schools and at work, and to swear loyalty to the Japanese emperor every morning. Instead of Korean, we had to study the Japanese alphabet and read Japanese books, and bow to the Japanese flag. Anyone who spoke Korean or read a Korean book in public was punished. Nobody could teach Korean to their students or use their Korean names in official documents. For thirty-six years, the Japanese extorted everything from us, our land, our natural and human resources, our women, our freedom and rights, and our political autonomy. They killed and tortured our leaders. If you ever see the torture instruments they used on the Koreans in the independence movement, you will faint."

From the beginning, the Japanese ruled the Koreans with violence. Teachers taught their classes with bayonets at their sides; the number of police officers tripled; the military police were given the right to punish suspects instantly and arbitrarily without due process in court. The penalty of caning a person's backside while he was bound and laid flat on a panel on the ground was revived. Strict censorship was practiced and any report unflattering to Japan was eliminated. Lands belonging to communities were forcefully confiscated and sold to the Japanese for dirt-cheap prices. Anything made of metal, including spoons and chopsticks, was taken away for the war effort. Most of the rice produced in Korea was shipped away to Japan, causing widespread famine. The Japanese turned the Korean Peninsula into a strategic military post, a road to Manchuria and China. They tried to conquer their neighbor country by wringing its very heart.

As the invasion of China and Manchuria became a full-fledged war, the Japanese went one step further. From the 1930s on, they started to implement "assimilationist policies," worse than the "bayonet policies," making it a national law for Koreans to speak and write in Japanese and to change their names into Japanese ones. By 1940, 80 percent of Koreans had been forced to change their names, and those who refused suffered severe penalties. Some Koreans even committed suicide rather than face the shame; to them, changing the names given by their ancestors was a blasphemy, to the same degree that disowning God in the presence of a gun would be to a devout Christian. But the majority of Koreans had to abide by the law in order to survive in their own country. The consequences of not adopting Japanese names included being: brutally beaten by the teachers in school; excluded from the rations list; denied legal documents; denied a chance to work or be promoted at a public institution; fired from one's job; denied admissions to school and to the next grade; denied delivery of letters and packages by the post office; and subject to the constant, close scrutiny of the police.

"Did Father change his name into Japanese?" I asked.

"Yes, he had to. His Korean name was Lee Chang Keuk, but the Japanese name he had to adopt was Kawamoto Hideyaki."

"What about Outside Uncle and you and your sister?"

"The Japanese viceroy declared that anyone with the last name of Nam didn't have to get a Japanese name because there were people with the same last name in Japan. The viceroy himself was named Nam, *Minami* in Japanese. His full name was Minami Chiro."

"Nam was the name for a small number of people."

"Yes," Mother said. "Those who were Nam had to translate their names into Japanese although we didn't have to change them. My brother's Korean name was Nam Sang Moon, but it was pronounced as Minami Sobun: my sister's name was Nam Sang Soon, but it became Minami Sojun: and mine was Nam Sang Sun, and became Minami Sojin."

Father told me of the Korean Language Scholars Association incident that took place in 1942. It started when a man named Chung Tae Jin, a schoolteacher and a dictionary editor for the Korean Language Association, was arrested for allegedly planting doubts in his students' minds about the validity of Japanese language education. He was tortured by the Japanese police to the point of false confession; he signed a report claiming the association was waging a secret movement to liberate Korea from Japan. The Japanese police then interrogated forty-eight members of the association and arrested thirty-three, sending sixteen to prison on indictment. Two of these members died in prison from starvation and illnesses caused by torture. It took the Japanese police four months to file a report on these scholars because they received a different confession from each of the suspects who, tortured beyond recognition, were forced to say whatever the police wanted them to say. Making a nonexistent case must have been difficult even for the Japanese police.

In 1944, nearly two years after the police had cooked up a charge —"conspiracy to create a civil war"—the Japanese court sentenced each of the final twelve defendants to six to twenty years in prison. Since the Japanese had been trying to brainwash the Koreans into believing that Japan and Korea were one nation, "conspiracy to create a civil war" was a truly grave crime. Given the fact that by 1940 the Korean language was totally excluded from the school curricula, these scholars' patriotic efforts to preserve our language were courageous and effective. Were it not for them, the Korean language would have suffered years of setback during and after the Japanese occupation.

*My maternal grandfather, head of the school ·
PTA, in front of his house*

"But you said your parents still treated the Japanese woman, the wife of your school's principal, as a friend," I recalled.

"Yes, they did," Mother replied proudly. "She was a young woman who used to come by our house with a pot of red bean soup. I can still hear the clop-clop of her wooden shoes, and I can still see the beautiful kimono she wore as she walked into the front yard of our house. She brought the red bean soup as a token of appreciation to your grandfather, the head of the PTA in my school then."

I filled in the next part of the story: "Grandmother and Grandfather said '*arigato*,' 'thank you' in Japanese, and she said '*komabsumida*,' 'thank you' in Korean. The three of them chatted in

Japanese and Korean, using their hands and feet and facial expressions, right?"

"They did. She learned to speak a few words in Korean and your grandparents spoke some very basic Japanese. The three of them laughed together. They were friends—even when the Japanese government tried to destroy our culture and language."

"You said her husband was the one who ordered the teachers in your school to teach only Japanese. He was the one who trained them to punish students who spoke Korean by mistake. And yet, your parents welcomed her."

"Yes, they did. They knew her husband was following orders from his government. They held no hard feelings against him or his wife. He had virtually coerced your grandfather, the richest man in the village, to serve as the head of the PTA. But your grandparents wouldn't have suffered any punishments if they had been cold to them."

I was quiet for a moment. "How did the teachers force you to speak Japanese in school?"

"They made the children turn on each other," Mother replied. "When I was in grade school, our teacher would give each of us ten cards. Whenever one of us made the mistake of speaking Korean, another would snitch. The teacher would take one card away from the child who spoke Korean and give it to the child who snitched. At the end of the week, some of us would have only one card left after speaking Korean nine times, and some would have fifteen after reporting on their classmates five times. Every Saturday, the teacher would give the students with the highest number of cards prizes such as pencils and notebooks, and scold the ones with the least. This 'card game' started in 1934, when I was a third grader, and continued through 1945."

I smiled mischievously. "Did you ever have your cards taken away?"

"No, never," Mother said, returning the same smile. "I snuck into the school outhouse when I wanted to speak Korean. I talked to myself. And I had a best friend I spoke Korean with. She was a short little girl. We would walk into the empty lot behind the classrooms to whisper. We cupped our ears and mouths with our hands, so nobody could hear us. The bullies who spied on us for the prizes couldn't prove we had talked in Korean. We got caught a few times and were scolded by our teachers, but we said it was secret girl talk."

"You weren't afraid your girlfriend would snitch on you."

"No, I wasn't. Nor was she. Our bond as Koreans was stronger than our desire for the pencils and notebooks we could get for snitching. Most Koreans, children and adults alike, shared the same bond. There were students bad enough to squeal on their classmates, but they were a small minority. In every group, there are those who go bad under the same circumstances, but they pay the worst price of all. They get shunned by their peers. When the Japanese left Korea in 1945, all the children in my village united in isolating those few children who had received prizes at our cost."

"That's why the Japanese failed so miserably in making Koreans Japanese."

Mother nodded. "A reign of terror goes only so far."

I shivered. I knew that terror tactics might not convert a person's heart to a cause, but they could certainly numb you in your tracks and freeze your blood. "Tell me what happened to Outside Uncle."

Mother was used to telling this story, too—the story of how her brother and his friends had fallen under suspicion for harboring seditious thoughts. The Japanese police knew they were among the intellectuals who resisted the occupation, and watched them closely. "Outside Uncle almost got arrested once. A friend of his traveled two hundred miles to tip him off, and he burned all his books in the backyard of our house. The Japanese police officer, who showed up two days later, found none of the seditious materials he had expected to find in your uncle's study, and after a thorough search, he left."

"What were his books about?"

"History, philosophy, political science—any serious literature that inspired questions about colonialism and international relations," she explained, echoing Father's language. "But the Japanese cracked down upon Marxist books especially hard. Marxism was the philosophical theory against colonialism and right-wing fascism, which were the backbone of imperial Japan, and Marxist books were especially popular with Korean scholars."

The Japanese police officer who searched Outside Uncle's home used his bayonet to poke the haystack, the grass in the cowshed, and the rice and barley in the grain storage. With his hands, he threw the quilts and mattresses upside down, took the lids off the big pots in the kitchen, and rummaged through the closets, tossing the clothes out and stepping on them.

"And he left with no apology?" I asked.

"He did apologize briefly, and we were surprised." Mother snickered. "Under the Japanese, we had no freedom of speech, no freedom of thought, but I guess we had the freedom to receive an apology."

I knew Mother and her family were lucky to have received any kind of apology, however curt. There were plenty who received none at all.

Women Whose Marriages to the Gods Were Successful

Bᴵɢ Sɪsᴛᴇʀ ᴡᴀs ᴛᴏ ʙᴇ ᴡᴇᴅ ᴛᴏ ᴀ ᴍᴀɴ ʜᴀɴᴅᴘɪᴄᴋᴇᴅ ʙʏ Fᴀᴛʜᴇʀ. This seemed like the worst possible fate in the world to me at sixteen. I wondered if I would ever marry. How could Father meet Big Sister's husband before she did? How could he see the young man just once and decide that this would be his son-in-law? How could he persuade her to marry this man, knowing little more than his professional qualifications? And although I wasn't surprised that Big Sister had played the dutiful daughter and agreed to the marriage with a man not of her choosing, I was still dismayed to see it all come to pass.

Producing a flattering picture of his candidate from a back pocket, Father told Big Sister how bright and diligent the young man was. In the end, with that dreamy look on his face, Father convinced her she was as crazy about her prospective groom as he was. In this way, he prepared her for her wedding, and nobody in the whole family—except me—had a shred of doubt that Father's decision was correct.

Big Sister was marrying a promising young man, to use the cliché the world bestows upon men who work from eight to five at an institution (usually a bank) renowned for its stability and prestige. He had numerous other qualifications as well, not the least of which was his noble heritage. His ancestors had occupied high positions in the Yi Dynasty bureaucracy for six hundred years, owned the most land among all the noble clans, and controlled the selection of influential

Big Sister's engagement ceremony.

leaders. Although his family had been impoverished for decades, the long prosperity they had enjoyed in the past was a spiritual backbone to be counted on, according to Father. Overjoyed with his own good judgment, Father recited the list of his future son-in-law's extraordinary accomplishments: his near-perfect grades in high school and college, his having put himself through school for ten years, his reputation at his work, and his polite manners and gentle personality. He was a perfect candidate for her.

But the truth I saw was that Big Sister was a victim of Father's hypocrisy. He had spent his life declaring his greatest desire was to see the dynasty replaced with a republic. But the procedure he followed in selecting his son-in-law was exactly the opposite; it embraced the old traditions and resisted the new. Father confined his attention to the man's achievements, never considering the subjective dynamic between a man and a woman—the bedrock of a relationship. Did he believe a democratic republic could be created when half the population was systematically repressed in their own homes? What could women with no choice teach their children about fighting tyranny and living in a free country?

I could see Big Sister was going to have a difficult marriage. People say marriage is a challenge for everyone, and we all know this is true. But something about Father's man pointed to a long, hard road for Big Sister. Tall and lanky with thick glasses and bookish manners, he failed to strike me as a man deserving of Big Sister. It would be a good marriage in appearance, but he had the quirkiness of a man who had to overcome too many hardships for too long.

Marriage through a matchmaker was an ancient tradition in Korea, and the majority of modern Koreans still practiced it in my childhood, although the original form was slightly modified. During the Yi Dynasty, a man and a woman were married to each other by their parents and stayed married until one of them died. When the wife died first, the husband remarried a virgin; when the husband died first, the wife remained as a widow for the rest of her life, whether she had children or not. They never met before they married. Since their union was a contract between the two families—signed by their parents, for the sake of perpetuating the good names of their ancestry—what mattered was a continuity of their heritage. The couple was expected to reproduce their parents' social class by giving birth to male children as soon as they were united; for the sacredness of the family and the lineage of the clan, love between two individuals was duly sacrificed, personal conflicts buried. Some couples fortunately found each other attractive and got along well, but many, even most, lived in the same house without love, and helplessly watched their marriage dissolve after the expected arrival of the male heirs.

Few men from powerful families lived without concubines or frequent trips to geisha quarters, unable to bring themselves to fall in love with their wives. While their wives lived alone without love, companionship, or the possibility of divorce, husbands spent their best days and nights in the arms of other women, whom they didn't even try to respect as their equals. Obtaining children from their wives, to whom they passed their glorious family names, they sought pleasure in the company of their mistresses.

At the end of the Yi Dynasty, some westernized Koreans bravely launched a new convention. They began choosing their own spouses before asking permission from their parents; a few went further and married without their parents' approval, while others went as far as marrying against their parents' wishes. But most Koreans followed the old tradition, choosing to be united with blessings from their families and clans. Father and Mother were members of this majority and were married with good will by their families. Father was one of the legions of men who obeyed the ancient rules and remained faithful to the woman chosen by his family.

In Father's case, it was his grandfather, my great-grandfather, who read the Confucian scripts under a leaking roof, who made the decision to say yes to the matchmaker. He had raised Father because his son, Father's father, had abandoned his legitimate children for his illegitimate ones. As happened in many situations, a lifelong marriage was based on a third-hand character referral. When an upstanding young friend of Father's proposed his younger sister as Father's bride, the old man assented without a moment's hesitation and encouraged him to come by again. Such a talented, charming young man, the old man thought, must have an equally smart and beautiful sister. Because he so much liked the young man—Mother's older brother, Outside Uncle, who wished to see his little sister married to his best friend—my great-grandfather had few questions about the qualifications of the prospective bride.

Mother's marriage to Father was predetermined by the men in her life. They knew each other well—or they thought they knew each other well—and that was enough. It never occurred to any one of these brilliant men that Father had no sense at all concerning relationships with women. In their generation, the ability to love and respect a woman was not only disregarded but also discouraged as a symptom of an effeminate mind. Like the kings of their country, men were admired for their accomplishments but were known for treating women as little more than baby-makers. How I admired all these men as Koreans and how I disrespected them as men!

Seoul Station, 1966.

In 1971, the year Big Sister was married, the ways of the Yi Dynasty were modified, so Father allowed his daughter to meet the man she'd marry—more than once. He offered her the semblance of choice, but the first and final decision was his. His daughter, a young woman with no knowledge of men, was not to be trusted to make such a serious choice.

According to Koreans, a woman had three different faces, the first of which was created by her father, the second by her husband, and the third by her sons. A lucky woman had a father who gave her a happy face by taking good care of her; a luckier woman had a husband who gave her a peaceful face by being a good provider; and the luckiest had sons who gave her a graceful face by accommodating her comfortably. In a fortunate woman's life, her face got successively better, making her the envy of everyone; but in an unfortunate woman's life, her face got progressively worse, turning her into an object of pity.

In all fairness, I must admit that Father was more enlightened than most of his friends. One of them, a professor of Western philosophy at a university in Seoul, told him that he was looking for a daughter-in-law whose eyes were seldom entirely open, as if she rarely had any thoughts of her own. Demonstrating, he impersonated a woman with sleepy eyes, his chin slightly lifted, his mouth agape, and his brows turned downward—making the face of a woman looking up to her husband with idiotic adoration. While teaching Kant, Hegel, Schopenhauer, Voltaire, and Nietzsche at a university, emphasizing the critical role of the Enlightenment in history, he envisioned a daughter-in-law happily confined in the Dark Ages. Another friend of Father's, a professor of English specializing in T. S. Eliot, Ezra Pound, and Marianne Moore, married his oldest daughter to a man neither she nor he had ever met. The young man was from a stable family of noble ancestry, currently working on a PhD at Oxford University. Since his daughter raised no objection—or couldn't raise any—the contract was sealed. Smiling, after a three-day honeymoon she flew to England with the young man she'd only just met.

I wished I knew how these women truly felt. Maybe, I thought, they believed they were marrying gods; only for gods could human beings abandon themselves so easily. Apparently, Big Sister believed that she ought to get married as firmly as a child believed that she ought to grow up to be an adult. It occurred to me she might have had spells of doubt, that she might have dreamed of a man of her own choosing. But I quickly suppressed these questions. They were treacherous misgivings, since she appeared to be content. Citing the fact that 80 percent of people her age chose arranged marriages, she represented herself as a "good daughter" following the norms of her culture. She took comfort in the fact that couples who chose to marry for love tended to be blinded by their passion and that many of them ended up in unhappy marriages. Quite possibly, she didn't know how she felt.

I didn't know how to express my disapproval besides with icy eyes and disrespectful glances. I pitted my taciturn antagonism against Father, who I was convinced was wrong. I reveled in watching him fly into piques of purple rage. He and I were constantly at odds after the announcement of Big Sister's engagement. I fought him over everything I could, and he became antagonistic toward me in return. One day, when he was talking about sending Big Brother to America for a graduate degree, I interrupted, "Well, let's just hope he won't get cancer." Father was outraged. "You damned bitch! You'll have your tongue cut off one of these days if you don't learn how to hold it."

Another time, he was talking with his boys about baseball in Japan and America, comparing the personalities of the two countries revealed on the fields. I jumped in, "Don't their differences show in their policies? Americans accept people from all over the world, but the Japanese don't like any who are not Japanese. They don't even give citizenship to Koreans who were born and raised in Japan." Father, deeply vexed, said, "We're talking about baseball. Why don't you keep your stupid mouth shut?"

I found a release in denigrating Mother and Little Sister, whom I perceived to be as powerless as I. Deliberately and recklessly, I abused the two women I loved the most. I would say to Mother, "If Father had married the girlfriend he had before he married you, Grandmother would have ended up in an insane asylum a long time ago. She was a college graduate from Seoul, not an uneducated country bumpkin like you. Only a woman like you would have grovel for such an evil mother-in-law and take care of her all these years." I would curse Little Sister, "You're going to be short and fat. I can see that in your bone structure. You'd better begin to exercise now if you don't want to look like a straggling duck." Mother and Little Sister didn't bother to retaliate, and I got away with my abuse. With these two women, I became Father.

One evening in 1973, Father came home seething with indignation. "I've just heard they kidnapped Kim Dae Jung," he announced

to the boys at dinner. Kim was a prominent, uncompromising dissi-
dent with a long track record of fighting Park Chung Hee's dictatorship. "He was in Tokyo, organizing an overseas political network to
establish democracy in Korea."

"I'm not surprised he was kidnapped," Big Brother replied. He
was obviously downplaying his shock. "Did they kill him?"

"No, and I wonder why. They could have killed him, but they
didn't." Father's voice faltered with helpless outrage. "It is truly evil.
After all the false charges—conspiracy, treason, sedition, communist
propaganda—now it's a covert attempt to assassinate him."

"The Yankee bastards won't allow Park Chung Hee to kill him,"
Less Big Brother said. "They want both of them alive. They arm Park
with weapons for his coup d'état and back him up financially, and
they've been secretly protecting Kim, too. They're guarding him now
because they have to keep Park under their control. They need their
toady and their rebel at once, and that's why Park can only bring
false charges against him."

"The Americans' double-dealing is probably why they had to
spare him this time as well," Father agreed. "The American ambas-
sador to Korea, Philip Habib, met Park and asked him to release the
victim the day they kidnapped him, and Kim was dropped off in
front of his house in Seoul. To remind Park that they can eliminate
him anytime they want, the Americans are protecting his enemy as
well as his friends."

"Thanks to Park, we have the anti-communist regime they want
and capitalism thriving on cheap labor," Less Big Brother raged.
"Foreign companies can pay dream wages in this country."

"They also feel obliged to practice their democratic ideals," Big
Brother added. He drew the corners of his mouth downward. "They
want to be able to say to themselves and the rest of the world that
they support freedom fighters and punish tyrants. But having to back
up dictators for economic and political reasons, they're in a dilemma.
So, they have to control both the dictator and the freedom fighters.
I just hope they don't try to kill him again."

"Would you please eat first and talk later?" Mother interrupted. "Dinner's getting cold."

"I'm worried they'll kill him and report it as suicide," Less Big Brother said, picking up a spoon of rice to relax Mother.

Father put a piece of kimchi in his mouth as he spoke. "Uncle Sam won't leave Park alone, but," he stopped to chew the kimchi and continued, "they won't do anything to get him out of power unless he crosses them, and he hasn't crossed them yet. He's been hurting only Koreans; he hasn't embarrassed the big men in Washington yet."

"He's going to soon," Big Brother said. "Students and activists are condemning them. Their placards read, 'Yankees go home!'"

"The U.S. has been backing dictators from the beginning," Less Big Brother fumed. "First, they set up Syngman Rhee, supplying him with arms to obliterate everyone in the opposite camp. Then, they helped Park Chung Hee with his coup d'état. But now with 'Yankee go home' signs all over the place, they may change their minds. He's testing their patience."

"Please stop talking and eat," Mother said again. "If you miss the right time for dinner, you'll get a sore stomach."

I started to get nervous, too, for a different reason. Ever since Big Brother had punched me in the face, I was always fearful of creating the impression that I wasn't helping Mother. If the dinner dragged on, the chores would be delayed and keep Mother up deep into the night.

"Can you talk about politics later and finish eating your dinner?" I echoed.

"Now is the only time we can discuss it," Big Brother snapped. "We've got important things to do tomorrow, so we should get to bed early."

"If you think your work is better than Mother's, you are wrong," I cried, surprising myself with the sudden outburst. "She's been working all day to keep you fed and warm. It took her time to cook dinner. If you wait until the food gets cold, she'll have to start all over again. Are you going to warm up the soup for yourself?"

"Why do you care when she doesn't care?" Father boomed.

"Because you are wrong," I declared.

Father looked at me, dumbfounded.

"A woman cannot say a man is wrong," Less Big Brother admonished. "She is fed by him. A woman cannot hate a man; her livelihood is dependent on him."

"You're not making a penny now!" I shouted. "You're dependent on Father and Big Brother!"

"Stop now." Mother was exasperated. "On a full stomach, you'll have a better discussion."

I was furious at Mother for bowing to their condescension, for giving her rights away. Overwhelmed by my contempt for her, I lost the words from the tip of my tongue. I wanted to cave in to a feeling of hopelessness.

When dinner was over, Father, Big Brother, and Less Big Brother broadened their discussion to political matters concerning China and Southeast Asia. But Mother suddenly returned to the topic of Kim Dae Jung while serving them apples and tea. "If Kim's life is under constant threat, I wonder how his wife and children make a living. Is he getting any money at all to support his family? How are they getting by?"

Father and his sons looked at each other, stunned by the woman's gibberish.

"We have two nostrils instead of one for someone like her," Father spat out. It was an expression Koreans resorted to when faced with a dumb talker; with only one nostril, the listener would choke from frustration. The gods gave us two nostrils, they said, so that we could breathe in the presence of people whose intelligence was so stiflingly low.

"Why? Why can't you answer her question?" I erupted in her defense. I thought Mother had asked an excellent question.

"Why don't you answer her?" Less Big Brother returned. "Is there anyone smarter than you in this world?"

"You're a man and I'm a woman," I flung back. "You *must* be smarter. You should answer her."

"Stop!" Mother yelled. "Stop, all of you! The apples will turn brown if you don't eat them now." She picked up a piece of the peeled, cut apple with a fork and put it in front of Big Brother.

"You're a woman and you do women's work," Less Big Brother continued. "You ought to be able to understand a woman's level of thinking."

"You can say so only when you do men's work, not when you haven't provided a penny for your women," I retorted. "Mother worries about buying food and clothes because Father's salary is far from enough. I would gladly wash your socks and underwear if you earned money to help Father." My words were burning like kindling in a fireplace. I couldn't stop until I burnt myself out.

"Why are you always on the pounce like this?" Mother tried to cool me down. "Silence is better than words. Keep yourself quiet."

I was choking with frustration. "Father's saying you're ignorant and his sons are accusing me of picking a fight. Don't you feel anything?"

"Don't you dare put your father down! He's your father!" Her wrath was frightening when one tried to pull her husband from his pedestal. She was more faithful to Father than he was to himself.

"What have I done wrong to you? Give me a list," Father demanded of me. The corner of his mouth was drawn, the muscles under his eyes in mild spasm.

My argument with him was doomed. I fell mute. Although I understood the validity in Mother's question—I, too, wondered whether Kim Dae Jung's wife was getting enough money for her children—I couldn't explain it. The Three Men of the Family were deaf to all but their own voices.

Mother was unhurt by any of it. To keep the family together, she chose to put everyone else's feelings above hers and to ignore the men's insults. She would impart her philosophy to me more than once: "When one party pretends to lose, the other party truly loses. Losing is winning, my dear."

In their condescending attitude toward women, the Three Men of the Family were no worse than most politically conscious and active men in my country. They knew how to systematically and quietly keep women from the center. Mother allowed her men to be who they were just as the women of my country allowed their men to be who they were.

In 1973, sexism prevailed even among the most progressive political movements in Korea. The male leaders of these movements treated women in their campaigns as secretaries rather than as partners, alienating them from the decision-making processes. The women on the campaigns were generally found to be too militant and assertive, so many progressive men didn't get involved in personal relationships with them, preferring more docile, feminine women not yet toughened up by men's work.

By the time I was in college in the seventies, the women's movement in South Korea was in full swing. Democracy for the nation was its top priority. The women in the movement often postponed the rest of their objectives in deference to the single most urgent task—overthrowing Park Chung Hee's regime. But this concession on their part was taken advantage of by men, who refused to accept gender-specific grievances as a legitimate part of the changes to be made. Women would have to wait until the country's political problems were solved and the men were satisfied with the social progress.

As I identified with Kim Dae Jung's wife, it occurred to me that she wasn't the only political woman whose sacrifices went unnoticed by men. Male political prisoners were objects of open admiration among their supporters; their wives, struggling to hold their families together, remained in the virtuous background. The husbands languished in indefinite but glorious political martyrdom, while the wives ran back and forth between home and prison, providing their husbands with clean underwear and decent food and news about their children while their homes sank into poverty. It was the wives who kept the men informed of what was going on in the world outside the prison, cheered them with visions of their coming liberation, and reinforced their faith in themselves. Inspiring their children with tales of their fathers' dedication to justice, these wives kept their families, with mere nickels and dimes, in good health and clear judgment.

But anonymity was the reward for all the routine heroics these women performed. For women in my country and generation, I longed for something better. "What more do you want?" girls at my school would ask me. "If a man's gratitude isn't enough for you, you should live alone." Seduced by the meagre words of praise men threw at women like coins for charitites, these women seemed to have lost sight of what really mattered.

Father never thanked Mother in his children's presence. For all the years she spent in the shadows of his once-active political career, he felt deeply indebted to her, but I never saw anything but indifference and even harshness in his demeanor toward her. It wasn't until the last months of his life that he confessed to me how much he had loved her and how impressed he had always been by her strength to combat the hardships brought upon her by his past. "Be nice to your mother when I'm gone," he pleaded. "She's a grand spirit who will jump into a fire to do what she has to do. If you have half of her resilience and intelligence, there will be nothing you can't overcome. I wanted to tell you about her for a long time, but you know how old-fashioned I am. I was afraid I'd seem a weak man if I said thank you to my wife."

As one of these fire-jumping, sacrificing women who opted to embrace the big picture at the cost of the small, Kim Dae Jung's wife was fortunate enough to live to see the eventual outcome of her husband's lifetime of tribulations. In 1998, he was inaugurated as the president of South Korea, and in 2000, became the first Korean to win a Nobel Peace Prize, and was both a pioneer in bringing North and South Korea together to a table of peaceful negotiation and a backbone in the effort to improve Korea's relationship with the United States and the rest of the free world.

When I was much older, I finally realized that I had never loathed or lacked respect for women who played a secondary role for their husbands' advancements. What I had long warred against was the notion that a woman was to be automatically relegated to second place, regardless of her choice or talents.

Battle Fatigue

WHEN I WAS SIXTEEN, A CHAIN OF EVENTS TOOK PLACE IN MY house. The first was Grandmother's accident. She broke her arm and was bedridden for a month, and drove Mother to the brink of insanity. In addition to spoon-feeding the old woman three times a day, Mother had to change her clothes and bathe her. She had to pull her up to sit, and Grandmother was no light load. Because the old woman could never exercise or sit straight for longer than an hour, she lay in bed all day, turning all the food she ate into fat. Her groaning reminded me of a dying bear I had once seen at a zoo.

What exasperated Mother the most was *how* Grandmother had broken her arm. In an attempt to eavesdrop on her son's conversation with his wife, Grandmother had crawled to his bedroom. Our winter sliding doors had been taken out from their grooves for the summer to keep the air cooler, and were leaning against the wall of the living room. Over the course of her illicit trek, Grandmother managed to upset the doors, which crashed down on her, breaking her arm.

Although Mother was used to dealing with Grandmother's jealousy, she had reached the end of her patience. After moving her back to the house from the doctor's office, she finally confronted Grandmother: "Were you afraid your son and I were conspiring to hurt you? I am not putting poison in your food. I am not starving you. I am doing everything I can for you, serving you like a daugh-

*My grandmother, father, and oldest brother in our Seoul
house. The man on the right is a cousin.*

ter. What's wrong with you?" It was the first time Mother lost control in front of the old woman.

Mother's stress hardly ended with Grandmother. Soon after
Grandmother recovered, Father was nearly arrested again. This time,
an operative from the Chief Intelligence Office came to his school to
ask the principal about his "seditious thoughts." Father had made the
mistake of saying during one of his classes that Park Chung Hee and
his men were hardly different from a bunch of gangsters, something
he had probably gotten too comfortable saying to his own family, and
one of the students reported it to the Intelligence Office.

When the intelligence officer confronted him about Father, the
principal improvised. He told the inspector that Father was Park's
childhood friend, an "abuse buddy," as we say in Korean, that they
had grown up in the same village, gone to the same school, drunk
from the same well, and spoken the same dirty words. Father, the
principal said, had the privilege to say whatever he liked about his
old buddy Park. The principal went as far as to make up stories

about how Father used to drag Park to half a dozen different bars in one night and get him into all kinds of trouble. When the agent refused to believe him and threatened to barge into Father's class and drag him out in front of his students, the principal bluffed, "If you harass him, I will personally call your boss, President Park, and have you seriously reprimanded. You don't interrogate someone's childhood pal. It's an insult. You think your boss would like to be insulted?" Father was lucky to have such a clever, convincing boss. Had it not been for the principal's wits, he would have been taken to the basement of the Intelligence Office and beaten senseless—or worse.

Shaken as she was by Father's experience, Mother maintained her composure until Big Brother came home late one night from the Intelligence Office. He had been kidnapped from campus by an intelligence agent who wanted to find out the whereabouts of his friend, an undergraduate at Seoul National University who had organized a series of student protests. Big Brother refused to snitch on his friend, and the agent beat him on the buttocks until he couldn't scream any longer, warned him about the consequences of hanging out with dangerous young men, and put him in a taxi barely before the midnight curfew.

After helping Big Brother to his room, Father could hardly breathe, and Mother broke down completely. For days on end, she couldn't shake the paranoia that her oldest son's life would be ruined as her husband's had been. Big Brother knew there was only one thing that could help her to recover: he promised her that he would never again attend student protests.

There was no guarantee, of course, that staying away from other activists could protect anyone. Every day, we heard of examples of how one's good public standing could suddenly turn. Because interrogations and tortures were conducted in secret chambers, there were only rumors of what was done to citizens who dared to speak up. The cases reported in newspapers represented only a fraction of the false confessions and manufactured crimes; most were whispered about with no verifiable source of information.

After Big Brother was kidnapped, I heard Mother and Father talk in low voices about a history professor who was rumored to have been punished for saying something far less offensive than what Father had said in his class. According to what Father had heard, this history professor explained to his students that Koreans weren't 100 percent homogeneous racially, that the myth of our racial pureness was created and perpetuated by the fascist government to unite us under the slogan of "one pure race." Someone at the Intelligence Office found this seditious and took him to the basement of his office, where he beat the professor until he lost consciousness. He was over fifty, and it took him many months to recover.

We heard the most gruesome stories of torture, such as of one man who had poured boiling water on his own face in order to wake himself up from the paralyzing pain and avoid giving names to the intelligence agent. In another story, a man who was unable to endure the torture threw himself out of a fourteenth-floor window; his family never got to see his body. A third man, a law professor, was pushed over a cliff by a hired assassin, and his wife was falsely informed that he had taken a wrong step while climbing a mountain. Men as young as nineteen were administered electric shock torture until they didn't know what was true anymore, and scholars in their seventies lay on the cement floors of icy jail cells, too cold to fall asleep, watching the water in their cups freeze.

"Get out of this country," Father would murmur to me. I was gratified he wished me the same escape he wished his boys.

At seventeen, my war with him was focused on one consuming subject: my prospective major in college. The Three Men of the Family decided I should aim for admission into the Fine Arts Department at Seoul National University. The rationale: Fine Arts was the easiest department to be admitted to in terms of test scores, so this was a way for me to get into the nation's most prestigious university despite my mediocre test scores.

Fine arts, besides, was a genteel field with the least potential to threaten men, and most of its graduates turned out to be good wives with painting as an unobtrusive hobby. They weren't women of Picasso-style genius, doomed to ruin the peace of their families with their careers and drive their husbands and children into misery. An amateur female painter could work on her art during her spare time, after all the household chores were finished. With such a woman as a wife, a man could kill two birds with one stone: he'd have a wife who could both keep a well-run home and exhilarate him with the kind of creativity that wouldn't threaten his sense of superiority.

Plus, Big Brother was a talented painter; therefore I must be, too. With such resolution as they had, they of course saw no need to consult me.

"You don't know if I have any artistic talent," I said, hearing the shrill in my voice. "You just want me to go into art because you think my scores are too low for any other program at SNU."

"If you were smarter, we wouldn't have to tell you to choose fine arts," Less Big Brother said. "You would be able to enter any department at SNU."

"I want you to go to SNU for your own sake," Father said neutrally. "A diploma from a first-rate college means everything. For a woman, it's a shortcut to marrying well."

"You just want to have a daughter who goes to SNU," I insisted.

"Ha!" I could tell Father was stung, that I'd hit the nail on the head. It was for his own benefit that he wanted me to have a prestigious university name on my diploma, even at the expense of my happiness. Did he care about my hopes and dreams at all? I was euphoric at my discovery.

"If you admit that this is for you, I will work as hard as I can to try to enter the glorious SNU," I pressed him.

He suddenly took a step down into the yard, to grab a jump rope lying there. "You stupid, self-destructive bitch!" he spat, climbing back up into the living room. "I will show you what happens to an evil child so thankless to the man who sacrifices everything for her."

I knelt during the beating, hiding my face between my legs, afraid of the marks the rope might make on it. "You reduce my sacrifice to bubbles, you stupid bitch!" he bellowed as he whipped me with the jump rope again and again.

The rest of the family stood by watching, convinced Father was right to beat me. I could not give them the satisfaction of hearing me scream. "You sacrifice yourself only for the boys!" I fired back, lifting my face from my knees.

"If I am sacrificing myself for the boys, it's for a reason you cannot see with your thick brain." His voice was trembling, hoarse from anger. "Look at your big brother. He's working two jobs to help me support you, going to school during the day and tutoring high school students at night. He's the one paying your tuition. Without him, you wouldn't be going to a private high school." In this reminder of my debt to Big Brother was a second reminder of my failure: I had failed to enter my first-choice high school, which, like many of the very best high schools, was public. The physical pain from the jump rope was nothing compared to the memory of the humiliation. "Your big brother wouldn't be selecting your major if you had worked harder and done better. You want to go one more round about this?"

"No matter what, he has no right to choose my future." My head hurt from shouting into my knees. "I'd rather not go to school than have him boss me around."

Even as I said it, I knew I didn't stand a chance. Half of high school girls in Korea had their college majors chosen for them by the men in their families. Big Brother had twice as much right to select my field, and I had little reason to complain. I ought to have complied without reservation, thanking him for his good intentions and generosity. But I was afraid and angry at the idea of a future defined by work I didn't want to do.

"You don't have the choice not to go to a good college," Father said through clenched teeth. "You don't have the choice to embarrass your family."

"You're a hypocrite," I cried. "You said earlier that you wanted me to go to a good college for my own good, but now you're admitting the true reason."

He was at the end of his words, and so was I. As the rope came down again, I was pushed beyond resistance, my endurance worn out. I begged him to stop and said I was wrong. I was humiliated by the defeat. But it was Father's eyes—not the jump rope, not even his words—that frightened me. They were the eyes of the very dictators who had destroyed his life, full of the same cold disregard for humanity. His were the eyes of Park Chung Hee, of Syngman Rhee, and of Kim Il Sung emanating from the television, from the front pages of the newspapers, and from the dark corners of my imagination. In a polarized society, only fear thrived, and suppression and brutality spawned more suppression and brutality in both the victims and the victimizers. The more the oppressed fought to liberate themselves, the more they came to resemble those who oppressed them. Father had turned into a tyrant wielding personal terror against his underlings.

I can't explain how long it took me to replace in my mind the coldness in his eyes with the warmth I saw a decade later. To meet the man who Father truly was—a loving man who knew how to restrict his denouncement to the few responsible individuals, a compassionate man who never extended it to the common people who served the dictators out of the need to survive—I had to wait. To *know* him, I had to see more of him.

Against his more radical friends, Father would often defend a distant relative of his, who became a member of the secret service for Pak Chung Hee and developed a blind admiration for him. "Minsoo didn't seek power or money. He found himself in the Presidential House to feed himself," he would explain. "He grew up in a starving family with only grade school education, and had to leave home at the age of twelve to support himself. Living in an impoverished, violent neighborhood, he did everything he could, including waiting tables, cleaning toilets, construction work, and delivering food. But one day, a taekwondo master happened to pass by while he was fighting the local street thugs, and impressed by his bravery and skills, he offered to train him free of charge. Little did the master know that he would be scouted by an agent from the President's House within six years. But then, he wasn't surprised a bit because Minsoo was a natural athlete, easily overcoming larger, more extensively trained opponents. Four years of surviving the dark alleys had given him the hunger and five years under the master the skills to feed the hunger. Eagerly, he advised his disciple to go with the agent, sure that it would enable him to make a decent living."

Considering that South Korea then was a polarized place, where one became either a fighter against the dictator or a member of the majority terrorized into silent complicity, Father's endorsement of Minsoo was a sign of an astonishingly generous attitude. As one of the individuals who had risked their lives to bring democracy in their country, he had every right to disapprove of anyone who didn't actively oppose Pak. But his personal empathy remained intact.

His love, however, didn't cloud his judgment. Contrasting Minsoo with another distant relative, he would flare up, his eyes glittering with righteous contempt, "Hyunsuk is an entirely different case. He voluntarily chose to serve as one of the right hands for his second cousin, Chun Doo Hwan, the self-appointed successor to Pak." Like Minsoo, Hyunsuk had been a welcomed guest in our house, but knowing how Father felt about Chun, he stopped visiting. "He wasn't living from hand to mouth like Minsoo. With more money than he could spend for the rest of his life, he wanted a big break. So, he went to his second cousin, who got him involved in a business importing weapons from the US. He knew Chun was going to use them to arrest, torture, and kill those fighting for democracy, but he didn't care. Do you see the difference between these two men? They served the same tyrant, but one did it to survive and the other to fulfill his greed."

"One is *guilty* in the sense that everyone is guilty and the other is guilty *and responsible*," I returned. By this time, Father and I could sustain a conversation such as this one; I had gained the language that could give voice to the complexity of my thought.

"Minsoo came to admire Pak as a homeless person would adore a man who rescued him from the street," Father said. "Out of gratitude, he became one of his most devout followers. He believed that Pak should be the president until he died, and he hated anyone opposed to him. He said to me once, 'I wish I could capture all those impure elements standing in his way, put them in a giant fishnet and drop them into the Pacific.' I wouldn't be surprised if he had touched the chief guards in the Presidential House with his zealotry and got handsome gratuities from them every now and then." He chuckled.

"Didn't you give him money, too, sometimes?"

"I gave him a little bit here and there until he found work at the Presidential House. I was the only friend he had during those days, and we still visit."

Father loved people—even those who violated the very marrow of his beliefs. I would be a liar if I claim that the trauma of his beating is entirely gone. But I believe I would be honest if I suppose that the trauma found a tougher surface, a stronger layer of memory that keeps it from flowing over to the top.

For several months after Father's beating, I played the compliant, smiling, and faithful daughter and sister. I was a good student for my teachers, and a loyal friend to the girls in my school. I sat down and talked with the Three Men of the Family.

"The fine arts exams shouldn't give you trouble, since there are no math or science components. You'll just have to take some exams in literature and history, and we can avoid your weaknesses," Big Brother instructed.

"But I'm still worried," I murmured, my voice feeble. I didn't want to give them the impression I was still resisting their good will. With my mind made up, I was seeking advice and help. "If I were talented in painting, I would know by now. I've never received any more than a passing grade in fine arts. I don't know how to hold a brush."

"Why are you always so negative?" Big Brother didn't sound reproachful. "You haven't tried. How do you know?"

"Don't sabotage yourself," Less Big Brother chimed in.

"I don't want to disappoint you." I no longer had to fight myself to keep my voice down. I was broken in.

"If you set your mind to it, you can do it," Big Brother said warmly.

"It's nice of you to encourage her so." Father came in, glancing at me with affection. By now, he had forgotten the jump rope, even if I hadn't. "But I'm concerned about money. Art lessons can be quite expensive."

"I can pay," Big Brother said confidently. "Next year, I'll be working at a bank full-time while going to graduate school to get a master's degree. Besides, I already talked to an experienced painter I met through an artist friend of mine. He offered to accept only a fraction of the fees he charges most other parents."

Father was still concerned. "You won't be able to save any money. How are you going to get the money to go to America and get a PhD? You know I can't give you any."

"I'll manage somehow. If I don't get a fellowship from one of those American universities, I'll receive some other financial aid. Something will come along." Big Brother had planned with his usual cautious optimism.

As always, my envy and admiration of him rose like silent waves on a lake. That quiet confidence of his—that ascending spirit characteristic of a person who has never tasted failure in anything he has tried—was impressed upon me again, and I was seized with a yearning to foster the same self-composure.

Big Brother flourished in spite of his own suffering. Chronic headaches and diarrhea, which eluded medical diagnosis, as well as the possible return of his tuberculosis, kept him constantly on edge. Obviously, his unwellness was due to ongoing stress. Ever since he was born, he was told that Father was the roof of our house and that he was the supporting beam. Living under the weight of such high expectations and responsibilities and, most of all, the pressure to live the life denied to Father, his tiger's stomach was just as stifling as mine. When I was seventeen, he was only twenty-two, a stoic young man who couldn't explain what was going on in his heart to anyone.

"It'll be just like having two full-time jobs," Father warned, "earning money at dear cost. I appreciate you wanting to devote part of it to your sister's education. But can your body handle it?"

"If I don't pass the exams, you won't get a penny of it back. I'll be so ashamed." My voice was as low as a mosquito's hum.

"Don't worry about it." Less Big Brother pointed at Big Brother. "You resemble him so much a blind person would recognize you're his sibling. If he grew his hair long and braided it, your friends would mistake him for you. They'd be shocked you grew a foot taller overnight. If you have an ounce of his genes, you've got a painter in you."

My situation was entirely my fault; had it not been for my lack of excellence, my brothers wouldn't have had to worry about me. Neither good enough to escape their interference nor obedient enough to be happy with their command, I was in a demoralizing limbo. I was a paper dragon. I cried secretly, falling into familiar destructive moods.

I started going out into the streets of Seoul at night, watching the street thugs bleed from fistfights, the denizens of the red-light districts luring customers in, and the secret lovers clasping each other. I felt an awesome thrill. Observing the groups of young, innocent-looking men and women rushing about together on open dates, I was aroused by an odd mixture of envy and contempt.

The place that drew me most often was the giant fish market, where hundreds of little partitioned stores stood in several lines. At each, a man in an apron cleaned fish on a huge cutting board, nodding and shaking his head at customers' requests. The air rumbled with the clopping of knives, the low haggling of buyers and sellers, and the splashing of water over fish—the rhythm of killing and the melody of life made possible by killing. Mesmerized by the sight of severed fish heads, I strolled along the back alleys of the stores. Most people wanted the heads removed, and the cleaners gathered them in a bucket below the cutting table to sell at the end of the day to farmers with livestock or to make soup for themselves. I knew fish head soup could be quite tasty, having eaten it almost every other day as a little girl.

I scrutinized the scared, wide-open eyes of the dead fish—thousands of them in a bucket. That's life, I thought. Killing to eat. Fish eat other fish, and humans eat fish. We eat everything that has eaten everything else—cows, goats, chickens, pigs, and birds. We eat vegetables that have eaten the nutrients in the dirt. Humans are the cruelest of all life forms on earth.

I didn't know what to do to control my crushing sorrow. I could neither cry in the crowd nor cast a condemning finger at the butchers. Fish in fact was my favorite food; I had no right to blame the people who worked hard to provide it. So I laughed, loudly and hysterically. I laughed at the bizarre, vicious cycle of living and killing, and at the callous indifference of all living beings. Then, I got on a bus, sat in the back row, and rode until I lost sense of where I was. Getting lost in the city on a bus somehow gave me the illusion of vanishing from this world.

I was ready to fight, determined to be healthy and to work hard. By entering SNU, I realized, I could show how capable I was and have a chance at a future beyond the kitchen. I had one year left to prepare, and I was to spend it in a very small tiger's very small stomach.

"You won't have a life for one year," the teachers at my high school would drum into us. "Think of yourself as being dead for this year. It'll help you to do nothing but study." I studied in school, at home, and at the painting studio Big Brother found for me, a sixteen-hour-a-day work schedule. I didn't even have to push myself; I didn't have time.

To boost my endurance, I decided to forget—for the time being, at least—how absurd it was to require girls to have college education since one needed no more than simple arithmetic in order to be a good housewife. We were expected to work ourselves to a breaking point to go to college, and then, the moment we graduated, to marry and drop all intellectual pursuits to be faithful wives and mothers. For the women of my mother's generation, grade school was a sufficient qualification for "marrying well," but for my generation, a college education was required, thanks to the Korean zeal for education. But because the Confucian patriarchy lingered on, once we'd cinched our degrees, we women were to give up excellence and confine ourselves to the kitchen. We worked hard to acquire knowledge and then were forbidden to use it.

Women went to college purely for the purpose of marrying well, to find men with matching degrees. Women with a college diploma married men with a college diploma; women with only a high school education married men with only a high school education; women with degrees from prestigious universities married men with degrees from equally prestigious universities; and women with graduate degrees married men with graduate degrees. There were few exceptions.

I tried to be thankful as I memorized my lessons. How lucky I was to be born in modern Korea! During the Yi Dynasty, most women weren't even taught to read and write; there were a few wealthy, noble girls who were privately tutored to read the Confucian scripts, but most didn't even know what a book looked like. And how fortunate I was to be raised in a middle-class home! I was indebted to Mother, who scraped pennies together so I'd be able to attend college, something girls from lower-income neighborhoods couldn't dream of.

But I was bored. None of the subjects in school interested me because I was being forced to memorize. Although I very seldom slacked off, I was mentally absent from most of my classes. Keeping my eyes fixed on the teachers standing before the blackboard, my face straight and held high, I blocked the class out, dreaming instead of James Joyce's Dublin. From the dust jacket of the book on Less Big Brother's stack, I could tell Joyce had had a bad eye, and I came to the conclusion that he got it from too much reading and writing.

At the studio, where a foolish, quirky old goat of a man was the official instructor, I was bored, surrounded by graduate students in fine arts. The charcoal pencil didn't stick to my fingers, as if it knew I wasn't cut out for the job. But I went to the studio every evening after school, sometimes skipping dinner. With less than an hour between the last class in school and the lesson at the studio, I had to grab a quick sandwich at a fast food stand and wolf it down in transit. I barely finished before the national midnight curfew—which was strictly enforced—and was fortunate if I found a seat on the bus and could fall asleep until I arrived at the terminal, where I got off to walk the two blocks home. If there was one thing that year I was more grateful for than the lesson fees paid by Big Brother, it was this hour of sleep I got on the bus.

Whenever exhaustion tempted me to complain, I gave myself a familiar pep talk. Every twelfth grader in Korea had to keep up the same breathtakingly regimented routines. By making college the single most important factor in a person's life, my country turned its teenagers' golden age into a prison of test scores, fear of failure, and sixteen-hour-a-day study schedules with very little physical activity. Every seventeen-year-old in my country was a victim.

My painting problems, however, did not solve themselves, even with all my hard work. It was a dilemma. I was unable to tell my brothers about my lack of progress. I knew they would accuse me of not trying hard enough, of being a defeatist. To add to my anxiety, the head instructor at my studio never tried to inform my father and brothers of my stalemate. It occurred to me that he perhaps couldn't bring himself to violate the family's conviction that I would make a good painter. Apparently, Big Brother's opinion had a mysterious hold not only on his family and friends but also on strangers. Even my studio instructor had been persuaded to believe in my talent.

"Don't give up hope," he told me. "You'll make it."

In my despair and exhaustion, I sometimes found myself laughing maniacally, waving my fist to and fro. At times, I heard Mother's laugh in mine, a deep, sonorous, heartwarming sound that pealed across the living room at our home whenever Big Aunt came over for a visit. I felt my stress was somehow deeply connected with these women's lifelong tribulations.

Big Aunt was a widow who had raised three daughters by herself. Her husband had been slaughtered at the beginning of the Korean War, along with at least two hundred thousand other men and women, by Syngman Rhee. "He was taken one day by two police officers," Mother explained to me years later, "never to come back. Big Aunt couldn't even give him a proper burial because she couldn't find his body. It was probably thrown into a mass grave and burnt with a hundred other bodies."

In 1949, Syngman Rhee and his government had ordered an ad hoc program called "Report to Amnesty" in hopes of subduing the remnants of the left. They called in as many as 330,000 citizens, some of whom had no affiliation with the left and had been coerced into joining Report to Amnesty by recruiters eager to fill their quotas. Because there was an overwhelming number of socialists in South Korea and because the prisons were already crowded with "thought criminals," Rhee's regime established a policy to resolve what had become an unmanageable problem. They would convert members of the left into supporters of the Rhee government, and would supposedly "help" them assimilate into the right-wing mainstream. Report to Amnesty was a means of seducing leftists with the hope that the Rhee government wished them well.

But during June, July, and August of 1950, the first two months following the outbreak of the Korean War, Syngman Rhee and his men ordered a round-up of many South Korean civilians to whom they had previously offered official pardons. Rhee issued an order to have all of these "converts" killed at once, afraid that they would join forces with the North Korean army and turn on them. Over two hundred thousand civilians on the list were massacred in less than two months of time, leaving a trail of mass burial sites along the roads taken by the retreating South Korean army.

Since the DMZ was drawn in 1945, North Korea reputedly started to prepare for the war in an attempt to reunify the Korean Peninsula. Given the cold war in the Peninsula, Rhee and his men perhaps had known that a violent conflict between the North and South was inevitable, but what surprised them was the swift, high energy with which the North Korean army moved. They were frightened to see that when Seoul fell in the hands of the North Korean troops immediately after the invasion, a number of its residents remained in the city to welcome them and to volunteer to serve them. The CIA reported that when the North Korean troops captured Seoul in June 1950, half of the student population in the city actively aided them, many of them even enlisting with them. Because they had been studiously preparing for the war for years, North Korean soldiers were highly skilled and motivated, earning the hearts and minds of the civilians remaining in Seoul.

Syngman Rhee and his men were particularly afraid that the political prisoners they had incarcerated would give credence to the North Korean claim that they were provoked by the South Korean government to invade the South. Undoubtedly, North Korea invaded South Korea in June 1950, but according to North Korea, the South Korean government during the years and months prior to June 1950 deliberately attacked some places in North Korea. North Korea alleged that their attack on the South was a justifiable response and that the Korean War was a breakout caused by the South Korean regime. Nobody knows what truly transpired in those very tense years prior to June 1950, particularly during the months and weeks immediately before June 25. North Korea possibly made up the story of the attack by the South Korean government, or it is in part based on facts; South Korea perhaps exaggerated the one-sidedness of the North Korean invasion, or it is true partly or entirely. But one thing remains true. Syngman Rhee and his men killed massively without a trial.

People died like swarms of flies before, during, and after the War, and to have a murdered husband hardly made Big Aunt special. What made his death particularly absurd was that it occurred as a product of Rhee's paranoia, and nothing else. Big Aunt's husband, who had not even signed up for Report to Amnesty, was taken one day along with probably tens of thousands of others who were not officially registered on any list. He died at the age of twenty-nine, leaving behind a twenty-four-year-old wife and three pre-school daughters.

Together with Mother, Big Aunt created a laugh made by adversities—a contagious sound of two women united against the evils of dictatorship. They laughed in spite of everything they had faced, in spite of what had been done to their husbands and families. Big Aunt was unable to express her grief for her late husband who had been killed at the prime of his youth and Mother for her husband who was socially buried during the peak of his life. Even with a child's ears, I could feel that it was a melody they invented instead of words, a festive song soaring from the knots in their souls that couldn't be unraveled by anything.

I wasn't surprised to learn that my peers considered me a friendly freak with my manic studying, wild scowling, and raucous joke-telling. Since the last thing I wanted for myself was mediocrity, I was secretly proud. In my scowl, the girls saw a deep-feeling skeptic whose questions went unanswered, and in my ear-busting laugh, they heard a wild freethinker whose exuberance was being choked by conventions—just like them. Pinned down by pressure, hiding their equally crazed feelings, the girls saw themselves in me. They welcomed me into their company like a kind of sacred clown.

I often performed comic shows for my classmates, partly to lighten the mood, partly to release some of my own stress. One day, during the second half of the lunch hour, when there was no teacher in the classroom, I took out the faerie queen costume I'd been working on for weeks each Sunday, the one day I had off from school. I pulled the costume on and began to dance.

"Terrific!" the girls sang, clapping their hands. "Go on! Go on!" A few girls started to dance with me, turning round and round, making a slow circle. "Fly! Spread your wings!" The girls surrounded me.

Lost in their attention and the ecstasy of my fantasy, I swung my torso to and fro, knocking together and parting my legs like a pair of Venetian windows. I waved my arms in the air like a music conductor, while moving my hands and fingers up and down and side to side like a drunken piano player.

"I'm afraid you'll turn into a real faerie queen!" a girl shouted. "After you've gone to the moon, who's going to make us laugh?"

"We'll get you a woodcutter to make you come back to Earth," another said.

"You idiot!" a third girl hollered. "The woodcutter didn't make her come to Earth. Boredom on the moon did. He just stole her garments. Get the facts straight! Look!" She took a handkerchief out of her pocket, folded it, and tied it around her head, and then dashed toward me to snatch the jump rope from my shoulders. She was impersonating the woodcutter who stole the faerie queen's garments. I struggled, grabbing the handles of the jump rope with one hand to keep the rope from slipping away. I had painted it in nine different colors, feeling a keen sense of irony that Father had used this very rope to whip me just a few months before. I applied the paint alternately to produce a rainbow pattern. The rope was supposed to represent the wings the faerie queen wore.

For the garments, I'd rummaged through Mother's closet, digging out a long, white cotton slip that came down to my feet. It was what Mother wore under her traditional Korean costume. The slip wasn't exactly fit to be a faerie queen's outfit, which, according to pictures, was longer than a wedding gown, dragging on the floor, billowing from top to toe like tall clouds whipped by the wind. I would have preferred to buy a long flare skirt at a pricey clothing store in Seoul, but I had nothing but a few dimes and nickels and a couple of bus tickets. The only thing I could afford was a box of white tinsel, which I glued onto the yellow bandannas that I'd sewn into a twisted sash. I'd stitched the whole thing together with a great air of subterfuge on Sunday afternoons, hiding in my bedroom with the door to the outhouse open across from me. Few Korean parents knocked before entering their children's rooms; in case Mother came in to call me away to other chores, I had to be ready to dart into the outhouse with the needle and the thread.

With my costume pulled over my school summer uniform, I looked as bulky and amusing as a comic-book monster. My coke-bottle glasses, which gave me a pop-eyed appearance, clashed with the assorted flowers pinned into my braided hair. Nothing could have been further from a faerie queen. I was a grotesque geek. Had it not been for the flowers—the daisies, tulips, dahlias, and roses a girl picked from the garden in front of the classroom to pin into my hair—I would have looked like a birch tree dancing in a sack.

But my performance, which so delighted all the girls, suddenly came to an end upon the chemistry teacher's entrance to the classroom.

"What the hell is this?" the teacher thundered, hitting the board with a stick. His name was Mr. Choi, but he called himself Mark Twain, taking pride in his acerbic, undiscriminating tongue. We privately called him Twain the Rotten. The class hushed at once, and we all hustled back to our seats.

"It's been five minutes since the bell rang for class," he bellowed. "If you didn't hear it, the show must have been great." Pointing at me with his stick, he ordered, "Hey, you! Come out here!"

I walked to the front and stood before the board, my head bowed in fear of punishment. He yelled at the top of his voice, "For a twelfth grader facing college, every minute should be cherished! Didn't I say that a thousand times already?"

I confessed my "crimes" to him. Twain the Rotten listened, gave me a sharp scolding, and motioned me to follow him. In the hallway, he told me to go to the bathroom to take off the costume, and when I came back, he examined me from top to toe, pointing with his stick at the one piece of tinsel stuck to my black skirt. I flicked it off, and he told me to sit down.

Had I done as I was told, I would have saved myself some trouble, but of course I didn't. With exaggerated slowness, I straggled toward my seat, making a distorted caricature of his face, sticking my tongue out and pulling up the ends of my eyes to add comic monstrosity. The girls burst into laughter. Sensing I was defying him, he called me back to his desk to demand an explanation. I complied by demonstrating my face for him, and, hearing the girls laugh again, he ordered me out of the class one more time. For the rest of the hour, I found myself sitting alone at a desk in the hallway, writing an apology:

> Dear Mr. Mark Twain,
>
> I am very sorry that I have offended a teacher, whom I ought to respect with all my heart. Our parents raise us and our teachers create us; as I love my parents, I respect my teachers. I deeply regret my disrespectful behavior toward you and will take the utmost care to change my attitude. If you exercise your tolerance and generosity, of which you have more than plenty, I will be forever grateful. Thank you for considering my apology. I look forward to being forgiven by you and your most magnanimous heart.

I wrote another letter for my own gratification:

> Dear Twain the Rotten,
>
> I am extremely glad that I insulted your sensibilities today. You are the last person who deserves respect from your students. You ought to be eliminated from the educational system. You didn't punish me for my poor academic performance, but you degraded me for trying to bring fun and humor in school. To you, making an effort to breathe some life into our gulag-like class atmosphere is a treachery.

I congratulate myself for the apparently revolutionary behavior I exhibited today, and I promise myself never to lose this spontaneity I was born with. It's a gift and I am determined to use it to fulfill my destiny. Thank you for being so deeply offended by me. Your anger tells me what a powerful tool I have. I look forward to offending you and your likes forever.

When the chemistry class was over, I handed the first letter to him, bowing until my back was almost bent in two, and inserted the second one in between the pages of the English textbook in my bag. I was going to take it home and use it as a bookmark for my copy of *The Dubliners*.

The bad news arrived as a shock for everyone but myself: I had failed the entrance exam for SNU. My family was humiliated and depressed. They looked at me but were incapable of *seeing* me. To make it worse, Less Big Brother kept saying, "You should have let us know early on that you weren't talented in painting. If you had, we would have helped you to apply for a different major right away."

I fantasized about inflicting various long, slow, painful deaths on Less Big Brother. In my fantasies, right before he gave up the ghost, he used his last breath to admit it was *his* fault, not mine, that everything had gone so wrong. But such fantasies were of only limited use.

I took to imagining a teenage girl on a boat adrift on a stormy ocean. Enjoying herself on the wild waters, she shouted to the unkind gods, "Hey, you! Thank you for making my life so interesting!" On her journey, bucking the tide was an elating daily business. Without hardships, she would have been bored.

They Were Nice Fellows

ONCE AGAIN, I WANTED TO REALIZE HOW INSIGNIFICANT MY troubles were. I askd Mother to tell me the story of the hungry soldiers. The soldiers were among the many North Korean stragglers abandoned in the South after the army withdrew in the weeks just after the American intervention in 1950.

"Nobody could keep me from feeding those soldiers," Mother remembered with pride. "They were from North Korea, but they were *Koreans*. They were my people, and they were starving."

"But the American choppers could have killed you," I'd cry each time she told the story.

"They shot at me, thinking anyone who was moving was the enemy, and some of their bullets missed me by only a foot. But they didn't hit me." Her eyes hardened. "The Americans were scared of me, of my will power. They could have killed us all easily, just by hitting the house once. The whole house would have been vaporized in one shot, since it was just a grass roof. But they didn't dare burn the house down because they didn't want me to put a curse on them. So while I was cooking, they just kept shooting the ground outside the kitchen."

I knew Mother's version of events had nothing to do with what had actually happened. Obviously, the pilot had been too soft-hearted to gun down a young mother; or perhaps he was afraid to be court-martialed for killing a civilian. But in my heart, I adhered to her version, where the pilot feared *her*.

*My mother as a young woman, sewing in our house
when I was a small child.*

"It was in the country," she told me, "the house where your great-grandparents lived. Grandmother and I were taking refuge in it after the North Korean army took Seoul and everywhere north of Taegu. We stayed there until the North Korean army retreated."

The Northern soldiers who walked in on Mother and Grandmother were on their way back North, taking mountain roads and back alleys, starved and exhausted. Rumors of the Northern soldiers' cruelty abounded, but this pair behaved like little children obeying their teacher, and Mother didn't report on them to the authorities. She had a way of meeting strangers, of seeing into their hearts and carrying their innermost feelings in her hands. She wasn't afraid, not even of being reported herself. She was a strong-willed person even then, and the whole village knew if anyone betrayed her, they would be cursed.

"The soldiers weren't your enemy," I said.

"Oh, no! Lord, no!" she said vehemently. "You were taught in school to believe North Korea was and still is your mortal enemy, but the truth is much different, my dear." Clearing her throat, she explained, "Korea was divided into the North and South for political reasons. The people didn't want to be separated. We are one country, one people. We always have been. Our national feelings run far deeper than our ideological conflicts. We see each other as brothers and sisters."

"Why were we divided then?"

"You're too young to handle the full truth." She was still telling me this when I was seventeen.

"Why did North Korea invade the South, though? Can you tell me that much?"

"Your father would chide me if he knew I told you this." Her voice dropped. "The first independent government established in modern Korea was socialist, so North Koreans believed they were getting their country back." She silenced my forbidden questions with her eyes. "Knowing more than this will get you into trouble."

Switching back to her original topic, I said, "Tell me how Grandmother greeted the straggling soldiers."

"She gave them wet towels to wipe their faces with. She told them we were one people."

"She didn't try to chase them away?" I could picture her showing small acts of kindness to people in unfortunate circumstances, but it seemed utterly against her character to risk the safety of her grandchildren to feed stray soldiers from the enemy camp. "They could have harmed Big Sister and Big Brother." At the time, Big Sister would have been two years old, Big Brother only one month old. "She wasn't afraid for them?"

"She didn't have to be afraid. They weren't dangerous."

"They didn't threaten to kill Big Sister and Big Brother if you didn't feed them?"

"No!" Mother was suddenly defensive. "They wanted to hold the babies in their arms, but Grandmother wouldn't let them. She was afraid they were carrying germs."

"So, what did you cook for those North Korean soldiers?"

"All I had was some leftover barley and a few hot peppers soaked in bean sauce. The barley was half-raw because I had to steam it so fast, but each of them ate two huge bowls in a wink, with the peppers as the sauce. You can imagine how hungry they were."

"Grandmother didn't complain?"

"Not at all. She even apologized to them that we didn't have any rice. During the war, rice was as scarce as trees in a desert, but barley we could get a little bit of."

"Did they make it to North Korea?"

"I don't know. They were so exhausted and hungry."

The soldiers didn't leave right after they ate. They napped for several hours with their boots on, snoring like wild boars. When they woke up, it was almost dark and they had to hurry. They bid Mother farewell, and told her, in tears, "We're forever grateful to you, ma'am. You risked your life to save our lives. If we meet again, we'll recognize you in a crowd of a million compatriots. Your children will be blessed—when they join our children someday, they will see that we are one people in one nation." They looked at Big Sister and Big Brother and said good-bye to them, too.

Mother stopped, lost in the memory. "I'll tell you. They were nice fellows."

Although I loved hearing the story, it always made me feel guilty that I wasn't nearly as strong as Mother. She braved firearms to feed soldiers. How could I complain? Grandmother had described to me how Mother had given birth to Big Brother in the midst of the U.S. Air Force's bombing, with almost nothing to eat and drink: "Until the moment she went into actual labor and had to lie down, your Mother didn't stop running around, blanketing the doorsills to keep the American choppers from seeing our candlelight. She practically delivered the baby all by herself; I couldn't do a good job of caring for her because I couldn't stand straight with my spinal disc."

Remarkably, Big Brother was born on August 15, 1950, the anniversary of Korea's emancipation from Japan in 1945. Emancipation Day is a national holiday celebrated by Koreans to remember the long, hard fight to liberate their country from the Japanese. Mother and Grandmother were convinced Big Brother would be a fearless achiever, having arrived on that special day in the face of bombs and firearms. He would grow up to keep his country safe, to be one of the strongest, brightest men to protect Korea from the threats of the superpowers.

Even now, six decades later, I can imagine from Mother's description the details of the house where Big Brother was born. Its backyard is parted into a cowshed and a pigsty, and its front yard opens to rice and barley pads. To the left of the yard, there is a well from which Grandmother used to carry water, and on the far right, an outhouse where farming tools and pig feed are kept. Under the grass roof, there are tiny rooms with low ceilings, a primitive kitchen with a dirt floor and walls of wooden dish racks. Behind the house I see green fields, hills, and mountains, birches, pine trees, and weeping willows, the furrows of farmlands, and the narrow, unpaved alleys along which children bring back the cows and bulls from grazing. I see the strong earth that refused to surrender to the bloodshed during the war, the natural energy that could not be extinguished by the bombs.

Only the gods know for how many centuries the village has been there, how many wars it has survived, and how soon and often it came back to green life. Only the gods know how long my great-grandparents' house has been there, with its grass roof and low ceilings and dirt-floor kitchen. I see Big Brother as a baby breathing in this tenacious air, flailing on the cotton blanket, moving his hands to grab this resilient spirit. "Your big brother has a glow in his eyes," Grandmother would say to his little siblings. "It comes from the will power he mustered to come out into a world ringing with the deafening sound of bombs."

No Gun Ri

CHILDREN OF MY GENERATION IN SOUTH KOREA GREW UP WITH A system of mythologies about our own history. We were told that the North Korean soldiers who had invaded our sacred homeland were red-horned devils who killed children, raped women, and slaughtered the elderly. The South Korean and American soldiers, meanwhile, were angels and heroes trying to rescue their North Korean brethren from the iron grip of the heinous communist tyrant.

Even now, I can vividly recall the arcade games we played in grade school, in those early, desperate years after the Korean War. We would insert coins in a machine and miniature plastic figurines would pop up for us to hit with a club. One of the figurines was the head of the North Korean dictator, Kim Il Sung, a grotesque mask with an overdeveloped forehead and a squashed, red nose. Kim's head was placed right next to similarly grotesque figurines of Al Capone and Joseph Stalin, completing a turning circle of the faces of great villains in human history. We yelped with joy as we pounded the faces down and they shot back up. Whenever one of us succeeded in hammering Kim's head, we would yell in unison, "Kill the red devil!"

When I was older, Mother and I remembered these games. "In the South," she said, "at least we had the freedom to make a farce out of a tragedy. We were free to laugh at a serious business. In the North, I bet they weren't even allowed that."

A view of the Korean countryside, 1972.

North Korean children surely grew up with similar, if opposite, demonizing stories about South Korea and the war. I've heard numerous eyewitness accounts of acts of sexual violence committed by South Korean soldiers in the North, but, among the women I have spoken with, not a single eyewitness testimony of sexual violence by North Korean soldiers in the South. I am sure rapes occurred on both sides, but I am also convinced that South Korean soldiers were not the angels that we were taught they were.

These eyewitnesses also remembered how indiscriminately the U.S. Air Force bombed South Korea as well as North Korea, and killed more civilians in the South than the communist forces did. Bombing, they recalled, was the American troops' way of staying in control because they were afraid of any possible movement on the ground, even that of innocent villagers walking to get some water from a well.

Although the war had ended only two years before I was born, and its fallout had shaped or even created the entire world in which I was brought up, it was hard for me to believe some of the stories Mother told me. For those of us fortunate enough not to have had to live through the war, it is impossible even to imagine the kinds of brutality that happened every day.

"Mr. Hong—you know Mr. Hong," Mother told me. "The man who owns the bakery at Susong Market. Well, one day during the war, he was waiting for his wife to come back from her sister's house, and was left behind in Seoul from the citywide evacuation as the North Korean army stormed in. He told me and your father about what he saw." She stared at the wall as she told me, and I could tell she was picturing the scene.

The North Korean soldiers, who had descended on the city, called out people like Mr. Hong—those who had been left behind, and some others who remained in Seoul voluntarily to welcome the Northern soldiers—and gathered them at K Plaza. They were going to stage a mass execution of "enemies of the people." They shot some, and then dragged out a half-dead South Korean loyalist bound hand and foot, tortured beyond recognition, and laid him down on the stairs with his feet up. Two of their comrades placed a noose around his neck and dragged him down the stairs, spattering blood all over. His head hit at least a dozen steps. "But you know what?" Mother's voice was full of wonder. "When he was laid flat on the ground, he was still breathing."

January 4, 1951, is known as the January Fourth Retreat, when Mao's Chinese forces crossed the border to aid the North Korean army. Fleeing North Korean civilians brought with them tales of horror, of random acts of vandalism, arson, torture, rape, murder, and execution. In a furor of self-righteous vengeance, South Korea turned American machine guns on the fleeing civilians while the United States dropped bombs on Northern roofs. North Korea was bombed until, literally, the terrain was flat and nearly all traces of buildings had been obliterated. The North had no bombs to use on the South.

Although the story of the My Lai Massacre during the Vietnam War is now fairly widely known in the United States and around the world, the fact that there were similar massacres perpetrated by allied American forces during the Korean War is much less widely known. Well over ten thousand innocent men, women, and children in South Korea met their ends at the hands of American soldiers, their ostensible allies. In July 1950, an indiscriminate bombing by the U.S. Air Force killed 360 civilians in a town called Iksan; around the same time, a naval bombardment by the U.S. Army killed several hundred in a city called Pohang. In both large cities and small towns—such as Masan, Sachon, Yuirung, Kumi, Chilkok, and Danyang—a total of about ten thousand civilians were massacred by the U.S. Army. All of these should have been tried as war crimes in an international court, but these tragedies remained largely unknown until the story of a village called No Gun Ri emerged at the turn of the twenty-first century and started to expose other sites of carnage.

In 1951, Pablo Picasso painted *The Massacre in Korea*, which depicts helmeted soldiers shooting at children and pregnant women. Although I was familiar with the painting, seeing the mangled bodies of the No Gun Ri survivors for the first time in 2000, I found myself at a loss for words. One survivor, who had lost his nose, resembled the archetypal victim of leprosy, and I found his plight particularly haunting. Now that the story of No Gun Ri has become better known, this man has come forward with a plea for the youth of the world: "Please do everything to prevent a war." In war, it is not soldiers alone who are killed. Civilians, too, are killed by the anger, frustration, and racism fostered by war. What happened in No Gun Ri is in many ways similar to what happened in My Lai eighteen years later.

No Gun Ri was a typical Southern Korean village with a largely peasant population. There was probably one paved road for traffic, a few alleys and dirt paths, and houses with pigsties and cowsheds. Just like my great-grandparents' house, most had tiny rooms with paper doors and thin, long strips of wood to sit on in the front. They had grass or tin roofs and hand-built stone walls serving as fences. With a little over 120 houses and 500 people, the village was surrounded with hills and low mountains. In 1950, just before the massacre, there were an additional 200 people who had come south from Taejon to escape combat, making the total population of No Gun Ri about 700.

On July 25, 1950, a U.S. regiment was retreating South, having lost the city of Taejon to the North Korean army. The soldiers were paranoid because one of the defeats had been at the hands of a North Korean guerilla unit, who had disguised themselves as refugees. In a kind of undirected retaliation, the retreating U.S. soldiers lined up the villagers of No Gun Ri, telling them they were being moved to a shelter. The unsuspecting villagers followed the soldiers to a railroad, where the eight GIs disappeared to send a message on a wireless radio to a U.S. Air Force unit. Shortly after, a bomb fell on the villagers and killed about a hundred people in a bloodbath. One girl saw her own eye pop out and dangle in front of her nose; a man felt the head of a child fall from the sky and hit his neck; another man watched a woman who was nine months pregnant split in two.

When the bombing was over, the GIs came back to tell the surviving villagers that they were going to take them to a safer place. The refugees, now homeless and injured, had no choice but to follow them—at gunpoint. The GIs herded them to a tunnel under a bridge and kept them there for three days. Dying from hunger and thirst but not allowed to go out to get water and food, they licked blood from the dead bodies. Starving babies sucked blood instead of their dead mothers' milk. Some people attempted to escape, only to be machine-gunned. Over the course of three days, another 300 villagers died in the tunnel.

The survivors could not tell what happened. In the spirit of fear and suppression in which Koreans lived during and after the war, they knew they would be branded as reds and taken to jail if they came forward with complaints against South Korea's American saviors. Those who were still alive in 1999—after half a century—were finally able to come forward and tell their stories to receptive audiences. They at least had the opportunity to break the silence and describe the horror.

In 1989, after nearly three consecutive decades of right-wing military regimes, South Korea saw, for the first time, the birth of a supposedly civilian government. But the two "freely elected" administrations, which governed from 1989 through 1997, were still tainted by long-lasting residues of the military dictatorship. It was not until 1998, the year when Kim Dae Jung entered the Presidential House, that the crimes of the U.S. Army during the Korean War began to be exposed.

The massacre was suppressed by the U.S. government as well. Charles Hanley, the Associated Press journalist who spearheaded the team of investigators, testified at the Second International Conference on No Gun Ri that he was pressured by his own colleagues not to pursue the story. He said the editor in chief swore to him that it would never be published, and some in the press agreed. They were afraid such explosive news would bring damage to the AP. In the end, Hanley and his team won the battle, winning a Pulitzer Prize in 2000 for their investigative series, "The Bridge at No Gun Ri."

There are variations in the numbers of the victims. Some Americans, particularly the US Army, claim that there were fewer killed, while the Koreans and the AP allege that there were more. Since nobody can be totally accurate about the numbers unrecorded in official history, I do not entirely believe any of the numbers gathered thus far. But since 1999, more and more victims and their families have come forward to provide good reasons to suspect that there were at least 300 people killed.

Reparations have been the subject of controversy for several years now. In fact, in 2006 the United States offered the victims' families four million dollars. The families rejected the offer, finding the amount pathetically low, like charity for beggars. To the survivors, what matters is a sincere apology. They know that when Bill Clinton issued the half-hearted statement—"On behalf of the United States of America, I deeply regret that Korean civilians lost their lives at No Gun Ri in late July 1950"—it was no apology. They know that the Bush administration chose denial. It is a proven fact that the soldiers followed orders to kill civilians, but Bush's office kept bluffing as if the massacre had been merely an unavoidable accident caused by combat hysteria.

To this day, the Korean survivors are waiting for a clearly worded, transparent, and responsible statement: *We apologize for what the U.S. Army did to the Korean civilians in No Gun Li. We acknowledge that the mass killings were done on purpose. We committed a war crime.* They are not waiting for more money; they are waiting for sincerity.

Meanwhile, the survivors and the victims' families are committed to breaking the silence by talking to reporters and investigators, and to the members of the various committees organized on their behalf. Over the past decade or so since Kim Dae Jung came to power, fourteen committees have been organized to examine the affairs of the past, all of which treat No Gun Ri as one of the central issues to be resolved. Now, few people are afraid enough to hide it from history.

Because of Father's experience and Mother's quiet storytelling, I grew up angry at what the Americans had done to my peninsula. But I've wondered how my opinion would have been different if I had grown up in North Korea, where I wouldn't have had the freedom to dislike the Americans. I might have wished to be a South Korean, as much as South Korea had suffered.

In terms of intellectual suppression, South Korea was as bad as North Korea. Books by famous authors who voluntarily went to the North from the South were banned; we never learned anything of them. Nor were we ever told about painters, musicians, doctors, actors, singers, and dancers, who chose communism over the so-to-speak democracy. The South was no different from the North where all traces of social ideas discordant with communism were eliminated.

Compared, however, to the volume of bloodshed on the northern side of the DMZ, the amount on the southern side was relatively moderate. Had I lived in North Korea, I might not even have known about the discrepancy; there was so much disinformation that it made South Korea look open and plainspoken.

Conjure the Devil

A T ABOUT THE TIME I FAILED MY SNU ADMISSION EXAM, I TOOK UP
drinking. The cheap beer I snuck into the house helped me cry
and laugh, helped me forget that I was a "repeat," a university
entrance candidate who had failed the first time around and had to
take another year to try again.

What drinking helped me to forget the most, however, was that I
was becoming like all the women of my family, which was my worst
fear. I had their pounding headaches, sore stomachs, shortness of
breath, frequent colds and bronchitis, and the chronic fatigue and
drowsiness that made me want to fall asleep the moment I sat at a desk.
These were symptoms of the constant depression and anxiety from the
overwhelming schedules I had kept in vain as a twelfth grader. All the
work I had done—all in hopes of finding an alternative to the kind of
life that the women in my family had always led—ended up giving me
the same poor health and unhappiness I was so bent on avoiding.

I often skipped the "repeat" academy I was attending, and on the
days I didn't skip, I was late. The academies, which were designed
specially for first-round exam failures like me, weren't as tough with
their discipline as the high schools were. They couldn't afford to
punish anyone and take the risk of reducing the head count if students dropped out. They didn't care whether I came to class or not,
so I didn't have to go at all. The classes, besides, were exceedingly
boring. Since the academy's goal was to keep reminding us of the
same content we had learned the previous year, they taught exactly

Men push a cart through the busy streets of Seoul in 1966.

the same subjects with precisely the same methods we had slogged through in high school. Solving problems with formulae and memorizing dates and names had always made me weary, but going over the same process all over again made me want to die inside.

But I was unable to forsake my conscience entirely. Father was paying my fees, and they accounted for more than a small part of his hard-earned income. After teaching high school for twenty-five years, he had just landed a position at a junior college, but his salary had increased only slightly. Big Brother chipped in, but he was helping to pay for Less Big Brother's expensive private university.

Sitting in the back row in the class, I divided my time between reading English novels and looking at the board, pretending to listen. That I didn't understand most of the novels I read didn't matter. I was pleased that I could grasp some parts at least, mark certain paragraphs, and recite a few lines that struck me. It was enough. I could always replace the true meanings of the passages that escaped me with my own random interpretations. And although Less Big Brother was always condescending when I asked him for clarification, his explanations were succinct and piqued my hungry mind.

What a mistake the Three Men of the Family had made by introducing these Western writers to me! They had ushered me into a world of knowledge that was the legacy of the West's freethinkers and rebellious minds. In fact, John Stuart Mill, the British philosopher and the author of *On Liberty*, was one of their all-time favorites. After reading the famous classic in English, Father suggested the boys read it, and the boys immediately picked up a Korean translation. I, of course, was burning with longing to join the Three Men of the Family in inspiring conversation.

I seized whichever books were available to an eighteen-year-old with a few coins jingling in her pocket. I went to public libraries to get hold of Hemingway and Faulkner; I sneaked into college bookstores in Seoul to pick up the brand new copies of the most recently edited versions of Henry James and Edith Wharton. I even borrowed an ID card from a friend of mine who was attending a prestigious college so I could make use of its extraordinary library. With only a few hours between the end of the day at the academy and the nationally enforced midnight curfew, I had to hurry. I was tempted to steal some of the books that I coveted, to cave in to the voice—ridiculous as it was—that whispered to me, *Nobody else could use these books as well as you could*. But I stopped myself, fearful of what the Three Men of the Family would do to me if I got caught. So I walked to the secondhand bookstores near the academy, where I could purchase a few of the cheapest pirated editions.

Poor and desperate to learn English, Koreans in 1973 cranked out massive numbers of uncopyrighted prints, using them in private and public as tools for improving reading skills. Some of them were even officially adopted as textbooks at a number of colleges, by many of those professors who saw English education as a shortcut to the nation's industrialization. Less than two decades after the Korean War, which ended in 1953, those English-speaking authors whom I was so passionate about were household names in Korea. They were topics of discussion among young adults who were trained to harbor a level of curiosity, however high or low, about the Western hemisphere. Although not everyone in Korea was as deeply consumed as I was, learning English was rising to be a number one priority in the nation, a collective obsession. In high school, students were taught to read selections from Eugene O'Neill and Tennessee Williams, to translate F. Scott Fitzgerald's *The Great Gatsby* and Willa Cather's *My Antonia* line by line, and to interpret T. S. Eliot and Marianne Moore. Although few of my peers went so far as to spend every dollar in their possession on discounted pirated editions, I was in essence no better or worse than anyone.

Father took a fiendish delight in reinforcing this obsession of mine. One day, having just walked in on me as I was sneaking out one of his cherished books, he smiled, asking, "Are you going to read it?" I replied in a loud, fearful voice, "Yes, I am, every line of it." As a repeat, I was expected to devote every ounce of my attention to exams for college. I was prepared to receive a sharp lecture regarding my foolishness.

Instead, Father said warmly, "It's a good book. If you can read it someday without a dictionary, that would be a sign that you have mastered the English language, the reading part of it at least." He then took the trouble of explaining to me the movie version of the book, the ways in which the integrity of the book had been compromised by Hollywood. "Unfortunately, Gregory Peck and Ava Gardner fail to bring the characters in the book to the screen," he said with disappointment. "In the book, they're much more complex than they are in the film. Perhaps it was because the movie was made too quickly after the book was published. As you can tell," he said, pointing at the copyright page, "the book was published in 1957 and the movie was released in 1959. I wouldn't be surprised if Hollywood started to crank something out on the very day the book was published. They wanted to cash in on it."

We were discussing Nevil Shute's *On the Beach*, a novel that was far from popular among Korean readers in 1974. Father was a fan of the author because he admired Shute's unhesitating criticism of the civilization into which he was born. "Nevil Shute," Father explained to me, "was a product of the most advanced elements of Western liberalism. The novel, as you'll be able to tell, is about a nuclear war, which always seems to be impending. You'll be able to understand why I admire his satire of the West, and why I think the West is lucky to have a mind so ready to attack its own parents. An advanced civilization thrives on condemnation by its own children, whereas a backward civilization perishes by it."

After a professor of his at Peabody College introduced him to the book, Father bought a copy of *On the Beach* at a bookstore in downtown Nashville. He shipped it, along with all the other books that he had purchased in America, to his Korean address, to read at night after teaching all day. "I didn't have the skills to use an English-English dictionary," he confessed to me. "I had to resort to an English-Korean dictionary, and it didn't do the job of teaching me the nuance of the vocabulary in the book. I hope you'll learn to use the English-English dictionary, the Webster that's sitting over there." He pointed at his stack, his eyes glowing.

I was struck by the many ironies of our conversation. He wanted me to read for pleasure in English, yet he was the one forcing me to memorize for university exams. How absurd it was that he had so many stacks of expensive books and yet couldn't bring home enough money to buy our winter clothes! His books, a small library occupying two entire walls in his bedroom, were worth several paychecks, but his house was small and shabby with no indoor plumbing. Moreover, all of these books were in English, in the language that had produced the Western liberalism that he so wished to adopt, yet he stubbornly remained a devout Confucian, an old-fashioned, patriarchal despot. Like most learned men of his time, Father was being pulled in opposite directions, trying hard to join the ranks of Western liberals and yet remaining exactly who he was supposed to be in his own culture. And unlike most daughters, I bothered to raise questions about this contradiction, to fight to erase it from my life.

In my late teens, I was mired in a kind of vulgarity of violent emotions and cheap beer. My family's poverty forced me to wear the same ill-fitting clothes every day, and nobody gave me any advice on how to mitigate the mark of cheapness I carried. Mother, who might have offered words of wisdom, was too overworked to pay attention. I was not a pleasant sight. To forget my lack of beauty and grace, I spent my time alone. On weekends, I went to the graveyards on the outskirts of Seoul, reading Yeats, Joyce, and Nabokov. In a place where nobody, not even my own family, could see me and my poor clothes, I could revel in my favorite hobby. I could envision for myself the life of the expatriates I read about in their books. How cool it would be to pack everything in my possession in one suitcase and float from one town to another as Nabokov did! How emancipating to leave Korea for America as Joyce left Ireland for Paris! How liberating to deliver myself from the medieval Confucian norms as Yeats did from the oppressive Irish Catholicism! The thought thrilled me so much that I was even able to forgive and appreciate my brothers for having introduced me to my favorite authors.

Thanks to Big Brother, I was far more advanced in English than any of my peers. Although my speaking, writing, and listening skills were weak, I could read just about anything, and English literature became the dot of sunlight in the dark sky. Big Brother didn't yet know of my hope to go to America as a graduate student, but he seemed to agree with me that mastery of the English language was bound to make me valuable.

So I studied English. I went to bars, at the end of the day and sometimes at noon, to drink and scribble English vocabulary from my new pirated books. Bars for poor young men and women, where one could sit for hours after drinking only a couple of beers, were the only places I could afford to visit. Holding an English edition in one hand and a Korean translation in the other, I checked my own translation sentence by sentence against the printed one, euphoric at my successes and frowning with concentration at my failures.

I wasn't surprised at all when I failed again after my repeat year. I seldom worked at any of the required subjects except English, and even in English, I was weak at the grammar questions that made up a large portion of the exam. Since all college entrance exams were designed to test one's ability to memorize, I was at a critical disadvantage. Despite my reading competence, I ended up with no more than slightly above-average scores in English. My dot of sunlight in the dark sky was gone.

I had only one option: to apply to a second-rate college. The family consensus was that I couldn't wait for another year as a second-time repeat. It would bring the family not only financial strain but also another chance to lose face. If a stranger asked about me, my family would have to say that I was going to an academy as a second-time repeat; the Lee family was a first-rate university family, and had never imagined having to endure that kind of shame. My brothers agreed I would turn in my application for the English Department at H University, a second-rate college they had been considering for me. If I tried for a higher-level school and failed again, it would be an irreversible disaster.

As they expected, I applied to H University and passed the exam. My freshman year in 1975 was a continuation of the repeat year except for one critical difference: I was no longer bored in classes, as I was now being asked to read texts to understand characters and plots rather than to regurgitate names, dates, and grammatical rules. I was free to choose my own schedule. On weekends, I still went to graveyards on the outskirts of Seoul for the quiet solitude, but during the week, I didn't have to go to cheap bars to compare English texts with Korean translations. Professors taught the works of American and British authors in both English and Korean. Going to classes excited me, and I did well in school for the first time in my life.

But before I had a moment to let out a sigh of relief, the Three Men started to put pressure on me to transfer to a better college. "None of the students at your school have the face of success. They all look like losers," Less Big Brother warned. "If you stay there for longer than a year, you'll develop that washed-up look, too."

"I'd rather have you abstain from dating before you get married, but if you must, date an SNU graduate, not a fellow at H University," Father advised.

"If you transfer to another college, you will increase your chances of marrying an SNU graduate," Big Brother reminded me for the thousandth time. "If you end up with an elite SNU graduate with a prestigious job and influential friends, you'll have a good, stable, upper-middle-class life guaranteed for you."

The girls around me at college were shallow. Their interests were happily confined to pretty clothes, provocative cosmetics, nice dates, and fashionable hairstyles. Undeniably, my disregard for my own appearance was, to a certain extent, a defense mechanism. I based a good part of my lifestyle on pretending that my family had enough money. How else could a blossoming young girl, who was always surrounded by temptation for luxuries, go to school in the same faded jeans and the same red shirt? My contempt for the other girls was nearly a product of false arrogance.

Watching them, I realized how much I owed my father and brothers, how much more I had over the countless girls my age who were incapable of perceiving, let alone criticizing, the sexism of their own fathers and brothers. They were left untouched by the eye-opening ambivalence I harbored. The Three Men of the Family were worthy, and I decided to follow their advice, to try to transfer to a better college. Although "marrying well" wasn't on my mind, obtaining superior credentials was. In order to go to a graduate school in America and get a PhD, I would need to attend a first-rate school with more competent professors and a stimulating intellectual environment.

Higher education was one of the few fields where women were treated equally to men. Law and medicine were the other two that allowed women to rise to the top, but neither of these suited me. The minority of female lawyers had to spend much of their time combating reluctant acceptance and half-mocking attitudes from their male counterparts, and medicine was impossible for me since I was no good in sciences. Process of elimination left me with only the option of obtaining a PhD and becoming a college professor. There was a matter of personal pride as well. Until I went to a better college, I knew I couldn't earn Father's approval. He took every opportunity to remind me of the shame I was causing the family.

I was fairly certain I could do it. Because the exams for transfers didn't include math and sciences, I had a better chance of scoring high and surpassing stiff competition. Transfer exams tested the ability to think rather than to memorize.

The more interested I became in my field, the more resolved I became to transfer to another college. English seemed to be the major created just for me, and I worked like a maniac. I would read thirteen hours a day until I couldn't keep my eyes open. Then, to work off the tension, I would take off a day or so for the sole purpose of losing my mind, drinking until I couldn't stand straight.

Sometimes, I dragged male classmates to the old bars around campus. They were good drinking companions, unlike the girls who took forever to get over their inhibitions and loosen up. Free from the pressure to be well-behaved and elegant, they were more easygoing. I knew my male companions talked behind my back, but their talk wasn't backstabbing in the way that talk among some of the girls in the department was. According to them, I was debasing myself by drinking so much with the men.

But I didn't pay attention. I binge-drank as a man might. It was an easy, inexpensive way of disarming myself from the routine. I needed to be boisterous, and I needed company to be boisterous. Being with men kept me physically safe as well, since a woman alone at a bar exposed herself to grave danger; she was seen as a reckless creature inviting a pickup or possible sexual assault.

Because I read at a graveyard during the day and studied at a small public library near the campus at night, few people saw me except when I was in class or in a bar. I was deliberately hiding my true self. Planning to surprise everyone by transferring to a first-rate college, I kept my thirteen-hour-a-day work schedule a secret. Everyone—even my own family, friends, and classmates—was going to be stunned. They would say, "That girl with the bottle! When did she study? Where did she hide such a brain?"

I passed three different exams for three different top-notch colleges within a month. This drew me one step closer to my goals, reducing the distance I had to travel to reach excellence. At nineteen,

I felt I was equal to my dreams for the first time since I was twelve, when I had entered the best junior high for girls in Taegu.

"Permission to transfer to any of three good colleges!" Father marveled. Overnight, his attitude toward me had changed. He now treated me like a precious child. Now that I had qualified for a school meeting their approval, the Three Men of the Family were ready to guide me toward further achievements.

"Now you just need to read *Moby-Dick* to be a master of English," Big Brother told me.

"What he means," Less Big Brother clarified, "is as long as you don't make the mistake of thinking Ahab is a hero, you'll make it."

"Good thing you told her," Big Brother whispered to Less Big Brother. "If you don't tell her to read a book forward, she'll try to read it backwards." They laughed, but their humor was warm.

I will read it backwards, I thought to myself. *It's my way.*

The day after I chose K University, the best among the three, I picked up *Moby-Dick* from Less Big Brother's bookshelf. All day I struggled with it, devouring it with my desire and vanity. I wanted to dig into the famous classic and grasp its mysterious, profound meanings, but I also wanted to brag. Picturing Ahab thumping on the deck with his one leg, I identified with him instantly. He was kicking in a tiger's stomach.

Engrossed, I forgot the temperature in my room was fifty-five degrees in freezing February. In a traditional Korean house, only the floor could be heated by coal briquette, so the inside air was hardly warmer than the windy outdoors. But I was sweating, laboring to figure out the inscrutable Biblical names and implications, staring at the printed letters until I lost focus. So slow indeed was my reading that a page and a half per hour was a job well done. I refused to recognize that the book was simply beyond my grasp at that time. None of my peers dared to pick up the formidable classic. It didn't occur to me that my brothers held themselves to abnormal standards. When I dropped the book, however, I knew that I would pick it back up someday.

My three years at K University were going to be devoted to rules. To acquire the skills to break them, I had to learn them by heart. I had to understand all the subtle nuances of words with the same dictionary definition. Although the workings of a language seemed as arbitrary as a child's doodle, they had to be followed to a tee. Each day, I studied for six hours at home after eight hours on campus. I wished there were more than twenty-four hours in a day so that I could move the gods with more sacrifice. My brothers, amazed at my diligence, called me Faithful One.

Lucid Dreaming

ONE NIGHT, LESS BIG BROTHER OVERHEARD ME FINISHING A PHONE conversation with a male friend.

"Who was it?" Less Big Brother wanted to know.

"It was a guy I met through a classmate of mine." Like a child caught with a hand in the cookie jar, I spilled out everything in one breath. "He wants to get together with me next Saturday over some English questions he's got. He has an essay and wants me to translate some sentences he can't understand."

He eyed me. "It may not be a good idea to see him alone. You'd better see him in a group setting." Any contact I made with a member of the opposite sex, whether it was for a potentially romantic relationship or just conversation, had to be reported in full detail to Less Big Brother. I was his little sister; my sexual integrity was his business.

"Unfortunately, I'm not attractive enough to warrant more than academic curiosity."

"It doesn't matter whether you're attractive or not. A man is a man. He's got to want something else from a girl."

"Like what?" I wanted to gall him. I was disgusted because I knew all about the innumerable phone calls he received from girls. He had a dozen girlfriends, and yet he believed it was his duty to impose a chaste life upon me.

"Is this a high school biology lesson?"

"I don't know anything," I fired back. "Why don't you teach me?"

"You are a prime target for a fellow to use and dump. For a

The Three Men of the Family with Mother.

homely, unintelligent girl like you, chastity is the only asset. I would be surprised if this friend of yours doesn't have secret designs."

"Why don't you ask him?" I suggested with a falsetto laugh. "You can demand that he sign a contract promising not to use me. Man to man, you can give your word to each other. Here!" I picked up the phone, dialed the number, and as Less Big Brother stood in the room, staring at me, his mouth twitching slightly from shock, I spoke to my friend on the phone. "Sorry to call you again, but there's someone dying to talk to you."

Before I had the time to hand over the phone, however, Less Big Brother stormed out of the room. When he reappeared, it was with a porcelain rice bowl, which he threw at me with all his force. He aimed for my face but hit the hand that was holding the phone.

I picked the porcelain pieces out of my fingers one by one, carefully pouring hydrogen peroxide and Mercurochrome on the wounds. Looking at myself in the bathroom mirror, I felt relieved that it wasn't my face that was scarred.

I started to pack a suitcase. I gathered a toothbrush, a tube of toothpaste, some underwear, and books to read while on the run from my family. I'd packed Simone de Beauvoir's *The Second Sex*, which, in my mind, was a summation of all the theories developed in the other books that I put in my suitcase. Each one—Thomas More's *Utopia*, George Eliot's *The Mill on the Floss*, Harriet Beecher Stowe's *Uncle Tom's Cabin*, Ralph Ellison's *Invisible Man*, and Walt Whitman's *Leaves of Grass*—seemed to have been born to find their culmination in her well-documented research. I carried these books because I was driven to use the knowledge they gave me for the good of women. The weapons with which the men in my family had armed me—the very words of the people who had fought for democracy—were to be turned against them.

That day, the day Less Big Brother scarred me with the broken rice bowl and the day I left my family, I decided on my life's work. I was going to reeducate all the brothers in my country, all the men who believed in their authority to supervise and own the sexual lives of their sisters. A typical man of his generation, Less Big Brother believed he was exercising a brother's love by conducting a moral surveillance over his little sister. Women, I believed, also had to be reeducated. Their thinking was so conditioned that they would be disappointed and distrustful when the men in their families didn't impose sexual double standards on them. They would say, "My brother doesn't care who I hang around with. Is he concerned about me at all?"

Fortunately, I wasn't entirely without help. Little Sister snuck necessities to me the entire time I was gone. As an eleventh grader facing college entrance exams, she herself was under horrendous pressure, but sacrificing her precious break during the lunch hour, she met me every other day at a coffeehouse near her school, where she could hand me some small bills and dishes of leftovers neatly packed in plastic containers. She never once failed me.

I squatted in an empty house without heat or running water. It was owned by a friend's parents and waiting to be remodeled. To keep the room warm, I had to add new lumps of coal briquette to the burnt ones every few hours. The house was old and large and looked haunted in winter, standing starkly alone on a secluded lot at the edge of northern Seoul. It attracted few people's attention even in summer. Occasionally, I would strain my ears to hear the footsteps of the rare passerby. Nights were particularly difficult, when the February wind would howl across the wide, barren front yard and the worn roof. As the skeletons of trees swished over the eaves, I would cover my face with a book, chanting aloud the same sentences over and over again, recalling what a peasant woman in Mother's native village had once told me.

"When I was a little girl," the woman had said, "evil ghosts roamed the streets, trying to talk living people into going with them. They would open gates, sneak into people's houses, and whisper to them. One night, one of these ghosts came before my family, separated from us only by the thin paper doors of our bedrooms. But you know what people say, 'You can get out of a tiger's cave in one piece if you don't lose your mind.' My mother knew how to stay alert. She yelled at the ghost from her room, 'You evil spirit! Get out of here or I will burn you alive!' After loudly singing a song her mother had taught her when she was little, she pushed the door wide open, inviting the wicked spirit to face-to-face combat. But it was long gone. You see the lesson in this story, don't you? Whenever you're afraid, sing, as loudly as you can, a song your mother taught you as a child."

So on the nights when the noises were too much for me, I would sing myself a ballad called "A Mother Conch and Her Children," which Mother used to sing for me. It went:

> Our mother, a beautiful conch,
> fed us all her flesh and now she has no more left.
> She is floating away on the water as an empty shell.
> Empty shell, empty shell, she is our mother.

I read all day long with no break, and stayed up thinking all night, consumed by the desire to learn about the world that created the Three Men of the Family. I worried I would go blind from all the reading. Father had told me, "Your name means Peace and Tranquility. It is the name of a Buddhist painter who lived in a tribal kingdom in Korea that thrived two thousand years ago. To achieve his visions of a utopia, he worked so hard that he went blind at the end of his short, productive life."

I dreamed of the painter one night. Quietly, he sat on the floor, facing my desk, his papers spread around him. Without a noise, he rubbed his ink slab on the stone. As he gazed at me, I could see his twinkling, blind irises, luminous with cleansing spiritual power. They seemed sad and happy at once because, I thought, the complete realization of genius never came without sorrow. He began to paint. The painting, which I recalled with haunting clarity, was about the making of a Buddha. Sitting on the lotus flowers on top of a muddy pond, He was looking down at the monsters in the water with love and compassion, while the monsters were wriggling and flailing with the wish to rise to the air and become parts of the lotus. They were ugly and soulless, with half-human and half-animal bodies, with rats' faces, wolves' torsos, or fish's tails. The Great Master, whose way of living encompassed not only every human but also every beast, was in the beauty that lived inside the ugliness of these monsters. He and they were kindred souls divided and joined by the darkness in the water and the light in the air.

In the cold, empty house, I called out to Peace and Tranquility, asking him to respond to my lucid dream. My voice echoed in the front yard. Silently, the painter took my hand and led me to the kitchen where my family was eating. He slid the door open and gestured to the empty rice bowl on the table—the one empty bowl placed among six full ones. With his chin, he pointed at Mother, who stood up to carry the empty bowl to the rice cooker on the sink and fill it with hot steamed rice. As she returned to the table to place it next to the sixth one, he looked at me and nodded. I said, "Mother has been serving dinner for all of us as if I were there. She's expecting me any time." Peace and Tranquility was telling me to go home. So I went back home to be welcomed back. In silence, my family greeted me.

Homeward Bound

WHEN I BECAME A JUNIOR IN COLLEGE, I BEGAN TO DREAM about a creative marriage free of the pre-established gender roles, reversing my childhood decision to never marry. It was a conventional marriage, after all, that I was dead set against.

According to most of my peers, I was being greedy, setting myself up for frustration. A man, they said, should pursue a family and a career, but a woman planning to have both was doomed to fail. Few men would want her, and even if she were lucky enough to meet a man willing to select her over the multitude of submissive, traditional women, the probability of her succeeding in either role—mother or worker—was extremely low. What was a simple, realistic plan for a man was a complicated and almost insurmountable challenge for a woman. A wise woman would not drag a man down in such a futile effort.

"It'll be just as difficult as it is for a rich man to go to heaven," Father warned.

"How do you know that? I haven't tried yet."

"It's obvious," he said, his brows arching sharply. "If you fail to achieve what you want, I'll be stuck with the responsibilities of taking care of you."

"You won't be. I'll be in America!" I announced.

It was the first time I openly declared my decision to leave the country, and Father was shocked. Familiar with all the prejudices and handicaps facing young, single women who had been to America for several years, he found himself at a loss for words. The women who "drank the American water" were looked upon with suspicion, branded indecent or whorish because of the loose sexual conduct and open, unregulated lifestyle believed to be rampant in America. To make it worse, most of these women were pitied, since they were past the marriageable age and were often unable to obtain husbands.

I could see the flicker of fear in Father's eyes. "If you don't make it in America, who is going to provide for you? And how are you going to find the money? Universities in America aren't free, as you know."

I had thought this through. "All I ask from you is the money you planned to spend to get me married. Once I finish a master's degree with it, I might be able to get some financial support from a school for my PhD work."

"So, you think you're PhD material?" He burst out laughing, the furrow between his brows deepening. "If you don't have any real talent, you'd better have overly exaggerated self-confidence, I understand!" Despite his words, I thought I detected a faint twinkle of delight in his eyes. It looked almost as if he were trying to bury his pride under the hard paternal mask.

"We'll have to find out, won't we?"

"If you think a husband and children aren't good enough to sacrifice a career for, you're grossly mistaken. Teaching your children well is worth a hundred PhDs. You contribute to shaping the future of your country and the world."

I was choking, but I knew it would be of no use to disagree with his cliché. I would have to challenge everyone I knew if I stayed true to my goal. So I refrained from telling Father about the two young men I had been dating, who pledged full support for my dream of realizing my potential in both love and work.

Alone, I compared the two men in terms of their abilities to help me to achieve my "greedy" dream. One of them, named

*My mother and father observe Less Big Brother's
marriage ceremony.*

Yongman, was a twenty-five-year-old college graduate from a middle-class family who was rapidly rising at a large company. The other, Dongwoo, was at twenty-four a partner at a small but stable firm. They were equals in educational qualifications and social class. Dongwoo had a dry, subtle sense of humor while Yongman made boisterous jokes. Both seemed cheerful and optimistic, envisioning for themselves and their future spouses new paths unhampered by tradition.

Yongman and Dongwoo, who knew nothing of each other because I went out with them alternately, liked me very much, and I cared for them as well. But in both cases we'd met through a matchmaker, a mutual friend, and we knew very little about each other except what appeared on the surface. When a matchmaker paired two people, it wasn't the inner person that mattered; it was the outer conditions that determined the possibility. The man was expected to be competent, to demonstrate the ability to provide a

stable income and desired social status, while the woman was evaluated for her potential capacity to devote herself to her husband
and his family. Chemistry wasn't entirely ignored since everyone
conceded that a man and a woman must be attracted to each other
to some degree in order to live together for the rest of their lives.
As long as the pair didn't find each other repulsive, they were
encouraged to consider the match. It was believed that once a man
and a woman shared the same bed together long enough, the natural law of attachment would eventually take over and bring them
closer physically.

Impressed by my background and education, the two men were
eager, professing they had no objection to my hope of mixing a
career and a marriage, and declaring their willingness to support me
in my choice to continue on to graduate school. Finding me beautiful, intelligent, independent, and, most of all, compellingly different
from any of the women they had ever met, they volunteered to make
exceptions for me. I was, they each told me, worth sacrificing the
convenience of having a warm dinner ready every evening. "You
don't have to go all the way to America. You can get what you want
here," they tried to persuade me. Somehow, they saw the faerie
queen hidden in my cheap, uncomely clothes.

As our dates progressed, we entered a stage where parents would
want to be introduced. In Korea, where the family mattered as much
as the individual, a married woman's well-being was largely dependent upon her in-laws' opinions of her, and by marrying a man a
woman also married his family. Yongman and Dongwoo each
assured me that my future in-laws were in touch with the trends
among the younger generations. Their siblings were enlightened
enough to embrace the idea of having a female in-law working outside the home. They believed a career woman would be an asset for
the family. If, in the worst possible case, they couldn't help me, the
young men promised that they would leave me alone.

But as convincing as they sounded, I had doubts deep down. I
knew they were talking about their dreams, not their plans. To ful-

fill their immediate objective, which was winning my hand, they were pushing all the potential problems aside to be taken care of in the future. They weren't lying; they were temporarily shutting their eyes to the power of their culture. Confucian patriarchy was like the air one had to breathe; no matter how resilient or competent, a woman could not avoid it, and this was why so many women with graduate degrees and professional certificates were eventually forced to stay at home, picking up the same dirty dishes every day.

In principle, my dates were being irresponsible—and deceptive. They were like salesmen engaged in a bait-and-switch scheme. Operating in a seller's market in which there was no consumer protection, they knew that once they sold me a certain picture of what marriage would be like, they wouldn't have to deliver the goods, and would be perfectly entitled to deny me a refund or exchange. Since divorce was unthinkable for most women, the men were calculating that, once betrothed, I would have no choice but to surrender to the lifestyle that fell upon a married woman. Once it was sealed, the marriage would neutralize the career woman in me. A Korean proverb stated, "If you hit a tree with an ax ten times, it'll fall. If you go after a woman ten times, she'll surrender."

As transparent as they were, these suitors amused and saddened me. I almost bought what they offered. I wanted to hope. A complete life with a man, a child, and a career seemed a reasonable wish to me. Wasn't this the natural state of existence for a man? Wasn't a man with such a life praised as an achiever? Why was a woman who wanted it branded a greedy bitch? My head began to spin. I began to wonder if I, too, was a dreamer, not a planner.

Father was outraged when he learned I was going out with the two men. Although the reason he gave me was my own safety, I knew better. He wasn't upset because I was exposing myself to danger by dating or going out at night. He found it unforgivable that I dared to meet men who were not selected by him and who were beneath his standards.

In his mind, Father had a picture of the kind of young man who would be his second son-in-law. This man was preferably four or five years older than I, with a PhD or a prospective PhD in a respected, competitive field. Although he wanted a candidate with an advanced degree, Father didn't want a lawyer or a doctor. A medical doctor was ruled out because he wouldn't have the money to offer "three different keys"—one for a luxury condominium, another for a brand new car, and the last for an office for private practice. An MD was ruled out—he brought his wife such high social sttus her parents were expected to provide for the couple's living—Father didn't have the money. Nor was a lawyer an option. Since the court was little more than a chain of executioners for the right-wing military regime, the only difference between a relatively "clean" lawyer and an "unclean" one was the degrees to which they participated.

Now that he had one daughter married to a promising banker and one son attending SNU graduate school, Father was busy moving on to the next stage of operation: finding spouses for his unmarried children. For Big Brother and Less Big Brother, he looked for bright women from first-rate schools who were "good-natured" enough to be without ambitions of their own. He certainly didn't want a daughter-in-law with an advanced degree. But for his second son-in-law, he wanted a man as impressive as his own sons.

He made no attempt to handpick my husband. He knew me well enough to know I would retaliate if I were unhappy. He had to resort to a more circuitous and effective stratagem—getting me to give up on graduate school. Repeating that many women far brighter than I chose marriage over career, he kept trying to make me feel that I was reaching beyond my abilities and that I would soon be lost in despair. He even cited names of several women as examples of feminine modesty and self-awareness. Of course, he never succeeded in changing my mind. In my youth, it didn't occur to me that Father and I were identical twins in the art of argument. Back then, I couldn't see why we had to fight so constantly and for so long.

Taking refuge, as usual, in the outhouse, I was a child again with cookies in her hand, but the cookies she was holding at the age of twenty-two were the plans to fly far away from her country. She knew if she didn't leap across the Pacific, her life would remain as limited and stifling as it was. Because most key positions at universities in Korea were awarded to those who brought their PhDs from America and Western Europe, homegrown scholars with Korean PhDs were relegated to marginal posts and fringe part-time jobs. While watching her colleagues from Western schools moving rapidly up the ranks, as a spinster with a Korean PhD, she found herself locked in one place. Old maids in academia, unable to wed because of their careers and unable to move ahead because of their degrees, were often disliked, driven to pettiness and jealousy by their situation. I would not become like that. I needed to leave Korea, and I felt ready.

There was only one way to combat the constant question, "Are you married yet?" and having to return the tired answer, "Not yet." It was escaping the question altogether by leaving the country. The best revenge I could wreak on my country for its stupid, pathetic pity for single women was to turn out to be a smashing success. Whether I would have a career, a family, or both, I was convinced that I would handle it well.

Of course, I had only a vague and imaginary idea of what America was. I pictured it as a huge tiger's stomach, a vast place where a working woman was blessed with far more chances to find love. As a nation governed by human beings, it would be as flawed as any other, but it seemed big enough to allow for the kind of lifestyle that I desired and found unrealizable in my country. I knew I would have to endure a long, hard journey filled with trial and error, but I figured I would be given more room to jump and kick around creatively in the process. Wasn't America a free country where thinking exiles such as myself found a home?

The Three Men, of course, remained unconvinced. "Nobody I know has yet heard of a Korean getting a PhD in English from an

American university," Father pointed out. "A few have tried, but only to reach the conclusion that English and Korean are so linguistically different that they couldn't conquer the gap."

Big Brother and Less Big Brother warned me, "A sparrow trying to imitate a crane is doomed to lose." Father spelled out the famous Korean maxim for me: "You may have read a few books, but it'll take you—a sparrow—longer than a lifetime to do as well in English as a native speaker—a crane—would."

I, too, was secretly afraid. Having heard of the losers who returned to Korea with nothing but a suitcase after years of hard work in America, I could almost picture myself as one of them. I silently wondered whether I was making the right move. But I slashed the doubts away.

I had to remind myself not to denigrate the women who chose the traditional path. These women were trying to buy their meal tickets. I knew that if I blamed them, I'd have to blame everyone who was trying to survive. A housewife made one choice, a career woman another, and neither was better or worse than the other. These were the very women who loved me and whom I loved—they were my mothers and sisters and friends.

But acknowledging my love for them didn't lessen my ambivalence. The selfless women who were willing to give themselves up to be obedient, conventional wives made my path much more difficult. What man would choose an often-absent working woman over a woman who would make it her lifetime profession to prepare a warm dinner for her husband every evening? Why would anyone want to hire an expensive worker when he could have a free slave? In a power structure so grossly unbalanced, a woman was forced either to join the empowered majority or to stand alone in a vacant lot.

To see the consequences of the grossly unbalanced power structure, I didn't have to go far. Big Sister was one of those superior women who volunteered to put herself in an inferior position. She served her husband first at dinner like a good traditional wife, and put his needs above hers at all times because he was the breadwinner. It hurt me to see her working so hard for him on tasks I knew she didn't want to perform, but she was happy to do them anyway, convinced it was her job.

Little did she know that he, the expected breadwinner, would turn out to be a habitual breadloser. On the day he brought Big Sister his paycheck for the first time, he not only presented less than half of the amount he had received, but also demanded that she kneel on the floor to receive it with groveling gratitude. "I've worked hard to feed you," he declared. "But you've been enjoying a break at home. You're getting a free ride." When Big Sister refused to kneel, he became angry. She flung back, "If you kneel for me, I will kneel for you. As you work in your company to make money, I work in our house to save money. I cook, wash, clean, and iron your clothes. You're lucky I don't ask for half of your check for my domestic labor." A fight ensued, but Big Sister won in the end.

When I left Korea in 1980 for the first time, the couple had been married for eight years. Big Sister confided to me that during those eight years, he had made more than fifteen thousand dollars a year but brought only about seven thousand dollars home. While Big Sister tried to scrape every penny to buy the groceries, pay the bills, and send the children to school in decent clothes and shoes, he ran up large bills on hobbies beyond his means. He played golf with rich people, partied with tycoons at expensive restaurants, and visited bars to drink imported wines with wealthy wine connoisseurs. In the seventies, seven thousand dollars a year was an extravagant sum to spend on hobbies, unless you were among the extremely few rich people in the country; few men in their right mind would have squandered such amount. In one year, Big Sister told me, he even borrowed a lump sum of seven thousand dollars from a bank to continue to binge-spend. She couldn't let him have a red mark in his credit record because the whole family's livelihood was dependent on him, so she broke open her cd account and paid off his debt for him.

Her husband was incapable of thinking about the consequences of his behavior. Like a three-year-old boy, he was constantly leaving behind messes, and Big Sister kept cleaning up after him. Because everything they had—from the house and the car to the couches and the stereo—was registered in his name, she had no choice.

So she took a small lump sum from what she'd scrambled together and began to play the stock market. Since he was head of the household, any money she made would be legally his, but at least she would be able to get them back into the black. "I didn't have the money to hire a broker, so I had to figure out all the rules by myself," Big Sister told me. "I made five thousand dollars in six months, but I nearly died of stress." Her husband didn't lift a finger to help her during these six months, but he had the thrill of watching her buy another house in his name and having another wad of bills in his hands to squander.

I knew why Big Sister catered to this man whom she so despised. Had she been a man, she could have run a corporation, but being a woman, she was running a kitchen instead. He was the only avenue through which she could obtain social status respectability. To upgrade her socioeconomic standing, she had to upgrade his, and in the process of doing so, she found herself caught in the vicious cycle of handing him more and more opportunities to exploit her hard work. She had to make an inferior man into a superior man. As much as I sympathized with Big Sister, I rejected her choice. I believed a woman *could* be superior in her own right.

To this day, I am not sure if I have entirely forgiven Father for having chosen Big Sister's husband as his son-in-law. I acknowledge that there was no way he could have foretold the way he turned out to be, that Father was not responsible for his son-in-law's financial behavior. "If you blame the matchmaker," Koreans say, "it's just like blaming your bartender for you driving drunk." Over three-quarters of the couples of Big Sister's generation had arranged and possibly difficult marriages. Nobody can tell, even in love marriages, what will take place between a husband and a wife.

Big Sister and her husband have now been together for thirty-eight years. Americans always ask me the same question about their arranged marriage—"Are they happy?"—and I always give them the same answer: "They don't think in terms of being happy or not. They think about accepting or rejecting their destiny." After hearing this response, some Americans still insist, "If you marry a spouse chosen by someone else, you must be miserable."

During such conversations, I point out that Americans believe in choosing their own spouses, but their marriages often don't last. Nearly half of married couples get divorced in this country because they think the decision is purely their own personal choice. This is why there are so many unhappy children being shipped back and forth between two different homes. Since nobody else is involved in the exchange of vows at the altar, couples are allowed to entertain the notion that their marriage is nobody else's business. Couples in arranged marriages, by contrast, are compelled to consider not only themselves but also everyone else involved in their marriage. Before they rush to divorce, they must stop to think seriously about violating the sacred contract brought to them by the loved ones in their lives. They worry about letting down their families and relatives, their in-laws and friends, each of whom played a role in trying to match them up with suitable mates. To the couples in arranged marriages, staying married is a *destiny* as well as a *choice*.

Each kind of marriage has its problems, of course. A relationship sustained by fear and social pressure can be oppressive and often tyrannical, while a relationship maintained only by personal commitment can be rash and careless, oblivious of its consequences. But the former also requires a woman's one-sided, unconditional self-sacrifice, while the latter grants a bit more room for a woman's autonomous wishes.

To young Korean adults in 2010, marriage is a choice rather than a destiny, and finding one's own spouse without a matchmaker is the norm. Arranged marriages are still an option for those who don't have the skills for dating, but most parents nowadays take the backseat while their children discover their potential mates through

*Big Sister hosts a dinner party, with tens of tiny
plates of individual dishes.*

professional as well as personal matchmakers. Of course, the more
free-minded couples find it easier to part ways later.

Thanks to Father, an old-fashioned Korean man who believed a
married couple must stay married for the rest of their lives, Big Sister
was able to endure a difficult marriage. "You're my adopted son,"
he told his son-in-law. "If you left your wife, you'd be leaving me.
You'd be leaving your own father." He then turned to Big Sister.
"You're my daughter. I don't think you'll walk away from my son."
Thus, Father effectively consolidated this marriage by appealing to
the sense of the family.

With the same firmness that Big Sister believed in her destiny of
being married with children, I believed in my destiny of being married to my work. We each obeyed our destinies, whether or not they
reflected our personal choices, and ultimately we found ourselves in
different ways.

Although I've defended the merits of arranged marriages to
Americans, I've never stopped hating them. In Big Sister's case—and

in most of the arranged marriages I've witnessed—the man has thrived on the blood drained out of the woman, growing stronger while the woman became more and more fragile due to the humiliation and the despair of being imprisoned. I do not know how Big Sister feels about her husband. She confessed to me that she's contemplated divorcing him at least a hundred times, but as far as I know, she hasn't actively pursued it yet. She said she stopped loving him a long time ago, but nobody can discount the power of accumulated time. Thirty-eight years is long enough to change the shape of a diamond, to seal a relationship hated by both parties. Yes, she fulfilled her destiny by staying married to him, and yes, her children grew up healthy and smart, but at what cost to *her*?

One day in April 1979, I presented Father with a package from an American university. Explaining to Father what was in the large manila envelope, I felt I was almost at the end of the tunnel.

"One of the schools gave me a tuition waiver," I announced, bracing myself for one of our usual battles.

He gazed at me in silence, his eyes full of that odd mixture of worry and pride. When he opened his mouth, his tone was gentle. "I wish we had enough money to send you to the U.S." He was trying to say no for a little longer to save face, and I sensed it.

"I've told you time and time again, all I need is the money you'd spend on getting me married," I returned just as mildly.

"If we scrape every penny together, we might be able to get you enough to last a year or so," he offered. "But most likely, it'll take you longer to finish a master's degree. What will you do in the second year?"

"I know you can give me more. Any fool can tell it would cost you more than a year's expenses to get me married."

"You know money matters better than I do." A soft chuckle escaped from him. He was stalling.

The following day, Father told me that he could give me three thousand U.S. dollars initially and possibly more as the year went by, although he couldn't guarantee the amount.

"Don't feel you owe us anything," he said. "If you can't go on any longer in America, you can come back any time. Having you back in one piece would be a lot more important than a piece of paper with a graduate degree on it."

"He means it," Mother interrupted. "He wants you to be happy. He heard you typing for six months to fill out those applications and he was proud."

I couldn't believe my ears. My father—the man who demanded of his children the best of the best—was telling me to take it easy. He wanted me to know that failure was acceptable to him, that success wasn't everything. I could almost see the extent of his unconditional support, and I felt ashamed. I would do anything to show how much I appreciated his thinking.

We both knew I was right about the money, however. He would have had to spend at least five thousand dollars to have me equipped with a bride's package. He was still paying off the bank loan he had taken in 1971 to have Big Sister "safely married." The bride's parents were responsible for buying household goods, including a washing machine, a TV, a refrigerator, a dining set, furniture for the living room and bedrooms, a fancy stereo and speakers, and other stock ingredients of a well-furnished home. The groom's parents covered the cost of the wedding, including the ceremony itself, the reception, and the honeymoon. Some well-to-do parents of a groom even pur-chased a condo or a house, hired a brand new car and experienced chauffeur, or secured the service of a full-time housekeeper for their son and daughter-in-law.

Regardless of social class, however, it was the bride's parents who generally provided more for the couple. Because they were "giving away" their precious daughter to the man and the family who were going to feed her for the rest of her life, they had to not only make a good impression on them, but also prove with their spending that their daughter was worthy of being her in-laws' burden. This system was based on the belief that women had to pay in advance for their economic dependence on their husbands. *Please treat my daughter well* was the request being made by the bride's parents. The bride's parents "owed" other gifts to the groom and his family—often fancy jewelry, expensive fabric, luxury items, and cash in a lump sum. They showered their future son-in-law's siblings with Rolex watches, envelopes containing large bills, name-brand leather bags and purses, pearl necklaces and gold earrings. Some extremely wealthy parents spent several thousand dollars on jewelry alone for their daughter's in-laws.

In nuptial politics, there was a power play between the two parties—between the bride's family and the groom's—and a display of wealth. Even when the bride was a self-supporting woman, her parents made the gesture of good will and gave their future son-in-law's family the items on the customary list. Because their daughter was an outsider who needed to be welcomed by her new family, her parents wished to give her away with a statement proving that she was equal or even superior to him in terms of social class. To be respected by her in-laws, she needed leverage over them, a reminder of the financial power her parents could exercise on behalf of her and her husband; she needed the advantage of her background. In fact, the process was so costly that some parents nearly went bankrupt after giving their daughters away at the altar. There is a saying in Korea, "With three married daughters, one's home gets uprooted." Patriarchy, family, and social class were the three interlocking factors that created the custom of such nuptial politics. They are still at work today, arguably more powerful than ever as South Korea has become economically richer and the gaps between socioeconomic classes have widened.

When Big Sister married, my parents couldn't afford to shower her husband and his siblings with designer gifts. Still, it cost them to pay for the newlyweds' basic household goods, including fancy quilts and embroidered pillowcases, a small washing machine and a smaller refrigerator, two lacquered tables inlaid with mother-of-pearl, a chest of drawers with hand-carved designs, sets of dishes with famous painters' brushwork, and a dozen pairs of silver spoons and chopsticks. My parents gave them what they needed to fill their tiny one-bedroom apartment. They didn't want their daughter to be entirely without leverage over her in-laws.

Why should my parents pay for me to be a slave for a man and his family? I thought. *If anything, my parents should be paid for giving me away. Instead, for the same amount of money, they'll have the glory of welcoming back a daughter with a PhD, not a college-graduated maid toiling for a bunch of people who may not even deserve her.*

In August 1980, I flew to America to start my graduate studies. I was exhausted, worn down by the twenty-hour flight and the fifteen-hour jetlag. I slept for hours on end, waking up barely on time for the orientation for international students. As I was getting dressed to go out, a wave of terror suddenly seized me. I'd never lived alone before, and I felt utterly forlorn. I wondered how long it would take me to transform the horrible silence of loneliness into a melody of self-sufficient solitude.

I dreamed of the painter, Peace and Tranquility. With a long, thick wooden club, he hit the bronze bell on a small Buddhist tower, making low sounds that pealed across the sky. As if one short melody were enough, however, he stopped, walking back down the same endless road until he eventually disappeared into a tiny dot. He never looked back. He was going East.

Waking up in an American city where I could see nothing but endless rows of two-story houses, I was finally awakened to the painter's meaning. Beholding the eastern sky from my dorm windows, I realized that it was the same sky that my family in Korea was watching, the same spot where Father had seen a blue dragon the night before Little Sister was born. I would return to Korea in the end, to the same house where I had stolen his dream for her. To be homeward bound, I was going to empty my mind of all that was me.

Love Made Me
Grow Tall

I T HAS BEEN NEARLY THREE DECADES SINCE I LEFT HOME. NOW, I once again find myself thinking of my grandmother, who was so determined to turn me into an obedient second-class citizen like herself, and yet was ultimately correct in her prophecy that I would eventually find my words. Although I never learned enough about Grandmother to understand and pity the old woman while she was alive, I can now can see clearly that she was the reason I ended up devoting my life to fighting the sexism of my country.

Grandmother was born at the end of the nineteenth century, when the Yi Dynasty was in the last decade of its reign. During her childhood, Korea was finally annexed by Japan after suffering decades of Western colonial interference. Stricken with a national sense of loss, many rural Koreans sought to retain their cultural heritage by strengthening the hierarchical Confucian norms that had governed Korea for half a millennium. Clinging to the only lifestyle known to them was their means of resisting the occupation.

The sexist mores Grandmother inherited were dramatically reinforced by the extreme poverty she endured. As a child, she had to be grateful for boiled barley husk on the dinner table—there was almost never actual grain or rice. The women in her family were rarely offered more than a few leaves of cabbage and a little dab of bean paste on top of a lump of steamed barley. Food was always in short supply and whatever they could scrape together had to feed the boys. When Grandmother created the DMZ on the dinner table, she was merely reproducing the rules she had grown up with. She was no different from most grandmothers of her time.

In all fairness, Grandmother was benign compared to some of her peers. In 1971, when I was fifteen, I heard that one of Mother's distant cousins had given birth to a third girl in a row and that her mother-in-law, steeped in grief and despair, got dead drunk on cheap rice wine before staggering to the hospital. "That bitch is ruining my son's life!" she screamed in the hallway at the top of her lungs. Everyone on the obstetrics floor—including the doctors, the nurses, the expecting mothers, and her daughter-in-law—heard her. For nine months, the old woman, her son, and his wife had been united in the hope of having a baby boy, and the shattering of this hope was unbearable for the whole family. The young mother wept alone in the hospital bed, the husband went to work in shock, and the children were sad, unable to understand why the old woman had had such an outburst in front of strangers. I never forgave Grandmother for calling Little Sister "a worthless pussy," but at least she didn't make a scene in public. After letting Mother starve all day, she didn't get drunk or curse her daughter-in-law. That she already had two grandsons alleviated her sorrow, but three grandsons—the magic number for boys in Korea—had been her lifelong wish.

Preference for boys over girls was a five-thousand-year-old tradition in Korea, from which even the most enlightened people weren't entirely free. My parents were only two of the legions of Koreans who celebrated the births of their boys loudly and the births of their girls silently. Some couples just kept having children until they produced a boy. When I was growing up, families with seven or eight girls in succession and one boy at the end were a common sight.

Even professors, doctors, and lawyers of my own generation continued to have as many children as it took to land a boy eventu-

Me in Kansas, where I did my Ph.D.

ally. One of them, a professor of Western history, went as far as to have his wife undergo an abortion when he found out she was pregnant with a fourth girl. Convinced that it was her duty to provide her husband with a male heir, she came up with the idea first. He initially objected on the grounds that abortion was murder. But she insisted, aware that only a son could earn a woman a firm place in her husband's family, and he acquiesced. Despite his humanism and love for his daughters, he secretly longed for a son as much as his wife did. No wonder some obstetricians and gynecologists amassed a fortune.

On January 14, 1997, *The New York Times* reported that in South Korea, thirty thousand fewer female babies were being "born each year than would be the case if there were no such abortions," and that in a coed elementary school in Seoul, there were only thirteen girls for twenty-three boys. Although the status of women had changed by then, thanks to smaller family size and advances in science, technology, and women's higher education, preference for boys was hardly dwindling. Rather, modern medicine was harnessed to pander to societal wishes. On a summer day in 1995, Little Sister read a newspaper report about the police investigation of an obstetrician's office, where all of the dozen children born on one day were male: "It couldn't have happened unless there was medical manipulation."

Despite their longing for boys, my parents never contemplated the medical option taken by many people. "It's a crime," Mother would say, shaking her head. Father, who had stood in the hospital lobby for ten minutes to overcome his disappointment after hearing that Big Sister had had a baby girl, condemned the dehumanizing use of technology. And Big Brother, during his wife's pregnancy, repeatedly and sincerely assured her that if they had a girl, he would raise her with absolutely no regrets.

By 1980, the year I graduated from college, many of the urban middle class with college degrees had learned to practice the charade of embracing girls. It became possible for expecting parents and grandparents to say with a smile, "I just hope the mother and the baby will be healthy. I don't care if it's a boy or a girl." In order to counter everyone's secret wishes for a boy, a few of them would go as far as to declare, "Actually, I'll be happier if the baby is a girl." I heard the husband of one of my cousins say in front of his relatives that he was expecting a baby girl who would melt everyone's heart with her pretty face. Only when my cousin gave birth to a boy and her husband made thirty-five phone calls to spread the news of his future heir did everyone realize how strongly he had hoped for a boy.

However, since the lower class continued to take advantage of modern medicine to select the sex of their babies, there is a gender imbalance among Korean children born in the seventies, eighties, and nineties. In my nieces' elementary school, there were disproportionately few girls, and that school was only one of the thousands of such schools in the country. From the 1960s on, the government launched a vigorous campaign for two children per family, which succeeded in reducing population growth, but also created a sense of desperation to produce a boy. Since couples were encouraged to have only two children, they couldn't just keep having children until they produced a boy, as families had done up through my generation. Medical interference came as a natural option under the circumstances.

To Mother, her daughter-in-law's health was a top priority. She was disdainful of mothers-in-law who cared more about the sex than the health of their grandchildren. Although she was raised in a village and had barely finished junior high, she was more advanced than many educated, urban women of her age, and determined not to repeat her mother-in-law's cruelty.

In 1978, we received a letter from Big Brother in Boston, announcing his wife's pregnancy. "Usually, it's the grandmother who prays for a boy," Mother chided Father. "In this house, it's the opposite; it's you, the grandfather, who can't stop being foolish."

"It has to be a boy," Father said. "Our oldest son is the third heir of our clan; we need the fourth heir."

Mother didn't relent. "Don't you dare put pressure on your daughter-in-law! She's already working hard to support him. Without her, it would take him twice as long to finish graduate school." Big Brother was then working on his PhD in economics at Harvard, going back and forth, as he confessed in his letter, between the joys of prospective fatherhood and the stress of long hours of study.

He had married his wife in 1978, half a year after meeting her through a friend of Father's who volunteered to serve as a matchmaker for the prospective couple. This matchmaker thought the young man and woman were well matched because they were both graduates of Seoul National University and from comparable social classes. His father was a teacher at a junior college and her father was a university professor; their siblings were either attending prestigious universities or had graduated from them; he was going to get a PhD from an American university and she was ready to follow him to America and be a good stay-at-home wife and mother. As predicted by everyone who came to the wedding, it turned out to be an ideal arranged marriage with an excellent personal as well as social compatibility. Big Brother and his wife fit each other like custom-made gloves. To prove it, they had a son a year after moving to Boston.

When Father heard of his daughter-in-law's pregnancy, he said, waving a piece of paper, "I have three names for three different boys here. I hope they have three."

"If you send that paper to them," Mother threatened, "I won't speak to you again. How many names do you have for girls?"

"One," he replied.

Mother snickered. "So, you hope they will have three boys in a row and then one girl in the end. Why do you want a girl at all?"

"After three boys, a spice daughter would be good." A spice daughter meant a girl among many boys, a luxury a couple could afford after obtaining enough necessities.

In the end, Mother was happy that Big Brother's wife had a baby boy. The news made Father euphoric for several months, and he waited in joyful anticipation for the next four years until his grandson came back with his parents from Boston.

"Your Father's happiness was the only reason I was glad your sister-in-law had a boy," she confided in me. Mother had taken a stance on her grandchildren, and she was going to defend it to the end. She told me later about how she had threatened Less Big Brother the summer his wife gave birth to a second girl. After sending his wife out for an errand, Mother warned him, "If you ever, ever raise a brow in front of your wife or show disappointment in any way in your girls' presence, I will not leave you in one piece. You watch!" He hung his head in silence. He obeyed, and Mother didn't hear any more complaints from his wife about his sullen looks.

For many years, I was oblivious to Mother's bravery. For the first decade or so of her marriage, she was unable to challenge Grandmother's domestic rule. By 1971, the year I entered junior high, however, she was no longer a young woman entirely under

My mother holds Less Big Brother's daughter,
a granddaughter of whom she is very proud.

her mother-in-law's authority. As the mother of five children, she was confident in her power, and she revolted. How relieved she was, Mother would confess to me later, that she had two boys! "Sons are virtually the only power a traditional woman has," she said. "No matter how bright or successful a woman is, she doesn't have nearly as much privilege if she doesn't have a son. If I'd had only girls, I wouldn't have been able to silence your grandmother." When Mother overthrew the dinner table DMZ, I could finally entertain the hope of rebirth in my family—and in my country as well.

My Father's Daughter

WHEN I WAS A CHILD, MY FAMILY SUFFERED POVERTY, PERSECU-
tion, and the relics of Confucianism, all of which kept us
struggling against one another when we might have been enjoying
and helping each other. But I was born into a family full of love,
whose love has shone through the test of time. Alone in America, I
cherished the precious memories of how much they had loved me. I
found myself no longer cheated by memories of the bad.

Mother, like most women in her generation, showed some preference for her boys as we were growing up. But she loved all her children tenderly. I remember when I was a small child she would chide
me gently for not washing myself, telling me to hop into the tub.
When I was eight, we had a traditional Korean bathtub that had to
be heated with wood from beneath, and we each took a turn in the
same hot water, rushing to bathe ourselves before the water grew
cold. As the washing pad in her hand went adroitly up and down my
back, I felt her love massaging me all over. I thought if there was one
thing for which I would sacrifice everything in my possession at that
moment, it was spending just a few more minutes with her in the
water. But I knew it was impossible. Big Brother and Less Big Brother
were scheduled for a bath immediately after my turn, and she had to
help them wash fast in order to have dinner ready before Father came
home. So I left the bathroom, hearing the boys climb into the tub.
They didn't bother to skim my dirt out, well aware that once the
water got cold, it would take several hours to refill and reheat it.

And there was Little Sister. Whenever I felt unloved, I told myself over and over again how much my parents must have loved me to create such a perfect creature for me. She was the outcome of my prayers, the pillow on my back come to life. Often, she was my victim, being on the receiving end of my pent-up anger at the Three Men of the Family and Grandmother. Grabbing her ponytail, I heaped on her the same mean words piled upon me by the others and chased her out of the house to the alley. But unlike me, she was a loving, forgiving soul. Smitten with remorse, I would take her to the little shop at the corner and buy her candies with the pennies I had secretly amassed in my pouch.

Perhaps I knew even then that I would someday take her to America with me in my heart. Collapsing in bed at the end of a long day at the library, I would imagine her as a child, with her little, soothing hands stroking my arms and legs. In the pictures I drew in my mind, she was smiling, lulling me into sleep, ironing my scowl with that nurturing softness in her ebony eyes.

As I lay tossing and turning in bed, harassed by worries about term papers and exams, I would ask myself, *Did Grandmother love me? Did she have another face that I missed?* My memory ushered me back to the day a relative had come to visit her with an ice cream cone. Instead of eating it herself, she had saved this gourmet snack for me, waiting an hour for me to return home. "I thought I would give it to you when you came home," she explained sadly, indicating the melted mess on the table. "I didn't know it would no longer be good." Using a spoon to scoop the lump into the wastebasket, she handed me the wheat cone and said, "You can eat this, though." It wasn't the only time, I realized, that she had volunteered to give up tasty food for me.

Whether my memory tricked me or not, one thing was clear: in America, I missed my family so terribly that it was torture trying to avoid the temptation to pick up the phone to hear their voices. Every now and then, I would call Mother on an impulse, forgetting that two o'clock in the afternoon in America was four in the morning in Korea.

*My father, ever the professor, pictured here with
his sons and young cousins.*

Strange as it may sound, I missed the Three Men of the Family,
too. They had tormented me to achieve, and I was grateful. Thanks
to them, I refused to become one of those women who without question followed the path that was paved for them. I was inspired by
their moral anger and perceptiveness about how governments had
misled and abused us. It was the Three Men of the Family who,
unknowingly and involuntarily, taught me how to read a newspaper
between the lines and listen to a politician's rhetoric with suspicion.
While the media cranked out glowing reports on the national economic growth, they opened my eyes to the paupers and industrial
accidents; while the parliament spun out rave reviews of Park's leadership, they tuned my ears to the silenced cries of the tortured dissidents in prison. My best friends and my best enemies, the Three Men
of the Family fostered in me the ability to challenge them.

This awakening eventually helped Little Sister become a fighter, too. Upon graduating from college in 1985, she embarked on a career in journalism, becoming one of the first female reporters in Korea to be assigned to political news and one of the first feminist columnists to be published in a reputable newspaper. Six and a half years younger than I, she comes from a slightly more progressive generation, a culture that is a bit more advanced than the one that raised me. But she is as driven as I am to bridge the gap between the haves and have-nots, as compelled as I am by a sense of justice. Fighting the same war to extend democracy for women, she is to this day a dedicated, unmarried woman on her own independent path. She is now writing a book on eco-feminism, one of the first in the country on the subject.

Two—not just one—very strong-minded feminists were born and raised in one relentlessly patriarchal family, and this ironic outcome proves to me what a great family it was.

"Forgive the Three Men of the Family," I remember Mother pleading with me years after Father had passed away in 1989. "They were just like the famous American president you told me about To—, Tomas—"

"Thomas Jefferson."

"Yes, Thomas Jefferson. As a man of his time, he understood democracy of, by, and for the landed gentry, while non-landed white people, black people, and women went unacknowledged," she resumed, reproducing exactly the language I had used to introduce Thomas Jefferson to her. "He wanted *his* democracy, not democracy. Korean men of your father's generation fought for *their* democracy, not democracy. They achieved justice for one party at the cost of another. Had it not been for such hypocrisy, they probably wouldn't have been able to accomplish what they did."

In the eighties and nineties, feminists were no longer a small army of privileged women strapped to the right-wing fascist government as they had been in my parents' generation. By the time Little Sister graduated from college, feminist women formed one of the most vocal groups against the right-wing dictators in South Korea. They contributed a lot to bringing democracy to this country. They've grown up tremendously—and in a different direction—since the women's movement first came about in the forties and fifties. Now, they criticize their foremothers, to whom they owe what they have.

"Your father almost turned feminist," Mother said, pausing to laugh. "Although not quite, as you know. When you were in America, he sometimes volunteered to wash the dishes, so that he could brag to you later that he had learned how to do it. But I didn't let him do it more than a couple times because he just messed up the kitchen and created more work for me. He had changed his mind about doing women's work but couldn't bring his hands to obey the order from his head."

"What a revolution!"

"You don't know him as I know him." I had heard her say this many times. "We see two different men in the same person."

Secretly, I knew she was right. She saw her husband, and I saw my father. That he cared about her in ways his children couldn't see occurred to me a dozen years later. Mother waited twenty-five years to tell me her side of the story, keeping her silence until his unexpected death. On a day in 1992, the year when South Korea saw a democratically elected, civilian-controlled government for the first time, Father as a person was finally revealed to me.

Mother's husband, as I came to see him after his death, was a brilliant, frustrated, and loving man whose life was driven by three different forces: one, anger at Korea's right-wing dictators; two, a longing for his children to achieve what he could not; and three, devotion to his loved ones. Although it was easy to see the first two, the third was difficult to recognize. For fear of spoiling his children, he concealed his tender feelings behind a father's stern, rigorous mask. He felt his presence was only necessary to enforce discipline. He was there as the awe-inspiring judge, to let us know that we had to either improve or receive punishment. We were seldom exposed to the self-sacrificing man who devoted his entire adult life to his children.

I reminisced on my own. In my own memory, I met the man who had struggled to *express* his love for me, the warm, sympathetic father who had tried to shine through the stern face. From his deathbed, Father was gazing up at me, his eyes like a pair of tiny, bottomless pools of water incandescent with meridian lights, and I thought I had seen them before. That indelible mischief of a scheming little boy—that untainted spirit of a youth I thought I had inherited—was in those eyes, sparkling with an emotional eloquence for which he had never found an expression except in actions taken without tender words.

I had seen that particular mischief in those eyes. It was when he came home from a trip he had taken to another city to buy a typewriter for me, when he saw how happy I was with that marvelous little machine named Smith Corona he had carried all the way to Seoul. Because he couldn't afford to pay a retail price for it, he had traveled for three hours on a train to a wholesale store far from Seoul, where he had picked up the last machine in stock, which had been reduced to half price for clearance. It was worth the cost for the transportation, he said, since the train fare was only a fraction of the amount of the money he had saved, and since he hadn't taken a taxi home from the Seoul Station, he had saved even more. Unfortunately, he had to stand for nearly an hour in a crowded bus, holding the machine in one hand and the rail on the ceiling with the other

As he started to unwrap the package, it was the look on his face that excited me as much as the machine itself, and I could feel myself with the same expression, pounding on the keyboard of what seemed to be an elaborate creator of magic. We, the father and daughter in one mind, were a pair of wild-eyed children discovering a cuckoo's nest, a set of twins in fiendish delight over the eventual arrival of what they had coveted secretly for a million days on end. In my soul, I was a Daddy's girl.

"You recognize the sacrifices he made for you, whether you admit it or not," Mother told me after his death. "He rarely spent more than a quarter on a cup of coffee and almost never stepped into

*My mother, left, pictured here with her father, my father, and
Little Sister, in front of the house my mother was born in.*

a restaurant where it would cost him more than a couple dollars for
a meal. While the other teachers at his high school went out together to have lunch at a restaurant, he alone ate in his office from the
lunch pail I packed for him. He saved every penny—yes, every
penny—for your education."

"Oh yeah?" I asked, with my habitual cynicism. Mother and I
never tired of studying the book that was Father.

"You love him in spite of yourself. When he was alive, the first
person you asked about in your letters from the U.S. was your father.
Now that he's dead, the first place you want to visit when you come
home for the summer is his grave."

"It's my duty to greet him, dead or alive. It's not because I miss
him so much."

"It takes seven hours to go to his grave on a bus and another seven to come back," she reminded me, "but you don't mind making the trip."

"All I remember about him is the fear he inspired. Why did he make us so afraid of him when he loved us so much?"

"It was the Confucian way. You know he was raised by his old-fashioned grandparents. To make it worse, he didn't know how to be a father, having grown up without one himself, and his mother was a bitter woman. He never had a real family."

"He was surrounded with Confucian men who told him that a husband should beat his wife once in three days. He was rough with you. He was trained to believe that a real man doesn't exhibit affection for his wife. To avoid being seen as a weak man, he hid his love for you."

"You understand!" she exclaimed.

"With me, he had to be particularly strict," I continued. "I was different from the other children, rebellious and stubborn, and he was afraid that if he didn't make me into a 'good girl,' I would grow up to be one of those disobedient, unhappy women abandoned by their husbands. He had to beat me down."

"Now you see!" she cried in approval. "And yet, he was exceedingly supportive of you when he saw you trying to channel your rebellion into achievement. While you were in Kansas, working on your PhD, he created a small altar for you in our living room."

"An altar?"

"He placed a miniature statue of Mother Mary beside your picture. It was the first place he looked when he got up in the morning and the last place he visited before going to bed. Twice a day, he stood in front of it for a minute or so, with his eyes closed, praying to Mother Mary to protect you."

"It's because he wanted to achieve through me. I was working on a PhD then."

"No, no!" She shook her head furiously, but her voice was light-hearted. "He just wanted you to come back from America, healthy and unbroken. He didn't care whether you got a graduate degree or not. Didn't he say that time and time again in his letters?"

"Yes, he did," I agreed reluctantly.

"Contrary to what you think, he loved you unconditionally."

Father's death did not sever the ties we shared. Rather, it brought us closer, strengthening the love and hate that used to make our interactions so very difficult and emotionally charged. In my dreams, he came as a nurturing, affectionate father full of smiles and encouragement, but in my waking hours, I was assailed by the usual memories of his tyrannical glare and disparaging remarks. Underneath, however, I was in touch with the truth. The loving face he showed me was the real one. Since his death in June 1989, Father's soul lived permanently in my company, guarding my path in my dreams, almost to the degree that I would be frightened by his ability to foretell what was in store for me.

In one of the dreams, he came to me to say, "Your front door is unlocked." And it was. But the dream I remember most vividly came immediately after the first time I talked about these things with Mother, in 1992. In the dream, it was a winter night in a blinding blizzard, and Father went out alone, leaving the rest of the family in the safety of the house. My brothers volunteered to go with him, but he waved them off, afraid that they might catch a chill and come down with pneumonia. It was okay for him to get sick, he said, because he was an old man and taking care of his children was his job. He disappeared into the forest to gather firewood, and we saw him straggling, his feet buried in the snow. Closing the door, we went back to sitting in a circle around the little woodstove, reaching our hands toward the fire. As the afternoon wore on, Father still had not returned, and we— the five children—went out together, shouting in all directions, "Father! Father!" and running to the forest. As the night closed in, we went back to the house to fetch our lanterns and continued to look for him until we stumbled upon his ax and shovel. But he was gone.

Waking up, I was seized with the haunting sadness of the farewell. I started to weep uncontrollably, making a pledge in between the sobs, "Dad, your sacrifices will not go unnoticed. I will preserve your memory. Go in peace!" I was brought closer to him in his death than I had ever been in life—I could finally call him "Dad." To make it up to him, I could do anything. Wasn't the famous Korean saying—"When a woman is bent on unraveling the knot in her heart, she can cover the sky in July with snow"— handed down from generation to generation to be proven true by a woman like me?

In my apartments in Kansas and Tennessee, I didn't put any of his photographs on display, for I was still struggling with my tortured ambivalence. The faces of everyone else in my family deco- rated my tables and stacks, smiling that faint smile Koreans are famous for making when their pictures are taken. "Americans look radiant with joy in photographs, but Koreans don't," Father used to say. "We just wear a tiny, barely visible smile on our little stoic faces." He took pride in having learned how to look rapturous in pictures while he was in America, but the ones Mother kept in her house in Seoul didn't demonstrate this ability. They showed the seri- ous, rigid mask that evoked my fear, and I avoided looking at them. The black-and-white enlargement in her bedroom made me particu- larly nervous. It was an exact copy of the solemn, grave portrait hung on the wall at his funeral.

Once, Mother caught me turning one of Father's pictures face- down. She propped it back up and lectured, "You know Miss Chang, the woman who used to work with your father at the library at his junior college in Taegu? She keeps a smaller copy of this pic- ture on her desk, along with one of her husband and children. She said he's just like a father to her. Your father, of whom you think so little, is admired so deeply by so many people. Miss Chang told me that in her entire life, she'd never met anyone with such integrity and honesty.

"When he was running the library, she said, he was so meticulous and accurate with the numbers that everyone, including the dean of the college, looked up to him in awe. Administrators at colleges and universities back then almost had carte blanche over their budgets, with chances to pocket as much of the public money as they wanted. They could order massive amounts of unnecessary goods, too, in exchange for the bribes and gifts they received from companies. Backdoor dealings were routine, and if your father had taken advantage of them, nobody, including his superiors at the college, would have minded. Corruption was the air people breathed at that time.

"But he would have none of it, and Miss Chang was amazed. She once saw him turn down a gift of a ballpoint pen from a publishing firm because he was afraid that once he accepted it, he might be expected to consider their products over everyone else's. That's how he conducted the book-buying business for the school, and the man who succeeded him was worried whether he would be able to measure up to the standards your father had established."

After that initial lecture, Mother, ever the believer that "losing is winning," stopped resisting my effort to keep his face from my sight. She let me have my satisfaction. "You're a mule!" she'd say. She would tell me a joke she made up, "You know how many people it takes to make a mule cross a bridge? The answer is none, because it has to move on its own." She knew that eventually *her husband* and *my father* would be the same man in my life, and that we, mother and daughter, would be of one mind in loving him. Mother was right to believe this, but she didn't realize that I had already loved him all along, in my own way.

When the old man comes back to me in my dreams, I ask, "Do you remember the nice little house where we grew up? Do you think it was worthwhile for us to live in an area that was beyond our means?" He declares without a shred of doubt, "You bet it was. Look where you are now." I wake up echoing him, laughing with him, living with a man who has been dead for twenty years.

Considering how things turned out for us, it seems all of our sacrifices, especially Father's and Mother's, were worthwhile. Big Brother earned a PhD in economics at Harvard with a full five-year-long fellowship. I became tenured in English at an American university—as a Korean woman who came to the United States for the first

My mother and father, looking younger than their ages.

time at the age of twenty-four. Big Sister, the oldest daughter whose feminine virtues were praised by the family, learned to play the stock market, and played it well. Little Sister is a pioneering and respected journalist.

"If I need a PhD to prove how smart I am, I must be stupid," I say to myself and laugh. I can clearly see how I kept going back and forth between the two standards—the one that was held for me by my family and my country and the other that was held up by myself. I am glad I thought I was smart. Finally, I acknowledge what I knew all along: my family said the opposite of what they really thought. They told me I was stupid to make me angry, to push me to achieve. Criticizing was a traditional Korean way of encouraging.

I now look in the mirror to see my father raging out of my own eyes. I have *him* in me. I am *him*. I am a product of his sacrifices and sorrows, his joys and mistakes and hopes, of the dreams he was never able to fulfill himself and of the wrongs the world dealt him. How I internalized the tyranny committed against me by the men who had internalized the tyranny committed against them! I believe there is only one way to rescue myself from this cycle of tyranny. I have to end it, and to end it I have to write it. Made of words, my court is an open book in which the crimes are reported, the criminals indicted, and the brave ones like Father who stood up to them are given their due place in history.

To end the cycle of tyranny, I also acknowledge his love. While I was in America, it shone through the hundreds of letters and the small checks he managed to send, which opened my eyes to his true feelings for me. Long after he had gone to the world of the dead, his letters of inspiration traveled with me wherever I went, neatly packed in a silk wrapping cloth from home. They lay on the top shelf of my stack to remind me of the reasons why I was working so hard to perfect my English.

I work hard to explain my brothers, too. If Father had been dishonest enough to join the right-wing dictators, his sons would have been given more chances to improve their attitude toward women. Too busy trying to survive, they had no choice but to repeat the traditional gender norms they had inherited. Men who actively supported the dictators in fact were kinder to their wives and daughters because, with plenty of money and power, they could afford to pay attention to what was considered a trivial issue in their country then. While they turned a blind eye to so many people being tortured in prison, these men could stay wide awake to the cries for justice and equality from the women in their own homes.

An Amaryllis in
a Stone Field

ONE SUMMER DAY IN 1996, ON THE BALCONY OF HER APARTMENT, Mother was watering her thriving plants, readjusting the spaces between the pots to give them more breathing room. "Look!" she suddenly exclaimed, "I totally ignored this one. It's been stuck in the corner, covered by another plant, but it bloomed beautifully."

She was pointing at the two blossoms of an amaryllis fighting through the leaves of an alien plant. I suggested, "The stems may need a little support. They look weak." As Mother took out a red silk sash from a chest of drawers and tied it around the stems, I peered at the orange flowers with their V-shaped rows of stamens. A mysterious sense of pride welled up in me.

Every morning before breakfast, Mother and I beheld the amaryllises—one in the pot and the other, which had fallen from the stem, in a glass of water on the chest of drawers. Even though Mother spent most of her energy tending to the rare crinum flowers around them, she never forgot the amaryllises; she crooned to them and prayed for them. With severe osteoporosis and spinal disc problems, which made it hard for her to take a few steps without a cane, she never stopped loving and nurturing. Sitting at the table with all the food she cooked for me, I was full of gratitude. She was still alive, with an alert mind and strong will power; and I, having beaten the haunting past, showed all the signs of a human being who had been raised with abundant love. There was no lingering sense of guilt—not even the need to make atonements—between us. There was only the sheer joy of celebrating, with one heart, all that we had loved in the past and all the moments yet to come. I, like Mother, was an an amaryllis in a stone field, one of those numerous women in my country who withstood the test of hell.

I remembered the second time Mother had attempted suicide, when I was a twenty-year-old college girl. Vividly, I heard again the cry echoing through my distant past, the sound leaking from my parents' bedroom, a hacking cough one might hear from a baby trying to spit out a fish bone she had swallowed. "What? What is this? An electric wire?" Father was screaming, forcing his voice down, but the choking sound continued. Mother had unplugged one of the electric cords in the room and tried to strangle herself on an impulse. It was a sequel to her attempted overdose of sleeping pills when I was twelve and half, of which Father was unaware.

At the sight of the amaryllis, the memory came back to me, and I realized that I had repressed it to protect myself. With her first suicide attempt still fresh in my mind, I hadn't wanted to handle the second one. But now, having no more reasons to keep it repressed, I recalled what had occurred to me as a twenty-year-old college girl with high hopes and dreams when I heard Mother's hacking cough.

When I was in college, I could tell Mother was suffering from clinical depression. There was no way I could find out whether she was born with an imbalance in her brain chemistry, but I was absolutely certain that anyone with her ability to feel and think deeply would have found themselves in the same abyss. She was truly a thinking soul, and she was maddened. With such a great capacity to realize how absurd reality was—and with such little language in her possession—Mother plummeted into a mute rebellion against her life and tried to terminate the pain that she couldn't bring herself to articulate.

For days after her second suicide attempt, I was haunted with questions I could not answer. How long can a human being live in one tiger's stomach? One must live in one tiger's stomach for a while if it's the human condition, I reasoned, but one needs another tiger's

*My mother waters her plants, accompanied
by Big Brother's son.*

stomach sooner or later. Mother lived in one tiger's stomach for too long. In her tiger's stomach, she was silently screaming at Father for the recognition that she so very much deserved. Just as I always wanted a self of my own, she, too, wanted a self of her own. But saying so was a sin for a woman in a Confucian patriarchy.

When I was in college, however, I became conscious of something else that drove Mother over the edge. In a Confucian woman's life, two things were necessary for her self-esteem, and Mother could see that both of these were in serious jeopardy. Her husband, with the sole power to define who she was, was doomed to the shadows forever. Also, she was almost certain that her native family—her *chinjung*, as it was called by a married woman—had been virtually destroyed, robbed of the name that should have been passed on for posterity. With her brother, Outside Uncle, disappeared in North Korea, her father remained heirless, his lineage abruptly and permanently terminated. Her *chinjung* suffered what Koreans described as *myulmun*—the state of having one's family name destroyed.

Although a married woman was an outsider to her native family, she still loved them. Also, her status among her in-laws was in part determined by the strength of her native family. Father, of course, never slighted Mother because of what happened to her *chinjung*. Outside Uncle had been Father's best friend and had served as a matchmaker for Father and Mother. Seized by her sorrow, Mother caved in and spiraled into depression. She wanted to articulate what she felt, the choking grief threatening to kill her. The electric cord was her language.

In 2009, Mother still refuses to give up hope for her siblings. "He'd be ninety years old if he were still alive," I tell her, describing Outside Uncle's most likely situation. "He'd be too senile to recognize you." I abstain from uttering the strongest—and the worst— probability in her presence, that he's in a gulag or died in a coal mine. I do not admit to her that I, too, hope to see him come back home, to show that her family name has not been obliterated.

Mother is now in a new tiger's stomach, having been freed long ago from the tiger's stomach that brought her to the brink of suicide. With three metal bars to support her spine, her spirit is as lively as ever. She has more joy than grief. She feels particularly accomplished when all of her offspring, including her baby great-grandson, crowd together in Big Brother's living room.

I've never entirely shaken the question I asked myself over and over again as a child: *If Father loved her so, why did he never show it to her?* I still remember pressing my pounding heart that night she tried to choke herself with the electric cord, feeling more afraid of Father's violent outburst than glad of Mother's failure to die. By then, I was used to the pain he disguised in anger, but on that particular night, I heard not only pain but also love suppressed under the fear he was trying to control. His whispered rebuke and callous tone belied a desperate sorrow and compassion. In the morning, his eyes were swollen, and I could read the tenderness concealed under his rigid, forbidding mask. He had been crying all night long.

For years after hearing the sound of Mother's electric cord, I thought I was the only one in the family who was making some effort, however ephemeral, to understand what she was going through. When I found out why the impulse to end her own life had gotten the better of her, I found myself surrendering to the same desire to vanish from the earth. Now we—Mother and I—can love, fight, and make up like other mothers and daughters.

Just yesterday, I had a huge argument over the phone with her, a continent away. "If you keep giving to that giant leech of yours"—I meant, as you might guess, Less Big Brother—"you'll be out on the street one of these days. You give him every dime and nickel you've got. Didn't he take all the underwear from you?" I resorted to the old Korean metaphor for stripping a person penniless—"taking one's underwear away"—begging her to put an end to what everyone else in the family sees as blind catering to Less Big Brother's corrupt way of life.

Mother protested, "I don't want to lose hope. There's good in him. He was smart enough to explain Kafka to his Big Brother when he was only fifteen. He'll come around one of these days."

"Big Brother was just as bad as you," I told her. "He spoiled his little brother silly, and protected him when he should have been punished." I knew I was slandering her god, and I was at once thrilled and downhearted. I chastised myself, *Are you going to spend your entire life trying to pull Big Brother down from his pedestal? How long are you going to be that little girl you used to be?* Before Mother could launch her defense of Big Brother, I crooned, "It's amazing how a man with such rigorous discipline could be of the same pack with such a loose canon."

I had finally learned to distinguish between the two men. I hadn't appreciated that my brothers differed so much in the most critical area of human discipline until Less Big Brother, a middle-aged man, became a monkey on the family's back by repeatedly going bankrupt with his business ventures. And yet, despite the heartache he causes, I still care for him. Didn't we, after all, bathe in the same water in the same tub?

My mother has made a point of nurturing her good relationship with Big Brother's wife, seated here on her right. Father holds his grandson.

If the subject of Less Big Brother comes up again when I call Mother tomorrow, I plan to say, "I hope you think about your other children, too. Once you're gone, he'll be a burden for his siblings. If you stop catering to him now, you can at least reduce the degree of the problem for the rest of us." As of now, I am not certain she will be able to turn him down, but I have hope. I know that she is capable of wisdom as well as generosity. I remember what she did for Big Brother's wife, whom she cherishes as one of her own children.

"There isn't anyone in this world who would know better than I," she used to tell me, "what it's like for a woman to live with her mother-in-law. I'd hate it if your big brother's wife had to suffer the same thing that I had to endure for forty years." Incredible as it may sound, Mother was successful in breaking the hate cycle, saving her daughter-in-law from the life that had nearly destroyed her. She never breathed one bad word about her to anyone or opened her mouth except to praise her "newly adopted daughter." She avoided sowing even the tiniest seed that might have sprouted into animosity. Nevertheless, there was as much tension between them as there was mutual admiration. I am convinced Mother had as many complaints about her daughter-in-law as the latter did about her. But the old woman never broke her vow of silence.

"Nobody is as grateful as I am to your father," Big Brother's wife confided to me once. "He made it possible for me and your mother to live separately. Without his pension, she'd be living with me and your big brother, and I'm afraid we might clash."

Acknowledging her point, I replied, "That's true, but it was Mother who made it happen. She was the one who spent carefully every penny he made, the one who enabled Father to accumulate enough money to buy a decent condo for you. She was also the one who insisted on letting you live separately from your parents-in-law."

In 1983, when she and Big Brother moved into a cozy little three-bedroom apartment in Seoul, more than half of the married youths of their age were living in the same house as their parents-in-law, either unable to afford a different setup or still attached to the traditional custom. With the arrival of the nuclear family, a large number of young couples, including oldest sons and their wives, had begun to live alone, but the old-fashioned lifestyle was still not only popular but also financially more feasible and culturally more familiar.

Mother was unusual because she volunteered to give up a mother-in-law's privileges. She refused to be served three meals a day by her daughter-in-law and live the rest of her life without housework. "Your mother has a large heart," Big Brother's wife marveled. "As if forty years under such a ruthless mother-in-law weren't enough, she had to play full-time nurse for the old woman in the end. For about two years before she died, your grandmother had to be spoon-fed in her bed and helped with her bowel movements. But I don't remember your mother uttering one word of complaint in those two long years. I offered to help her once when I saw her cleaning the old woman's stool smeared on the quilt, but she waved me off, closing the door on me. What amazed me more, though, were the genuine tears that were still left in her for that old woman when she died. Your mother cried more than anyone else in the family. I'm telling you all this because you were in America during Grandmother's final years."

Hope for Reunion

O N June 13, 2000, Kim Dae Jung, the president of South Korea, went on a three-day summit to meet Kim Jong Il, the famously mysterious leader of the North. Fighting tears of joy, I cried silently, *Father, you'd be happier than anyone else on earth today. Thank you for all the sacrifices you and your friends made for your family and your country. You—the invisible men and women who lie buried in our history—taught us how much work democracy takes. You are the ones who made Kim's visit to North Korea possible.*

Although Kim's administration was far from perfect, it was the first one to be entirely free of the residues of the right-wing military, and this was one of the key political factors that made it possible for him to initiate the peace talk with North Korea. Father had been right in predicting that at least half a century would have to pass before South Korea would see the evolution of a completely civilian government.

"Your father would be ecstatic if he were alive," Mother said, as if she had read my mind. Mother and I watched and re-watched the same scenes on TV, the rendezvous between the two Kims being rebroadcast endlessly on every channel. Anchorpersons, pundits, and commentators contended vigorously to reexamine and re-explain the same ceremonies and meetings, analyzing time and time again the historical significance of the same speeches and conversations. In

The sprawling metropolis of Seoul, as it was in the 1960s.
In the last 40 years, it has grown physically and
financially, and South Korea is currently the 7th largest
economy in the world. Yet we are still divided from
our family and friends in the North.

mesmerized excitement, the whole country was watching and listening. For three days, Mother and I did nothing but stare at the TV. How glad I was to be at home that summer! Since I had left Korea for the first time in 1980, I had been back home a few times, but that summer of 2000 was made particularly unforgettable by the two Kims' visit.

And how impressed I was by my people in the North! Some estimated six hundred thousand people came to the Pyongyang Airport to greet Kim, lining both sides of the road to his hotel for miles, waving little paper flags, their faces radiating ecstasy. Echoing the crowd, Mother and I shouted, "Mansei!"—Hurrah!—standing in the living room with our arms raised high and our backs straight with pride. The North Korean women in the crowd were wearing brightly colored traditional Korean costumes and plain-looking low-heel shoes, with their hair cut in straight lines above their chins without bangs or curls. Their faces beamed heartfelt celebration and their body language manifested tremendous relief, their eyes transfixed on the car carrying the two Kims.

"I can see how relieved they must feel now," Mother observed. "Their state was condemned as the nest of evil by the world. Now that they have opened their door to South Korea, they can prove themselves to be otherwise."

To help North Koreans step out of the humiliating isolation, South Koreans moved first. They gave unsparingly to their brothers and sisters on the other side of the DMZ, happily competing with one another to raise the amounts of their donations. "The starving children in the North could be ours when you think about it," they would say. "Had we been born and raised there, we could very well be living in a house with no heat and electricity in freezing January." These givers were responding to Kim Dae Jung's Sunshine Policy, the strategy of familial love and support, the purpose of which was to touch North Koreans' hearts with generous economic aid and diplomatic good will.

Each year, Mother donated a small sum of money, hoping it would buy hot soup and warm rice to fill children's empty stomachs. "If I eat one less apple a day, a child will have two more meals a day," she would say. Living on Father's retirement, she barely had enough for herself, but sharing it with her brethren in the North brought her a sense of comfort. In a way, she felt she was helping her own brother and sister in North Korea, whose children and grandchildren, she was afraid, might be suffering from hunger and cold—if they have children at all. Of course, we cannot know for sure.

June 2000 taught me a final important lesson about my country. After all the blood and hell suffered in the South and the North, the Korean people in the two states have never stopped and will never stop seeing themselves as one. Mother's family story constantly reawakens me to the fact that Korea is the only country among the several tribes and kingdoms that rose and fell in the vicinity of China for thousands of years that succeeded in maintaining its national identity. All the rest, including the powerful Mongols and Manchurians, were culturally and politically assimilated into China, a nation well known for its skills in absorbing its neighboring rivals

by either force or seduction. Korea indeed is distinct—and distinguished—in its talent for preserving itself amidst the superpowers
that are always harassing and trying to destroy it.

"I'm sure Father is applauding your generosity in his grave," I
assured her.

"If he were alive, he'd be receiving a full-time salary and we'd be
donating three times as much. He predicted North Korea would
experience such destitution. He said that after Kim Il Sung's death,
there would be catastrophic events to make the internal fractures in
the regime."

"It wasn't difficult for him to foresee the death of socialism."

"Not at all. He could clearly tell the difference between the
socialism in his youth and the socialism in his old age. The former
was based on the ideals of justice and equality for everyone and the
latter was dysfunctional and corrupt."

I had heard many people say the same. "That's why socialism in
our country was doomed to fail."

"Your father would agree with you. But what he resented was
that our idealistic plan was destroyed before it had a chance to run
its course."

"A country should be left alone to go through the process it is
bound to go through. When its dialectic is interrupted by superpowers,
it sheds blood. Although," I said, "realistically, no country has ever
been and will ever be free from another's interference. For a small country like ours, to exist without outside interference is a mere dream."

Just a couple years later, George Bush would call North Korea an
"axis of evil," making America a villain in the Korean Peninsula all
over again, hounding the North into reactivating its nuclear facilities. Totally oblivious to the long, tortuous history of the tension
between the United States and North Korea, its mortal foe across the
Pacific, Bush and his henchmen once again stirred up the Americans'
ancient hatred, founded mainly on ignorance and blind Cold War
consciousness. In their terrifying rhetoric, they seemed utterly
unaware of the nuclear terror under which the North Koreans were

forced to live for half a century.

In 1950, Douglas MacArthur seriously contemplated dropping atomic bombs over the northern tip of the Korean Peninsula, and during the Korean War, the Joint Chiefs of Staff came close to using them several times over North Korea. In 1951, the U.S. military also dispatched to Pyongyang a solitary B-52 bomber in an attempt to terrorize North Korea, the state that never used bombs in its warfare with South Korea. I wondered if Bush-supporting Americans knew that it was their own country that had placed a pile of nuclear weapons near the DMZ in 1957 to intimidate the then non-nuclear North. I also wondered if the American people ever knew the open secret that their own country had continued its rehearsals for a long-range bombing strike upon North Korea until 1998—for at least seven more years after the nuclear weapons were withdrawn in 1991 under the pressure of the South Korean peace movement.

During the past thirty years of my life in the United States, I have never met an American, Bush-supporting or not, with any awareness of the nearly half-century-long assault upon North Korea by their own country. The American demonization of Kim Jong Il is quite self-righteous, lacking any knowledge of or reflection on the events that have led the North and the South down the roads they have gone. I vigorously agree with these Americans that Kim Il Sung was a heinous dictator, and that Kim Jong Il, his son, is an equally heinous one. But I must offer them a footnote—that unless they look at both sides, they will continue to make the mistake of yielding to their government's propaganda. As the saying goes, "It takes two to fight."

Chased to the edge of a cliff, North Korea had few options other than to play its nuclear cards. After having complied with the Clinton administration by entering the process of freezing their nuclear arms, they had virtually no choice but to fall back on the same weapon to cope with Bush's belligerent attitude. Even now, nuclear arms remain the only bargaining tool they are allowed to exercise. With no economic power and no dependable ally, they have nothing but the fearful recognition they can command by being a dangerous presence.

Talking to Mother in June 2000, I was worried about the prospect of George Bush becoming the next president of the United States. Smaller countries are, sadly and inevitably, always prey to the interests of bigger and more powerful ones, but there are individuals who push this ugly reality to an extreme. As I had feared, during Bush's residence in the White House, the peace talks between North and South Korea were dramatically slowed down. The reunions of divided families over the DMZ were stalled, in some cases permanently; Koreans in their seventies and eighties were forced to envision rejoining their loved ones only in heaven. "If people in Mississippi couldn't find their siblings in New England after the end of the Civil War because some dumb-ass president from Korea called their country an 'axis of evil,' then Americans would know how I feel," Mother raged. "When Clinton was in charge, I could at least entertain some hope of finding my siblings, but now I am reduced to wishing to see them in the other world."

But during those three mesmerizing days of the historic June 2000 peace talks, Mother and I wanted to do nothing but rejoice. From the thirteenth floor, where her home was located, we saw dozens of college students standing in a circle on the ground in the middle of the apartment complex, cheering loudly and sipping from bottles of soju, Korean vodka. One of them was holding a placard that read, "From Seoul to Pyongyang, the taxi fare is only twenty dollars," and another was waving her arms like a bird in imitation of a traditional Korean dancer, a uniquely Korean gesture of celebration.

"Godspeed the reunification!" they sang in chorus. "And long live the Korean Peninsula!"

"We'd better celebrate, too," Mother suggested. She took out a bottle of soju from the kitchen cabinet and popped the cork. It was three o'clock in the afternoon, but neither of us had any reservation about getting tipsy.

"Damned if you do; damned if you don't," she went on, gulping down her glass of soju in one draw. "If you don't fight for your country's interests, you'll have nothing left of your own; if you do, you'll be ridiculed for being unrealistic. But thanks to people with your father's courage, who fought to keep the principle alive, we still have our country. He and his friends were hardly different from the Chinese students facing the tanks in Tiananmen."

I sipped at the soju. "While I've never heard of an American ridiculing the Chinese students at Tiananmen for being unrealistic, I have personally met several Americans who openly sneered at the socialists in the Korean Peninsula for being foolish."

"None of them had a clue of what happened in the Korean Peninsula, why there had to be socialists," Mother said. "If their own government tries to set up a left-wing toady in China, they'll condemn it in a moment. But Uncle Sam set up one right-wing toady after another in Korea, and virtually created the monster named Syngman Rhee."

"There were other men the Americans could have used. Why did they select Rhee?"

"Your father said he had skills to interface with the Americans with the greasy efficiency of an experienced Washington lobbyist. His fluent English and staunch anticommunism won them over."

"Rhee used Uncle Sam for his own power in the end."

"Malice wasn't one of the Americans' motives," Mother said wisely, "but when power is exercised in conjunction with ignorance and misguided ideas, it inevitably leads to malice. A nation, just like an individual, should be judged only by its actions, not by its intentions. Evaluated by its actions, the United States was criminal."

By the time we finished the bottle, it was dinnertime. With a reddened face, Mother started to make a pot of soup, chopping a chunk of choice beef on a cutting board with a bunch of green onions, mixing hot pepper with soy sauce and garlic powder. I washed the bean sprouts and peeled the onions, my eyes teary. In a hurry to go back to watching TV, we ate quickly, finishing another half bottle with the meal. Then we fell asleep to the pundits' familiar analyses. The next morning, we woke up to another anchorman's voice and again enjoyed the same scenes over a pot of coffee and a tray of French toast. A little North Korean girl with a face like a China doll sang a song for Kim Dae Jung's wife, which went, "Our teacher, our teacher, who inspires us to love our family and country . . ."

"Although they don't admit it," I picked up. "most Americans like to think we owe them. They believe they helped us to thrive on rich capitalism. They know nothing of Korea before the birth of its capitalism."

"When your father was in America, he was often asked, 'Would you rather be in Kim Il Sung's hands?' He didn't know what to say."

"We modeled our capitalism after the American style," I said with a cynical laugh, "Maybe, we do owe them."

"Your father used to say that in South Korea, we can at least put the food on the table. In North Korea, a grain of rice is a luxury. In the end, capitalism turned out to be more effective than socialism."

But the methods the Americans used to plant capitalism in South Korea were absolutely horrible. Thanks to their "benevolent" intention, nearly three million people, including two million Korean civilians and thirty-three thousand of their own soldiers, were killed during the Korean War. Including the unreported number of the civilians slaughtered by Syngman Rhee and Kim Il Sung before, during, and after the war—which is estimated to be well over a million because the number of civilians killed in South Korea alone is between 600,000 and 1.2 million—over four million people died during the violent decade surrounding the war, and for this enormous casualty, the United States was at fault.

Shaking their heads in disbelief over Khmer Rouge's butchering of an officially documented million and half Cambodians, the Americans didn't bother to be nearly as disturbed about the deaths of over twice as many human beings in Korea that was caused by their own government. The evils of the communists in Cambodia were worthy of their attention, but the evils of the capitalists in the Korean Peninsula were not. To them, communism is bad, but capitalism isn't.

No-Name State

FOR THE NAÏVE ADOLESCENT I WAS, FOR THE SPIRIT ALWAYS LEAPING to distant horizons, America seemed to be the place at the end of the sky, and English happened to be the language spoken there. I couldn't have realized that it was merely a bohemian's language that I was working so hard to master. Now, having lived in this huge, often indifferent country for more than half of my life, I have discovered a sad truth. Although I saw much of the good that I had imagined, I was often seized by spasms of loneliness I couldn't control. Yes indeed, I was blessed with opportunity, by the privilege to create a niche of my own in a country where I was neither born nor raised. But there was always the gnawing awareness in my mind that most Americans failed to perceive me as one of them and that I, too, failed to perceive myself as such. Always, I found myself pushed out to seek a country within a country. Always, my soul was anxious to plunge into an unmapped land.

Sometimes, I even cherished the fact that Big Brother had dictated fine arts as my college major. I never wanted anyone to dictate my major, of course, but over the long years of living in America where individualism spawns indifference, I began to appreciate the intention with which he had selected my field. He cared about me enough to believe that my future was his future. He proved this to me.

In fall 1991, I was frantic, about to take my doctoral exams to find out if my decade-long effort was going to be fruitful. I dreamt of Big Brother holding a giant transparent water tank against a wall, his torso and outstretched arms clutching the huge glass panels and his legs spread in perfect balance on the ground. Upon waking, I knew I was going to pass my exams, to celebrate and move on to the next stage.

Big Brother grew to be a man I could admire. On more than one occasion, he was invited to contemplate joining the inner circle of the political power of South Korea, urged by some to try to obtain a seat on the presidential cabinet. He was not only well-qualified but also well known among the core members of the upper administrative tier. But whenever the suggestion came, he shook it off, declaring in one clear word his decision to stay away from the temptation of political power. For several years after his return to Korea from Harvard, the powers running the country were still tainted by the residue of the right wing dictator, and for another span of a decade or so, the infrastructure of the political system had to be cleansed to accommodate the demands of democratization.

But he would have turned down any suggestion that he consider taking part in the policy-making process in the Presidential House. Political power, coveted by so many men of his stature in his country, was the last thing he wanted. To this day, Big Brother is a professor at a university in Seoul, imparting ideas for economic justice and equality, an academician with clean hands and a clear head. With the same moral integrity and behavioral consistency that he inherited from his father, he has dedicated himself to educating the youths of his nation.

As Big Brother was his brother's keeper, I tried to be my sister's keeper. I was able to help my parents to make the financial circumstances for Little Sister a bit easier, taking little more than bus fare as my daily allowance. If I spent less, I reasoned, she would have more—however much or little it might be—and if she had more, I would be in her life what Big Brother was in mine. She would have colorful silk and splendid cotton. I could also be what Big Sister was, the one to whom my siblings and I were always grateful for the sacrifices she had made as the oldest child.

I wanted to be a pilot in Little Sister's path, to help her to taste the magic of knowing. When she was thirteen, I gave her my copy of Albert Camus's *L' Étranger*, as Big Brother had introduced me to

Margaret Mead when I was sixteen. I told her about the suffragists, too, and she listened with the same avid attention I had paid to Big Brother while he explained to me about the long fights women had to wage to gain basic human rights. How proud I was of the intellectual tradition in my family! Its beauty and power worked again as I helped Little Sister to reap its harvest.

When Peace and Tranquility came to visit me in my dream three years after my arrival in America, I was seeking a different—and yet the same—answer. "The America I came to is nowhere to be found," I complained, as he drew an invisible map of the United States—one with fifty-one states, which I was to keep in my mind from then on—on the blank wall of my apartment. As a square-shaped state—a vast virgin land without a human trace—appeared between California and Oregon, he took a giant step forward into the mapped wall, and I followed him in equally long strides. Covered with forests, hills, lakes, rivers, and animals, the land was pleasantly quiet, with the occasional melodies of waterfalls cascading through the cliffs and mountains. He and I were the only human visitors, following a thin trail through the pine woods overlooking a creek. Since the weather was breezy and summery year-round in the state, we strolled comfortably and leisurely, breathing slowly and never breaking a sweat.

Peace and Tranquility, who was blind, knew the trail as well as a seeing person would recognize the worn path to his home. In silence, I walked beside him, peering at his profile in an effort to figure out how he could see so clearly. Before I could get a good look into his eyes, however, he lifted his finger to point at something ahead of us, a roe deer sauntering toward us without fear. I was incredulous, having never seen a forest animal unafraid of people. Because there was no human being in the state, there was no hunting, and the four-legged creature was only delighted to see the two-legged ones.

"What a lovely animal!" I exclaimed.

"Hush!" Peace and Tranquility brought a finger to his lips, turning toward me.

I looked at the man. With my eyes transfixed on his and my mouth dropping, I heard myself cry, "Dad!" The ancient painter was Father, blind and smiling, his still, calm gaze piercing into mine.

"Behold!" he hummed in a low voice, pointing at the deer again.

In shock, I watched the beautiful animal become covered with snow in an instant. The woods, too, turned white, freezing in the sub-zero temperature that turned the whole state into a giant ice mountain. Everything died in a wink, leaving me to shudder in the infinite white terror.

Waking up, I thought I could decipher the meaning of the dream. The state—which I was to call No-Name State for the rest of my life—was an imaginary United States to which I had moved from Korea, a utopia where human beings could not live. It was a place where everything was perfect and nothing could survive, a country reigned by death and governed by a flawless—and hence lifeless—logic. Father, whom I never called Dad except in my dreams, came to tell me this simple truth, to utter the words that Peace and Tranquility offered to his soul mate only in silence. Father was the artist who had given his eyes to paint visions of a perfect world, the warrior who had devoted his youth to doing what was right for his country—and the first one to realize that the world he had fought so hard for was merely an *idea*.

As I was finally awakened to the truth that the America I had constructed in my head was only an idea, I, too, was afraid that I was going blind, tormented in my soul by the price I had to pay. I found myself hanging in the air between the two homes, living in the wind that blew across the Pacific. Yet, ironically, it was this vain search for the America I had come to that was going to keep me on my toes, and I knew it. Because I would never find this neverland, I would forever search for it, refusing to give up. I would stay on in America, looking every day for a country within the country.

Acknowledgments

I OWE HEARTFELT THANKS TO JOELLE DELBOURGO, MY AGENT WHO surprised me one day by leaving a voice mail on my phone, and to my editor Juliet Grames, without whom I wouldn't have been able to deliver the content and style that I had tried to create initially. In some places, she virtually wrote for me the expressions I was looking for. Peter Mayer, my publisher at The Overlook Press who rescued *To Kill a Tiger* from the pile of obscurity, is another person to whom I am indebted. These individuals joined the ranks of the people who live in the most cherished place in my heart, who patiently and graciously nourished me through the most difficult stages of my professional life.

I wish I could describe my gratitude to Sylvie Grignard, my best friend from France who knows—and welcomes—the best and the worst of me. David Walker, too, another friend from the heart of the Southern United States, deserves my sincere acknowledgment. He never tired of listening to me. I have Patrick Enright, a fellow English professor who introduced me to Gustav Mahler's symphonies, and Elvira Casal, a friend in English Department at MTSU, who generously offered her time to advise me on matters of teaching and service. I also have Ellen Jordan, an English faculty at MTSU, who always called me back, and two dear gentlemen named Tom Strawman and Bob Petersen, both professors of English at MTSU, whose constant willingness to listen to my woes was amazing. I have colleagues upon whom I love to unload my anxieties, whose names in alphabetical order appear in the following order: Kirsten Boatwright, Will

Brantley, Jimmie Cain, Sandra Cavender, Laura Dubek, Jill Hague, Jan Hayes, Elyce Helford, Allen Hibbard, Kathy Kirkman, Alfred Lutz, Joseph Mitchell, Michael Neth, Sharon Parente, Jan Quarles, Jean Rhodes, John Sanborn, Michael Sniderman, and Steve Walker. Some additional persons, however, must be remembered since they played a critical role in my life in more ways than one: Terry Birdsong, Jimmy Carter, Duane Coon, Sukhee Cho, Michelle Curl, David Curl, Neil Hanson, Felicia Holman, Joy Mitchell, Marnie Mitchell, Michael Ray, and Atsuko Yoda.

I have five women in New York whom I mustn't forget. I am permanently grateful to Carolyn Kim, a former literary agent who, after reading my rough draft twice, brought me the good luck of being introduced to Elisabeth Dyssegaard, the very rigorous, highly skilled editor who helped me to create an entirely new narrative frame. I owe many thanks to Charlotte Sheedy, too, who worked closely with Carolyn Kim and generously gave a chunk of her time to reading my rough draft. Susan Zeckendorf, another literary agent in New York who impressed me with the time-consuming attention she paid to my writing, deserves my gratitude. There is then Carrie Cantor, whose painstaking editorial insights helped me to achieve the level of writing that I possess now.

Finally, I thank my sister In Hwa in Korea, who always and very promptly found the information I needed. I also thank the historian Bruce Cumings for the generous permission to use some of the same terms and vocabulary that he in *The Origins of the Korean War* created in an attempt to translate the historical events that took place in the Korean Peninsula immediately prior to the Korean War.

Index